FM 3-90.31

Field Manual
No. 3-90.31

Headquarters
Department of the Army
Washington, DC, 26 February 2009

Maneuver Enhancement Brigade Operations

Contents

DISTRIBUTION RESTRICTION:. Approved for public release; distribution is unlimited.

Figures

Tables

Preface

Doctrine provides a military organization with unity of effort and a common philosophy, language, and purpose. This field manual (FM) provides doctrine for the tactical employment and operations of the maneuver enhancement brigade (MEB).

FM 3-90.31 is intended to facilitate the operations and training requirements of the MEB as they organize, prepare for, and conduct operations. This initial FM will evolve after lessons learned from training and operational experiences are incorporated into future Army doctrine. This FM provides doctrinal guidance for commanders, staffs, and subordinate leaders to plan, prepare, execute, and assess MEB operations.

The other intended audience for this publication is those leaders and staff sections within units that will employ an MEB or may operate under the command and control (C2) of the MEB. This publication should also be used to guide joint, interagency, and multinational higher headquarters commanders and staff on the employment of the MEB.

FM 3-90.31 reflects and supports Army operational doctrine. It is based on the doctrine and operational concepts described in or emerging in selected documents to include—

- FM 3-0
- FM 3-07
- FM 3-11
- FM 3-19.1
- FM 3-34
- FM 3-90
- FM 71-100
- FM 5-0
- FM 7-15
- FMI 3-0.1
- FMI 5-0.1
- TRADOC Pamphlet 525-3-25

This manual is organized into nine chapters and three appendixes to provide additional detail on selected topics. A brief description of the chapters and appendixes is provided below:

- Chapter 1 examines the operational environment (OE) and the nuances that apply to the MEB headquarters.
- Chapter 2 provides a description of the key tasks of the MEB headquarters, its organization, and its role in support of the division and echelons above division. It also highlights the special role of the MEB in conducting maneuver support (MANSPT) operations.
- Chapter 3 discusses C2 within the MEB, the relationships to task-organized forces, and the relationships of the MEB to the division, other units within the division, and to echelons above division.
- Chapter 4 describes consideration for the MEB to integrate and synchronize its conduct of operations using the Army operations process. This includes the nuances of providing MANSPT operations support to various echelons of command, and integrating and task organizing the variety of capabilities that the MEB may receive to perform its missions.
- Chapter 5 discusses a key task of the MEB—conduct maneuver support operations.

- Chapter 6 discusses a key task of the MEB—conduct support area operations.
- Chapter 7 discusses a key task of the MEB—conduct consequence management operations.
- Chapter 8 discusses a key task of the MEB—conduct stability operations.
- Chapter 9 discusses sustainment of capabilities within the MEB and its subordinate elements. Successful MEB operations depend on effectively incorporating sustainment support. This chapter describes the integrated sustainment effort required to support MEB operations.
- Appendix A provides organization and manning chart information for the three organic elements of the MEB.
- Appendix B discusses command posts of the MEB.
- Appendix C provides information on the Army battle command system (ABCS) and its impact on the MEB.

FM 3-90.31 provides operational guidance for commanders and trainers at all echelons. It forms the foundation within the established curriculum for employing the MEB within the Army's education system. It applies to Soldiers in the Active Army, National Guard, and United States (U.S.) Army Reserve. Information contained in this manual will assist multinational forces and other Services and branches of the Army to plan and integrate MEB capabilities. This doctrine also will assist Army branch schools in teaching the integration of the MEB capabilities into Army and joint operations.

Terms that have joint or Army definitions are identified in both the glossary and the text. Glossary terms: The glossary lists most terms used in FM 3-90.31 that have joint or Army definitions. Terms with an asterisk in the glossary indicate that this FM is the proponent FM (the authority). Text references: Definitions printed in boldface in the text indicate that this FM is the proponent FM. These terms and their definitions will be incorporated into the next revision of FM 1-02. For other definitions in the text, the term is italicized, and the number of the proponent FM follows the definition. This publication applies to the officers and Soldiers assigned to operational headquarters; commanders and staffs of joint task forces (JTFs), corps, and divisions; Active Army, the Army National Guard (ARNG)/Army National Guard of the United States (ARNGUS), and the United States Army Reserve (USAR) unless otherwise stated.

The proponent for this publication is the United States Army Training and Doctrine Command (TRADOC). Send comments and recommendations on Department of the Army (DA) Form 2028 (*Recommended Changes to Publications and Blank Forms*) directly to Commander, United States Army Maneuver Support Center (MANSCEN), ATTN: ATZT-TDD, 320 MANSCEN Loop, Suite 220, Fort Leonard Wood, Missouri 65473-8929. Submit an electronic DA Form 2028 or comments and recommendations in the DA Form 2028 format by e-mail to leon.mdottddengdoc@conus.army.mil

Introduction

The Army is in the midst of a transformation process to move it to modularity—by adopting the six warfighting functions and creating new and special organizations. One of those new and special organizations is the MEB. As one of the five multifunctional support brigades, the MEB is designed to support division operations (also echelon above division operations within Army, joint, and multinational C2 structures) and to respond to state or federal authorities as a part of civil support operations.

The MEB is designed as a C2 headquarters with a robust multifunctional brigade staff that is optimized to conduct MANSPT operations. *Maneuver support operations* **integrate the complementary and reinforcing capabilities of key protection, movement and maneuver, and sustainment functions, tasks, and systems to enhance freedom of action**. The MEB contains no organic units other than its headquarters and headquarters company (HHC), network support company (NSC), and brigade support battalion (BSB) (see chapter 2 and appendix A). The staff includes chemical, biological, radiological, nuclear, and high yield explosives (CBRNE); engineer; and military police (MP) functional operations/planning cells. The staff also includes a fires cell, area operations section, and airspace management section which support the capability of the MEB to be assigned an area of operations (AO). Each MEB is uniquely tailored with augmentation for its directed mission. An MEB typically includes a mix of several types of battalions and separate companies which may include civil affairs (CA); chemical, biological, radiological, and nuclear (CBRN); engineer; explosive ordnance disposal (EOD); and MP units. It may also contain other units to include military intelligence (MI) assets and a tactical combat force (TCF) when assigned an AO with a level III threat. In certain circumstances, the MEB may also include air and missile defense (AMD) units.

An MEB is a combined arms organization that is task-organized based on mission requirements. The MEB is not a maneuver brigade although it can be assigned an AO and control terrain. The MEB receives, commands, and controls forces to conduct operations. These brigades will typically be called upon to control terrain and potentially facilities as well. While the MEB has no direct antecedents in today's force structure, it combines many functions previously performed by the division/corps rear operations centers, division engineer brigade, and other division-level engineer, EOD, MP, and CBRN assets when supporting a division. MEBs provide capabilities to enhance freedom of movement and maneuver for operational and tactical commanders. The MEB has a combined arms staff and C2 capabilities that optimize it for many missions and facilitating necessary and frequent transitions between those missions or in the conduct of multiple concurrent or consecutive missions.

MEBs conduct maneuver support operations, support area operations, consequence management operations, and stability operations for the supported force. These four key tasks comprise the core capability for this organization. Typical supporting tasks related to these four MEB key tasks are listed below:

- Perform mobility and maneuver.
- Perform protection.
- Perform sustainment.
- Conduct operational area security.
- Conduct response force operations.
- Perform area damage control (ADC).
- Conduct terrain management.
- Perform fire support coordination.
- Conduct airspace management.
- Respond to CBRNE incident.
- Provide support to law enforcement.

- Conduct post incident response operations.
- Establish civil security.
- Establish civil control.
- Restore essential civil services.

The supported headquarters provides the MEB with protection priorities while continuously updating threat estimates. After carefully assessing self-protection capabilities of the supported headquarters subordinate units, the MEB commander allocates assets to meet the supported commander's priorities. There will never be enough capability to make the supported unit invulnerable to threats. Therefore, the MEB commander must balance the needs of acceptable risk, self-defense, passive protection measures, and proactive elimination of threats.

The MEB is normally assigned an AO in which it performs a portion of its missions. It can also perform support missions outside of its AO. Normally, the MEB AO is also the supported echelon's support area. A *support area* is a specific surface area designated by the echelon commander to facilitate the positioning, employment, and protection of resources required to sustain, enable, and control tactical operations. (FMI 3-0.1) The support area normally includes the echelon's main supply routes. For each echelon, the support area is annotated with the echelon size, such as a brigade support area or a division support area. If the supported echelon has more than one MEB assigned, then the support area may be split into two or more AOs, one for each MEB.

When assigned an AO, the MEB performs terrain management, movement control, clearance of fires, security, personnel recovery, ISR, stability operations, ADC, and infrastructure development. The MEB does not perform movement control on movements through its AO on higher headquarters designated main or alternate supply routes. An MEB is not responsible for the supported echelon's unassigned areas. For example, movement control of sustainment operations in the division AO as a whole stays the division transportation officer's responsibility even when it passes through the MEB AO. The division transportation officer coordinates those movements with the MEB.

This FM introduces the use of movement corridors to apply protection to movement. The MEB is organized and trained to execute selected area security missions including route and convoy security. It is not designed to conduct screen, guard, and cover operations. These operations are assigned to brigade combat teams (BCTs), or in the case of screening operations, possibly to a combat aviation brigade. The MEB coordinates and synchronizes the collective self-defense capabilities of bases and base clusters within its AO. When the situation requires, the MEB provides the C2 and is able to execute limited offensive and defensive operations, using response forces and/or a TCF, against threats within its AO. The TCF may include ground maneuver, aviation, and fires assets. Division and higher commanders should employ a BCT or armored cavalry regiment (ACR) when an AO will require more than a single maneuver task force (TF) to secure the AO. The MEB is not designed to C2 multiple maneuver battalions.

The MEB does not supplant unit self-defense responsibilities. Units remain responsible for self-protection against level I threats. The MEB provides reaction forces to respond to level II threats in its AO. If the brigade is assigned an area security mission, it may need to be task-organized with a TCF when the likelihood of level III threats is high. Those portions of a division's supporting sustainment brigade or other tenant units positioned in the MEB AO remain responsible for their own unit security and base and base cluster defense operations. To accomplish this task, one method to consider is to place the tenant units under tactical control (TACON) of the MEB for certain aspects of security. The MEB oversees area, not local, security operations in its AO. This includes response and TCF operations directed against level II and level III threats.

The MEB conducts operations in areas external to its previously assigned AO when directed to do so by its supported commander. This decision requires the supported headquarters to either temporarily change boundaries for the AO of the MEB or have some other headquarters assume AO responsibilities for the terrain on which the MEB units are tasked to conduct operations. One of these solutions allows the MEB to conduct route security or convoy security operations along a ground line of communications (LOC) between portions of the division AO and the AO of a subordinate BCT through what may have previously been unassigned area within the division AO.

The supported MEB higher headquarters may assign missions for assets assigned or attached to an MEB executed outside its AO, such as CBRN, CA, engineer, MP, and EOD assets. This requires careful coordination between the tasked unit, the MEB headquarters, and the headquarters of the unit in which the mission occurs. As an example, a fragmentary order may direct the MEB to provide an EOD capability in direct support (DS) of a BCT for a specified period or mission. This capability would allow a BCT to safely inventory a newly discovered ammunition storage facility. The order authorizes direct liaison between the MEB and the BCT to coordinate numerous tactical and sustainment issues. These issues could include but are not limited to movement routes and times, linkup points and times, recognition measures, location of supply points, maintenance collection points, medical treatment facilities, and communications-electronics operating instructions. Another approach would be to place MEB capabilities operational control (OPCON) (or TACON) to the BCT for a specific mission profile if conditions require more than just a support relationship.

The number of MEBs supporting a headquarters depends on the factors of mission, enemy, terrain and weather, troops and support available, time available, civil considerations (METT-TC) and the critical considerations of span of control and functional area focus. A joint force commander (JFC) may place an MEB in support of another Service or functional component, such as a Marine expeditionary force (MEF). An MEB may also be placed in support of multinational forces.

The MEB provides a staff trained to C2 many of the key constructive capabilities required to conduct consequence management. The consequence management could be conducted during any full spectrum operation. The robust C2 and modular capabilities of the MEB make it effective in responding to disasters.

When the supported headquarters is task-organized with functional brigades, the MEB may also be required to provide support to these brigades. An example of this might find the MEB providing support to an MP brigade focused on providing control of dislocated civilians and handling detainees. In this case, the MEB may be tasked to provide general engineering support to construct detainee facilities for the MP brigade.

To effectively understand the doctrinal employment of the MEB, it will also be important to understand the keystone and other specialized CBRN, CA, engineer, EOD, and MP doctrine. The MEB is an evolving organization that fills a critical role as a unique brigade headquarters optimized to perform MANSPT operations in support of the division and echelons above division. Its unique staff organization is designed to facilitate organizational flexibility for the echelon that it supports. At the BCT level, the brigade special troops battalion (BSTB) can provide a similar role as a multifunctional headquarters to support MANSPT operations in support of the BCT and its subordinate elements.

Chapter 1

The Operational Environment and the Army's Operational Concept

Understanding the OE and how Army forces conduct operations within it as part of an interdependent joint force underpins mission success and lays the framework for the roles and mission of the MEB within the OE. This understanding requires a broad perspective of operational problems and their relevance to each mission. The OE must be understood from the perspective of land operations and the role of Army forces in unified action. (See FM 3-0.) This chapter includes a brief discussion of the continuum of operations, the Army's operational concept of full spectrum operations, an overview of the elements of combat power, and the linkage of MANSPT operations to the elements of combat power and the operations process. All of this is framed, where applicable, to the specific and unique capabilities and roles of the MEB. The following chapters will address the specific considerations for the role of the MEB and how it conducts operations.

OPERATIONAL ENVIRONMENT

1-1. Joint doctrine describes the *operational environment* as the composite of the conditions, circumstances, and influences which affect the employment of capabilities and bear on the decisions of the commander (joint publication [JP] 3-0). The OE encompasses physical areas and factors (geography, weather, infrastructure, and population factors) and the information environment, to include information concerning enemy, friendly, and neutral forces; and other variables relevant to a specific operation. Understanding the OE is essential to the successful execution of operations. To gain a broad understanding of these influences, commanders will normally consult with specialists in each area.

1-2. Operations on land are complex, dynamic, and uniquely tied to the geography and airspace of the area of responsibility (AOR). The complexity of land combat stems from the geography, from the large number of Soldiers and weapons platforms involved, and from the close, continuous interaction of land forces with the enemy, noncombatants, and each other. Complexity is also a function of the combined arms and joint nature of land combat, involving the interaction and mutual support of different arms and services. Instantaneous global communications multiplies this complexity. Uncertainty and chaos characterize operations on land. Technology, intelligence, and the design of operations can reduce uncertainty. However, regardless of the effort allocated to intelligence, commanders still have to make decisions based on incomplete, inaccurate, or contradictory information. An understanding of the OE underpins the commander's ability to make decisions.

THREATS

1-3. The threats faced by the MEB will be the same threats faced by other Army organizations and included in the four major categories of traditional, catastrophic, irregular, and disruptive. (See FM 3-0.) Preparing for and managing these threats requires employing all instruments of national power—diplomatic, informational, military, and economic. The MEB must be prepared to support operations against each of these threats. The organizational design of the MEB fills a previous void in Army and joint force structure. The MEB is uniquely optimized to conduct MANSPT operations in support of Army, joint, multinational, and interagency operations. The MEB is also designed to C2 forces to defeat level II and level III threats within an assigned AO. (See paragraph 1-7 below and FM 3-0 for a more detailed discussion of the threat.)

1-4. Military forces will face a range of threats that extend from smaller, lower-technology opponents to larger, more modernized conventional forces. It is likely that both will employ asymmetric methods that avoid or counter U.S. strengths, without attempting to oppose them directly, while seeking to exploit weaknesses. One technique to defeat the challenges associated with using improvised explosive devices (IEDs) may be by using movement corridor operations. (See chapter 5 for more information on movement corridor operations.)

1-5. Our adversaries will attempt to leverage the environment to achieve maximum advantage. To defeat our adversaries, Army and joint forces must equip, train, and operate in complex situations impacted by multiple variables. In addition to traditionally organized military forces, friendly forces will encounter fractured governmental structures, terrorists, and armed gangs when committed. The standing government may have lost control over sections of its country, allowing the free flow of weapons, drugs, and other contraband across state boundaries. Criminal and terrorist elements, with transnational interests and links, take advantage of the decay in state control and even attempt to accelerate it. Police, constabulary, and other elements of state control are often under resourced, corrupted, and/or dissolved. The MEB conducts operations to support the shaping of the OE and mitigate its negative effects on friendly operations.

1-6. The MEB has an organic staff that is optimized to provide for the planning and execution of key tasks associated with protection, movement and maneuver, and sustainment. It uses attached and OPCON units to conduct MANSPT operations in its AO and within the broader AO of the organization it supports. The MEB's capability to conduct support area operations in the assigned echelon support area provides added security and defense for other units and enhances freedom of action for the supported echelon. The capability to synchronize MANSPT operations and support area operations under the MEB provides a unique set of capabilities to other Army, joint, and multinational elements for addressing challenges presented by the threat.

THREAT LEVELS

1-7. Using threat levels assists commanders in managing risk, identifying vulnerabilities, and allocating forces and resources in time and space in the OE. At the tactical level, enemy threat activities can be generally described and categorized in three levels (see FM 3-90 for additional detail). Each level or any combination of levels may exist in the AO.

1-8. More than one level of threat may be active in an AO and may operate in either an independent or a coordinated fashion. (See chapter 6 for a discussion of how the MEB organizes to defeat these threats during the conduct of support area operations.)

- **Level I threat.** A small enemy force that can be defeated by a unit's organic resources.
- **Level II threat.** Enemy activities that require the commitment of a reaction force to defeat them.
- **Level III threat.** A threat that requires the commitment of a TCF to defeat it.

OPERATIONAL AND MISSION VARIABLES

1-9. Operational and mission variables complement each other and support the common purpose of describing the OE. The operational variables include political, military, economic, social, information, and infrastructure that collectively create the joint memory aid of PMESII. The Army adds two more operational variables (physical environment and time [PT]) to this joint construct to create the memory aid of PMESII-PT with a total of eight operational variables. The mission variables are grouped into the time-tested memory aid of METT-TC, which captures the six variables of METT-TC.

1-10. Each variable affects how Army forces combine, sequence, and conduct military operations. Commanders tailor and task-organize forces, employ diverse capabilities, and support different missions to accomplish military objectives. An analysis of these variables assist commanders in defining the conditions, circumstances, and influences that affect operational options considered to plan, coordinate, support, execute, and sustain operations. (See chapter 4 for a discussion of how the MEB may apply these variables.)

Operational Variables

1-11. Joint planners describe the OE in terms of operational variables. Operational variables are those aspects of the environment, both military and nonmilitary, that may differ from one operational area to another and affect the campaigns and major operations. Operational variables describe not only the military aspects of an OE, but also the population's influence on it. Joint and Army planners analyze the OE in terms of operational variables.

1-12. The variables provide a broad view of the OE that emphasizes its human aspects. Since land forces always operate among populations, understanding the human variables is crucial. They describe each operation's context for commanders and other leaders. Understanding them helps commanders appreciate how the military instrument complements other instruments of national power. Comprehensive analysis of the variables occurs at the joint level; Army commanders use the comprehensive joint analysis of the variables to shape their understanding of the situation.

1-13. A quick look at the eight Army operational variables is discussed below to highlight potential implications for the MEB. The examples are not meant to be all-inclusive treatment of MEB concerns or applicability for each of the variables. (For more information on the variables, see FM 3-0.)

- **Political**. Understanding the political circumstances within an OE will help the commander recognize key actors and visualize their explicit and implicit aims and their capabilities to achieve their goals. The MEB view might add challenges associated with political circumstances permitting or denying access to key ports of entry or critical sustainment facilities. Opportunities in the form of alternative access routes might be added. The MEB would be interested in the effect of laws, agreements, or positions of allies that might affect planning and operations. The political variable, always important, takes on a more prominent role during stability and civil support operations.
- **Military**. The military variable explores the military capabilities of all relevant actors in a given OE. The MEB view adds a MANSPT focus to the view of the OE that integrates CA, CBRN, engineer, EOD, and MP capabilities. Its multifunctional organic staff is concerned with the aspects of movement and maneuver, selected sustainment, and many of the tasks associated with protection and their effects on the force that the MEB is supporting. Using task-organized units and other specialized staff augmentation, the MEB responds to those challenges presented by an adversary's capabilities in its own AO and the more extensive AO of the unit that it supports. The MEB view might add the challenges associated with an adversary's capability to employ CBRN, explosive hazards or other obstacles, and the capability to challenge traditional survivability standards of protection.
- **Economic**. The economic variable encompasses individual behaviors and aggregate phenomena related to the production, distribution, and consumption of resources. The MEB view might add challenges associated with production or availability of key materials and resources.
- **Social**. The social variable describes the cultural, religious, ethnic makeup, and social cleavages within an OE. The MEB view would incorporate aspects of stability or civil support and the necessary support to the stability or civil support plan provided by the units task-organized to the MEB. The MEB must overcome the challenges associated with specific cultural or religious buildings or installations and a host of other potential social concerns. Opportunities in the form of the potential to provide for culturally related activities or building requirements might be a consideration.
- **Information**. This variable describes the aggregate of individuals, organizations, and systems that collect, process, disseminate, or act on information. The MEB uses information engagement to shape the OE as part of its operations.
- **Infrastructure**. Infrastructure comprises the basic facilities, services, and installations needed for the functioning of a community or society. The MEB view might add challenges associated with specific deficiencies in the basic infrastructure. Opportunities in the form of improvements to existing infrastructure and specific new projects might be added. The organic staff of the MEB provides for a detailed understanding of infrastructure by subcategories in the context of

combat operations, stability, and civil support operations. Several manuals that include more detailed information on this are FM 3-34.400 and FM 3-34.170.

- **Physical environment**. The defining factors are complex terrain and urban settings (super-surface, surface, and subsurface features), weather, topography, hydrology, and environmental conditions. The MEB view might add the challenges associated with natural and manmade obstacles. Insights into environmental considerations are also a concern (see FM 3-100.4). Opportunities in the form of existing routes, installations, and resources might be added. The organic staff supports a broad understanding of the physical environment through geospatial engineering which is discussed in detail in FM 3-34.230 and JP 2-03.

- **Time**. The variable of time influences military operations within an OE in terms of the decision—cycles, operational tempo, and planning horizons. The MEB view might add challenges associated with completing required CA-related plan missions in the time allotted because of the impact on perceptions of civilians during civil support or stability operations. Opportunities in the form of potential to accelerate priority projects might be added for the positive effect it would have on civil considerations and the perception of mission success.

Mission Variables

1-14. Analysis of the OE in terms of the operational variables provides the relevant information that commanders can use to frame operational problems. While such analysis improves situational understanding (SU) at all levels, land operations require more specific information. When commanders receive a mission, they require a more detailed mission analysis focused on their specific situation.

1-15. The Army uses the mission variables identified in the memory aid of METT-TC as a framework for this detailed mission analysis. When used together, mission and operational variables help commanders visualize their situation. (Chapter 4 provides a more complete discussion of analysis using the mission variables in terms of planning MEB operations.)

UNIFIED ACTION

1-16. *Unified action* is the synchronization, coordination, and/or integration of the activities of governmental and nongovernmental entities with military operations to achieve unity of effort (JP 1). It involves applying all instruments of national power, including actions of other United States Government (USG) agencies and multinational military and nonmilitary organizations. Combatant commanders play a pivotal role in unified actions; however, subordinate commanders also integrate and synchronize their operations directly with the activities and operations of other military forces and nonmilitary organizations in their AO.

1-17. Unified action includes joint integration. Joint integration extends the principle of combined arms to operations conducted by two or more Service components. The combination of diverse joint force capabilities generates combat power more potent than the sum of its parts. Joint integration does not require joint commands at all echelons; it does require joint interoperability and an understanding of joint synergy at all levels of command. Joint synergy extends the principles of combined arms to operations conducted by two or more Service components. The strengths of each Service or functional component combine to overcome the limitations or reinforce the effects of the other components. The combination of multiple and diverse joint force capabilities generates combat power more potent than the sum of its parts. Integrating the variety of MANSPT capabilities requires an understanding of the various capabilities and limitations of those MANSPT assets available for any given mission. Integration also requires a common understanding of the C2 structure and processes in place to employ the various MANSPT capabilities in unified action.

INTERAGENCY COORDINATION

1-18. Because of the leverage of their wide range of expertise and funding resources, USG agencies can support the JFC's mission objectives and can greatly expand the capabilities of the joint force. This is true whether the response is international in nature or within the United States (for example, during consequence management in the United States, MEB forces may respond to incidents, which require close coordination with other USG agencies). Coordination and a clear understanding of the commander's intent are critical when synchronizing operational efforts involving multiple USG agencies. The JFC will be required to coordinate with USG agencies to achieve overall U.S. objectives. The MEB staff must have an understanding of the capabilities of these agencies and their support functions. While USG agencies may increase the resources engaged in a given operation, they may also increase and complicate the coordination efforts. Stability operations are now regarded as a core U.S. military mission and are given priority comparable to combat operations. Because integrated civilian and military efforts are key to successful stability operations, the MEB staff must be prepared to conduct or support stability operations by working closely with U.S. departments and agencies, foreign governments and security forces, global and regional international organizations, U.S. and foreign nongovernmental organizations, and private sector individuals and for-profit companies. The MEB may routinely participate in interagency coordination during the conduct of consequence management operations within stability and civil support operations.

1-19. The intricate linkages among the instruments of national power demand that commanders consider all capabilities and agencies to help achieve the common end state. Interagency coordination forges a vital link between military operations and activities conducted by such organizations as U.S. government agencies; agencies of partner nations; nongovernmental organizations (NGOs); and regional, international, and United Nations (UN) organizations, and agencies of a host nation (HN).

1-20. CA activities are fundamental to the execution of full spectrum operations. Designated CA units, other military forces, and other government agencies, or a combination of the three perform and conduct activities for the commander to establish, maintain, influence, or exploit relations between military forces and other nonmilitary forces (see FM 3-05.40). CA operations assist in coordinating activities of engaged military forces, and other USG agencies, NGO, and regional and intergovernmental organizations to facilitate military operations and achieve objectives. These activities enhance the relationship between military forces and civil authorities in areas where military forces are present. CA operations also involve the applying functions normally the responsibility of local, regional, or national civil government, but for various reasons, are not being accomplished.

MULTINATIONAL OPERATIONS

1-21. Multinational operations are conducted within the structure of an alliance or a multinational. Achieving true unity of command is difficult in multinational operations and in many cases unity of effort is the best that can be achieved. Agreement among the multinational partners establishes the level of command authority vested in a multinational force commander. The President of the United States retains command authority over U.S. forces. Most nations have similar restrictions. However, in certain circumstances, it may be prudent or advantageous to place Army forces under OPCON of a multinational commander. To compensate for limited unity of command, commanders concentrate on achieving unity of effort. Consensus building, rather than direct command authority, is often the key element of successful multinational operations. The MEB may provide the C2 for Army and potentially selected joint forces supporting a multinational force.

1-22. During multinational operations, U.S. forces establish liaisons with multinational forces early. Army forces exchange specialized liaison personnel in fields such as aviation, CBRNE, fire support, engineer, intelligence, MP, public affairs (PA), and CA based on mission requirements. Missions to multinational units should reflect the capabilities and limitations of each national contingent. Some significant factors are relative mobility and size; intelligence collection assets; and long-range fires, special operations forces (SOF), and organic sustainment capabilities. When assigning missions, commanders should also consider special skills, language, and rapport with the local population, and the national pride of multinational partners. Multinational commanders may assign HN forces home defense or police missions, such as sustainment area and base security. Commanders should give special consideration to "niche" capabilities such as mine clearance that may exceed U.S. capabilities.

1-23. Due to its multifunctional C2 capabilities and the ability to conduct multiple MANSPT operations, support area operations, consequence management operations, and stability operations and tasks (see chapter 2), the MEB may be a unit of choice for the employment of Army forces in support of joint or multinational operations. Its organic staff ability to integrate CBRN, engineer, EOD, MP, and other units also makes it ideal for use in stability or civil support operations and situations where interagency coordination will be high.

CONTINUUM OF OPERATIONS

1-24. The continuum of operations frames the application of land power and links the OE with the Army's operational concept of full spectrum operations. It includes the full spectrum operations and operational themes. Each of these has described major categories but they are not discrete; they overlap; they occur simultaneously. There are three tools for understanding and visualizing operations—continuum of operations, full spectrum operations, and operational themes. (See FM 3-0.)

1-25. The full spectrum operations are the backdrop for Army operations. It is a tool to understand and visualize the level of politically motivated violence and the corresponding role of the military in resolving a conflict. It places levels of violence on an ascending scale marked by graduated steps from stable peace to general war (see FM 3-0). While the MEB operates across this spectrum, it is uniquely capable of performance on the lower side of the spectrum. It is also designed to effectively operate and adjust to transitions within the spectrum.

1-26. The MEB conducts operations to shape the OE, lower the level of violence, set conditions favorable for conducting subsequent operations and tasks, and to enhance freedom of action for the supported force.

1-27. An *operational theme* describes the character of the dominant major operation being conducted at any time within a land force commander's AO. The operational theme helps convey the nature of the major operation to the force to facilitate common understanding of how the commander broadly intends to operate (FM 3-0). The theme of a major operation may change for various reasons. Operational themes have implications for approaches, task organizing, resource allocation, protection, and tactical task assignment. The MEB may support operations within each of the operational themes.

OPERATIONAL CONCEPT

1-28. The Army's operational concept of *full spectrum operations* is the core of its doctrine. Army forces combine offensive, defensive, and stability or civil support operations simultaneously as part of an interdependent joint force to seize, retain, and exploit the initiative to achieve decisive results. They employ synchronized action—lethal and nonlethal—proportional to the mission and informed by a thorough understanding of all dimensions of the OE. Mission command that conveys intent and an appreciation of all aspects of the situation guides the adaptive use of Army forces (FM 3-0).

> *Note*: FM 3-0 discusses simultaneity and synchronization, lethal and nonlethal actions, and mission command in detail. Each of these affects the role of the MEB in full spectrum operations.

1-29. Full spectrum operations are the purposeful, continuous, and simultaneous combinations of offense, defense, and stability or civil support. Operations conducted overseas simultaneously combine three components—offensive, defensive and stability operations. Within the United States and its territories, operations simultaneously combine offensive, defensive, and civil support operations.

1-30. MEB operations contribute significant combat power, both lethal and nonlethal in nature, to all of the components of full spectrum operations. Based on a METT-TC analysis, the MEB will be task-organized with additional modular capabilities to meet mission requirements. The MEB conducts only very limited offensive and defensive operations as a brigade and typically supports other organizations in performing them. Staff augmentation by CBRN, CA, engineer, EOD, MP, and other capabilities may be necessary to C2 the mix of modular units and capabilities task-organized to the MEB. These same capabilities may be employed at division, corps, and theater echelons to conduct MANSPT operations tasks and provide other support to the force. Force tailored MANSPT capabilities can provide critical nonlethal capabilities to conduct or support stability or civil support operations.

1-31. The MEB can simultaneously support the elements of offense, defense, and stability (or civil support) in support of a higher echelon or focus on a single element of full spectrum operations during a phase of a larger operation or within a specific AO. The MEB provides the C2 of multifunctional units and is designed with staff capabilities and robustness to complement and reinforce any combination of full spectrum operations. When specific functional requirements or magnitude of mission exceed the capabilities of the MEB, functional brigades or multiple MEBs are employed to properly focus and C2 those actions. The unique design of the MEB, based on the factors of METT-TC, postures it to be a potential unit of choice when conducting stability or civil support operations.

COMBAT POWER

1-32. Full spectrum operations require the continuous generating and applying of the eight elements of combat power, often for extended periods. Joint doctrine defines *combat power* as the total means of destructive and/or disruptive force which a military unit/formation can apply against the opponent at a given time (JP 1-02). Army doctrine adds "Army forces generate combat power by converting fighting potential into effective action. Combat power includes a unit's constructive and information capabilities as well as its disruptive and destructive force." (FM 3-0) The MEB generates combat power to conduct operations in its own AO and supports and enables the generation of combat power within the unit it supports.

1-33. .Six of the elements of combat power—movement and maneuver, intelligence, fires, sustainment, C2, and protection—are collectively described as the warfighting functions. Commanders apply combat power through the warfighting functions using leadership and information (see FM 3-0). The MEB provides complementary and reinforcing capabilities across the warfighting functions with support that is primarily focused on the protection, movement and maneuver, and selected sustainment functions.

1-34. Commanders use the warfighting functions to help them exercise battle command. A *warfighting function* is a group of tasks and systems (people, organizations, information, and processes) united by a common purpose that commanders use to accomplish missions and training objectives (this definition was shortened; the complete definition is printed in the glossary). Decisive, shaping, and sustaining operations combine all the warfighting functions to generate combat power. No warfighting function is exclusively decisive, shaping, or sustaining. The Army's warfighting functions are fundamentally linked to the joint functions. They also parallel those of the Marine Corps.

1-35. Commanders use combined arms to generate and increase the effects of combat power. Army forces obtain combined arms through force tailoring, task organization, and mutual support. Mutual support takes the form of complementary and reinforcing capabilities. Commanders balance the ability to mass the effects of lethal and nonlethal systems with the requirements to deploy and sustain the units that employ those systems. Sustaining combat power throughout the operation is important to success. Tailored force packages maximize the capability of initial-entry forces consistent with the mission and the requirement to project, employ, and sustain the force. Follow-on forces increase the entire force's endurance and ability to operate in depth. Employing reserves, focusing joint support, arranging rest for committed forces, and staging sustainment assets to preserve momentum and synchronization all assist in applying combat power effectively over time and space.

1-36. *Combined arms* is the synchronized and simultaneous application of the elements of combat power to achieve an effect greater than if each element was used separately or sequentially (FM 3-0). The term combined arms is not reserved solely for close combat or maneuver units. Combined arms employ each of the warfighting functions and its supporting systems. Used destructively, combined arms integrate different capabilities such that counteracting one makes the enemy vulnerable to another. Used constructively, combined arms multiply the effectiveness and the efficiency of Army capabilities used in stability or civil support. The MEB uses combined arms to generate combat power and applies it to conduct operations. It routinely supports divisions and echelons above division and their subordinate headquarters to generate and maintain combat power. Based on METT-TC, the MEB may create combined arms battalion TFs or company teams from its assigned CBRN, engineer, and MP battalions and other units to facilitate operations within its own AO, and in support of other units within the higher headquarters to which it is assigned.

1-37. Combined arms use complementary and reinforcing capabilities. Complementary capabilities protect the weaknesses of one system or organization with the capabilities of a different arm or warfighting function. Reinforcing capabilities combine similar systems or capabilities within the same warfighting function to increase the function's overall capabilities. The MEB may use task-organized CBRN, EOD, engineer, and MP elements (TFs or company teams) to conduct route reconnaissance and use MP, engineer, CBRN, and EOD elements to perform various tasks primarily subordinate to the movement and maneuver, protection, and sustainment warfighting functions. In these examples, the combined arms applications of these elements are both complementary and reinforcing and provide MANSPT operations support to the force as a whole and specifically to the echelon headquarters they are supporting. (See FM 3-0.)

1-38. *Task organizing* is the act of designing an operating force, support staff, or logistic package of specific size and composition to meet a unique task or mission. Characteristics to examine when task organizing the force include, but are not limited to training, experience, equipage, sustainability, operating environment, enemy threat, and mobility (JP 3-05). To the joint definition, Army doctrine adds: The act of designing an operating force, support staff, or logistics package of specific size and composition to meet a unique task or mission. Characteristics to examine when task organizing the force include, but are not limited to, training, equipage, sustainability, operating environment, enemy threat, and mobility. For Army forces, it includes allocating available assets to subordinate commanders and establishing their command and support relationships (FM 3-0).

MANEUVER SUPPORT OPERATIONS AS PART OF FULL SPECTRUM OPERATIONS

OVERVIEW

1-39. *Maneuver support* **operations integrate the complimentary and reinforcing capabilities of key protection, movement and maneuver, and sustainment functions, tasks, and systems to enhance freedom of action**. The MEB conducts MANSPT operations and then integrates and synchronizes them across all the Army warfighting functions to support offensive and defensive operations and to conduct or support stability operations or civil support operations. The integration and synchronization of MANSPT-related tasks shape the environment to protect the force, enhance survivability and other protection tasks, enhance mobility and countermobility and other movement and maneuver tasks, provide selected sustainment support, and generally expand the freedom of action of the supported echelon while denying it to the enemy. This allows combat power to be applied at the decisive point and time and facilitates simultaneous combinations at the operational level and rapid transitions at the tactical level. (See Chapter 5 for a more complete discussion of MANSPT operations and their application in the MEB.) While other units may provide aspects of MANSPT operations, the MEB is uniquely designed and staffed to conduct MANSPT operations for the units that it supports.

1-40. The primary functional branches representing the core of MANSPT operations capabilities are found in the CBRN, engineer; and MP branches, but other critical and essential participation comes from the focused areas of CA and EOD, and in selected situations, the air defense branch. Each of these branches and focused areas has significant capabilities that contribute to the conduct of MANSPT operations. MANSPT operations require multifunctional and multibranch integration. The MEB and the other functional brigades (CBRN, engineer, and MP) are the primary units that conduct MANSPT operations at the division echelon and above. At the BCT echelon and below the BSTB and selected CBRN, engineer, and MP battalion headquarters may be designed and trained to C2 combined arms MANSPT capabilities. This is similar to how the MEB receives complimentary and reinforcing capabilities to and from the functional brigades The MEB may provide reinforcing capabilities to the BSTB.

1-41. MANSPT operations provide the commander with capabilities to be predictive and proactive while at the same time provide the ability to react to enemy initiatives. The commander must understand the OE and its implications to friendly and enemy operations. This understanding allows the commander to predict enemy actions that leverage the environment, to take proactive actions against the enemy to deny him the means to do so, and to avoid areas of highest risk or engage the enemy in those areas within enhanced situational awareness (SA). The commander may also shape the OE using the integrated capabilities of MANSPT operations to enhance the operational performance of each unit in support of full spectrum operations. MANSPT operations not only enable the performance of units but also seek to deny the enemy options—including the ability to maneuver freely. To develop and maintain this understanding of the OE, the commander applies a wide range of dedicated and collateral sensors. The commander also considers the physical, human, and informational factors when considering the impact of the OE on MANSPT operations.

PROTECTION

1-42. The protection warfighting function is presented along with the other five warfighting functions in FM 3-0. MANSPT operations integrate many of the tasks within this warfighting function, but not all of them. (When revised, FM 3-13 will address information protection.)

1-43. The *protection warfighting function* is the related tasks and systems that preserve the force so the commander can apply maximum combat power (FM 3-0). Preserving the force includes protecting personnel (combatants and noncombatants), physical assets, and information of the United States and multinational military and civilian partners. The protection warfighting function facilitates the commander's ability to maintain the force's integrity and combat power. Protection determines the degree to which potential threats can disrupt operations and counters or mitigates those threats. Protection is a continuing activity; it integrates all protection capabilities to safeguard bases, secure routes, and protect forces. The protection warfighting function includes the following tasks:

- AMD.
- Personnel recovery.
- Information protection.
- Fratricide avoidance.
- Operational area security.
- Antiterrorism (AT).
- Survivability.
- Force health protection.
- CBRN operations.
- Safety.
- Operations security.
- EOD.

1-44. Those tasks within the protection warfighting function that are best integrated by the MEB in MANSPT operations and support area operations are discussed in chapter 5. The integration and synchronization of MANSPT-related tasks shape the environment to protect the force, enhance survivability and other protection tasks, and expand the freedom of action of friendly forces while denying it to the enemy. This allows combat power to be applied at the decisive point and time and facilitates simultaneous combinations at the operational level and rapid transitions at the tactical level. (FM 3-90 provides a discussion of many of the tasks included in the movement and maneuver warfighting function.)

MOVEMENT AND MANEUVER

1-45. The *movement and maneuver warfighting function* is the related tasks and systems that move forces to achieve a position of advantage in relation to the enemy. Direct fire is inherent in maneuver, as is close combat (FM 3-0). The function includes tasks associated with force projection related to gaining a positional advantage over an enemy. One example is moving forces to execute a large-scale air or airborne assault. Another is deploying forces to intermediate staging bases in preparation for an offensive. *Maneuver* is the employment of forces in the operational area through movement in combination with fires to achieve a position of advantage in respect to the enemy in order to accomplish the mission (this definition was shortened; the complete definition is printed in the glossary). Maneuver is the means by which commanders mass the effects of combat power to achieve surprise, shock, and momentum. Effective maneuver requires close coordination with fires. Movement is necessary to disperse and displace the force as a whole or in part when maneuvering. Both tactical and operational maneuver require logistic support. The movement and maneuver warfighting function includes the following tasks:

- Deploy.
- Move.
- Maneuver.
- Employ direct fires.
- Occupy an area.
- Conduct mobility and countermobility operations.
- Employ battlefield obscuration.

1-46. Those tasks within the movement and maneuver warfighting function that may be best integrated by the MEB in MANSPT operations and support area operations are discussed in chapters 5 and 6. The integration and synchronization of MANSPT-related tasks shape the environment to provide mobility and countermobility, provide or enhance other movement and maneuver tasks, and expand the freedom of action of friendly forces while denying it to the enemy. This allows combat power to be applied at the decisive point and time and facilitates simultaneous combinations at the operational level and rapid transitions at the tactical level. The movement and maneuver warfighting function does not include administrative movements of personnel and materiel. These movements fall under the sustainment warfighting function. (FM 3-90 provides a discussion of many of the tasks included in the movement and maneuver warfighting function.)

SUSTAINMENT

1-47. The *sustainment warfighting function* is the related tasks and systems that provide support and services to ensure freedom of action, extend operational reach, and prolong endurance (FM 3-0). The endurance of Army forces is primarily a function of their sustainment. Sustainment determines the depth and duration of Army operations. It is essential to retaining and exploiting the initiative. Sustainment is the provision of the logistics, personnel services, and health service support necessary to maintain operations until mission accomplishment. Internment, resettlement, and detainee operations fall under the sustainment warfighting function and include elements of all three major subfunctions. (FM 4-0 describes the sustainment warfighting function.)

1-48. Sustainment is discussed in several ways in this manual—the sustainment warfighting function, sustainment operations; and sustainment tasks. The sustainment discussed as part of MANSPT operations only includes the sustainment operations performed by the MEB with task-organized forces. The MEB provides support to the sustainment warfighting function primarily through its focus on tasks associated with general engineering support and internment and resettlement operations.

FREEDOM OF ACTION

1-49. MANSPT operations are intended to enhance freedom of action for the supported force. Gaining and maintaining freedom of action is necessary during all full spectrum operations. Freedom of action in this context focuses on providing the commander with options that would otherwise be unavailable if actions by the threat were successful. These actions include, but are not limited to, tactical security, mobility, countermobility, survivability, CBRN operations, and other aspects of the movement and maneuver, protection, and sustainment warfighting functions. They include moderating or eliminating effects of obstacles (primarily terrain and weather) to enable the commander to deploy and maneuver where and when desired, without interruption or delay, to achieve the mission. Protection, movement and maneuver, and sustainment each have proactive and reactive actions associated with this focus.

1-50. Initiative is directly impacted by the freedom of action that a commander has. A commander may be impacted by many things to include constraints, restraints, and operational limitations (or control measures) imposed because of primarily legal, political, or C2 decisions. MANSPT operations may not directly affect these, but they do contribute capabilities for the supported commander to seize, retain, and exploit the initiative as the surest way to achieve decisive results. MANSPT operations emphasize creating options and opportunity for the commander.

1-51. There is no approved definition for freedom of action in either joint or Army doctrine. It is currently used as a part of the definitions for the terms *centers of gravity*, *constraint*, *operational limitation*, *restraint*, *space control*, and *tactical security*. FM 3-0 highlights only the sustainment warfighting function as providing freedom of actions but so do other warfighting functions. MANSPT operations contribute to the commander's freedom of action to decisively exercise his/her will to complete the mission, protect the force, and to affect movement (of both the enemy and his/her own forces). The MEB is specifically designed to conduct MANSPT operations for the commander at division and echelons above division and provide the supported commander with capabilities that contribute to freedom of action as a result.

This page intentionally left blank.

Chapter 2
MEB Mission and Organization

The MEB is a unique multifunctional C2 headquarters designed to perform MANSPT operations for the echelon it supports. Task organization is based upon identified mission requirements for the echelon it is supporting. It may be placed in support of Army, joint, interagency, or multinational headquarters. The headquarters is staffed and optimized to conduct combined arms operations integrating a wide range of MANSPT related technical branches and combat forces. The MEB can organize, provide, or employ unique battalion TF and company team combined arms technical experts to conduct MANSPT operations across full spectrum operations. The MEB may include a mix of CBRN, CA, engineer, EOD, MP and potentially AMD and/or a TCF. The number and type of organizations placed under a MEB depends on the mission, threat, and number and type of battalions or companies that require C2. Peacetime task organization may vary due to stationing and the type of units that are collocated under the MEB for C2. The MEB is optimized to provide staff planning for and C2 of the units required to conduct maneuver support operations, support area operations, and consequence management operations.

CAPABILITIES

2-1. The MEB is designed to C2 forces from multiple branches but especially those that conduct MANSPT operations for the force. It employs them to conduct full spectrum operations in support of Army division, echelon above division (EAD), joint, interagency, or multinational headquarters. More than one MEB may be assigned to a higher headquarters. The MEB is capable of operating across the full spectrum operations to support, reinforce, or complement offensive and defensive major combat operations and can support or conduct stability or civil support operations. It can enable the decisive operation or lead shaping or sustaining operations with a focus on general engineering or internment and resettlement (I/R). In special situations, the MEB may conduct the decisive operation. The MEB is not a maneuver brigade; however, it is normally assigned an AO and controls terrain. The only maneuver the MEB is capable of is defensive maneuver and very limited offensive maneuver by employing its reserve to counter or spoil a threat. The MEB does not typically maneuver as a brigade. The MEB is designed to be assigned an AO and C2 with higher headquarters designated TACON for security and defense of tenant units. (See chapter 6.)

2-2. The MEB shares these characteristics with the other support brigades—

- Tailorable—can be task-organized based on the factors of METT-TC.
- Modular—easily attaches/detaches subordinate units.
- Expeditionary—can be quickly deployed in modules.
- Networked—has an organic signal company and liaison officers (LNOs) to link with other headquarters/forces.
- Joint interdependent—uses and contributes to other Service capabilities.
- Agile—can reinforce other brigades with subordinate capabilities.
- Multifunctional—headquarters employs multiple branch capabilities to accomplish multiple types of mission tasks.

2-3. Unlike other support or functional brigades, the MEB is staffed and trained to C2 an assigned AO and to control terrain. In this regard, it is similar to a BCT, without the inherent maneuver capability of a

BCT. It has the added staff to perform the tasks needed to operate an AO to include conducting selected combat operations within that AO. Many of the units not staffed to control terrain become tenants within the assigned AO (especially if the AO is the echelon support area) of the MEB. (See chapter 6.) The MEB can also conduct up-to-battalion-level close combat within its AO when assigned a TCF. It provides an "economy of force" capability so BCTs/maneuver units can focus on combat operations. It directly supports and synchronizes operations across all six Army warfighting functions.

2-4. The MEB has limited organic structure and depends on other organizations for some additional capabilities. Detailed mission analysis and running estimates identify requirements. Examples of MEB dependencies include fires (counterfire radar, forward observers, and ability to lase targets, Air Force TACON party), sustainment (forward support company, area support medical company, aerial medical evacuation), and intelligence, surveillance, and reconnaissance (ISR) capability (unmanned aircraft system [UAS], MI units, geospatial staff).

KEY AND SUPPORTING TASKS

2-5. The MEB's key tasks include conduct maneuver support operations, conduct support area operations, conduct consequence management operations, and conduct stability operations. The following paragraphs include the typical supporting tasks for each MEB key task.

2-6. Conduct maneuver support operations (see chapter 5) includes—
- Perform mobility.
- Perform protection.
- Perform sustainment.

2-7. Conduct support area operations (see chapter 6) includes—
- Conduct operational area security.
- Conduct response force operations.
- Perform ADC.
- Conduct terrain management.
- Perform fire support coordination.
- Conduct airspace management.

2-8. Conduct consequence management (see chapter 7) includes—
- Respond to CBRNE incident.
- Provide support to law enforcement.
- Conduct post incident response operations.

2-9. Conduct stability operations (see chapter 8) includes—
- Establish civil security.
- Establish civil control.
- Restore essential civil services.

MEB ORGANIZATION

2-10. The MEB is designed to perform MANSPT operations in support of the division and its assigned elements and EAD organizations. The MEB is optimized to conduct operations and C2 those elements that conduct MANSPT operations (primarily focused on combinations of CBRN, engineer, EOD, and MP capabilities/units). The brigade also conducts combat operations up to the level of a maneuver battalion when task-organized with a TCF or task-organized with other maneuver forces. The compact size of the organic elements of the MEB facilitates rapid deployment, enabling strategic responsiveness while maintaining enough capability to provide C2 and the functional expertise necessary for rapid tailoring. The unique staff provides the MEB with the capability to conduct the other key tasks in ways no other brigade may do. This is discussed further in the chapter on each MEB key task.

2-11. Beyond its three organic units (HHC, NSC, and BSB), the MEB has no fixed structure. When assigned or attached in support of a theater specific operation, OPORD, OPLAN, or CONPLAN, the brigade staff will conduct a mission analysis to determine the capabilities, task organization, and command and support relationships necessary to accomplish the mission. The organization is tailored to respond to the elements of METT-TC. It receives a mix of modular units from detachments to battalions. Figure 2-1 depicts possible units task-organized to the MEB for a specific mission. In many cases, the broad geographic responsibilities and extensive functional capabilities that the MEB represents will require a variety of subordinate, functionally based formations, mission tailored for the environment.

2-12. It will be a challenge for the MEB to integrate task-organized units and employ them as cohesive tactical formations the way units with organic subunits, leaders, and Soldiers can. The trust and teamwork required to conduct close combat with combined arms formations (both technical/functional and maneuver) is difficult to develop quickly. The Army force generation collective training events and continuous in-theater training will be essential to prepare the unit, develop trust and teamwork, and certify leaders.

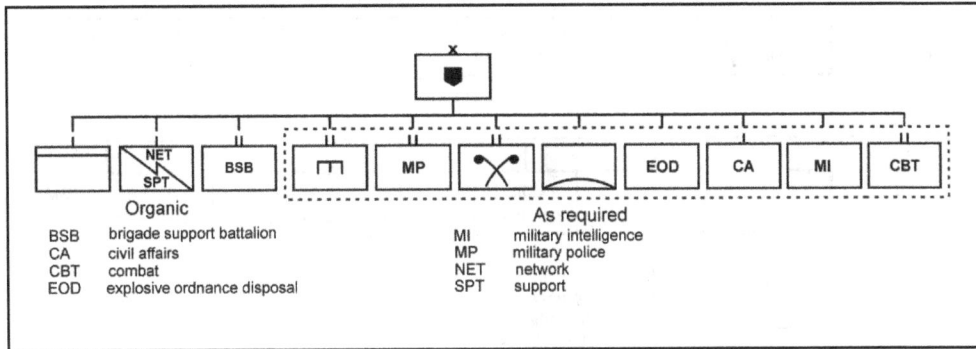

Figure 2-1. A possible MEB task organization

HHC, MEB

2-13. The HHC provides the basis for effective C2 in support of the MEB commander. Its primary mission is to provide C2 capabilities for the MEB across full spectrum operations in both complex and urban terrain and against conventional and asymmetric threat capabilities. This is accomplished by core staff from the MEB HHC and their associated signal support. See figure 2-2, page 2-4, for the major elements within the HHC organization.

2-14. The MEB staff is unique in its capabilities to C2 many of the tasks associated with its mission. No other brigade level organization has such a large and complete organic staff with the capabilities required to conduct these operations.

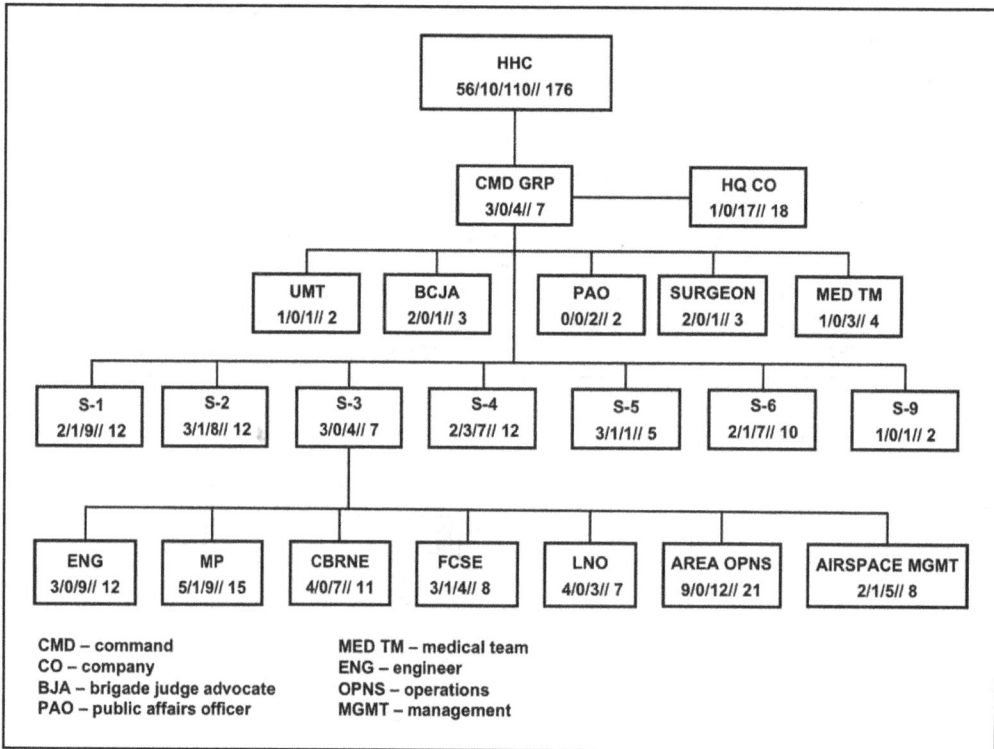

Figure 2-2. MEB HHC organization

2-15. The command group contains the commander and deputy commanding officer (DCO) and provides continuous command presence at one location or the ability to provide C2 for split-based operations. The executive officer, command sergeant major, and three enlisted members complete the command group.

2-16. The headquarters company contains the company commander and first sergeant and 12 other personnel to include a food management team, supply personnel, and an administrative noncommissioned officer (NCO). The company provides sustainment support for the MEB headquarters and staff.

2-17. The area operations section and airspace management section, along with the fires cell (FC) under the operations staff officer (S-3), gives the MEB the ability to be assigned an AO and control terrain. The area operations section includes engineer, area security, protection, ADC, infantry, and CBRN staff members. The airspace management section includes airspace command and control (AC2), electronic warfare system operator, and tactical airspace integration system operator staff to provide the MEB with the ability to control Army airspace within its assigned AO.

2-18. The FC includes a fire support coordinator (FSCOORD), fire support officer (FSO), and targeting staff. The MEB depends upon indirect fires and counterfire radar support from a fires brigade or BCT and must be augmented with forward observers and the ability to lase targets within its assigned AO. Based on METT-TC, the MEB may have an artillery element in a command or support relationship to provide indirect fires in support of its AO.

2-19. The S-3 operations section is unique due to the depth and breadth of its capabilities. It contains engineer, MP, and CBRNE cells that provide a staff that is designed to integrate and synchronize the conduct of MANSPT operations. This capability allows the staff to perform the MANSPT tasks associated with full spectrum operations in a more complete manner than any other brigade level staff. The engineer operations cell includes combat engineer, reconnaissance, terrain data, and power system technician staff that provides the MEB with the ability to conduct most engineer operations. The MP operations cell staff includes maneuver and mobility support, protective services, and I/R expertise that provides the MEB with the ability to C2 most MP operations. The CBRNE operations cell includes intelligence, CBRN, and the fusion of EOD staff to provide the ability to C2 many CBRNE operations. The liaison team can provide three 2-person liaison teams and a construction inspector. These assets give the MEB the ability to integrate with other organizations and inspect construction performed in their AO by military units, HN, or contractors.

2-20. The typical S-1, brigade surgeon section, medical treatment team, chaplain, public affairs, and S-4 logistics section, along with the organic BSB, provide the MEB with sustainment capability.

2-21. The S-2 intelligence section includes vulnerability assessment, intelligence analyst, criminal intelligence staff members, and UAS operators (but no assigned UASs). If there is a significant threat, the MEB must be augmented or task-organized with ISR capability, normally from the battlefield surveillance brigade (BFSB), when assigned an AO.

2-22. The S-5 plans section includes engineer, MP, CBRN, infantry, and power systems technical staff members to provide the necessary expertise to produce plans that capture both operational and tactical considerations.

2-23. The S-6 communication section and the organic signal network support company provide the MEB with communications connectivity that most functional brigades do not have.

2-24. All of the sections within the headquarters will be organized according to METT-TC factors to support the organization and operation of command posts (CPs). The MEB will normally field two CPs (a main CP and a tactical CP). The brigade will also have the capability to deploy command groups for short or limited duration requirements as CPs. The MEB can also use the tactical CP as an early entry command post. (See chapter 3.)

2-25. Key command and staff positions within the MEB organization will be uniquely identified as requiring the special skills of the chemical, engineer, or MP branches. The staff must synchronize and integrate many unique functional branches into brigade level operations. The range of employment options requires the staff to have an understanding of the joint operations. The Army has established a new special reporting code (SRC) 01C (chemical/engineer/MP immaterial) to identify the duty positions of commander, DCO, executive officer (XO), S-3, S-3 operations officer, LNO (team chief), and headquarters company commander.

NETWORK SUPPORT COMPANY

2-26. The NSC is intended to establish the organic communications for the MEB and provides the following communication capabilities:
- A tactical internet (TI) supporting Force XXI Battle Command Brigade and Below (FBCB2) SA and C2 data exchange capabilities to maneuver, logistics, and C2 elements.
- Combat net radio retransmission of voice using—
  - Single-Channel Ground and Airborne Radio System (SINCGARS).
  - Improved high frequency radio.
  - Single channel tactical satellite (TACSAT) for C2.

Note: The NSC has a secondary role of data retransmission where enhanced position location reporting system (EPLRS), TI, or Army Common User System capabilities do not exist for the MEB.

- Global Broadcast Service with the ability to receive high bandwidth products such as imagery, logistics data, and digital map information to support ABCS employment by commanders and staffs.
- Multichannel TACSAT to extend the range of the MEB's communications services.

- Management of the MEB C2 network.
- Establishment of primary command post voice/video capabilities for the MEB.
- Field level maintenance of organic communication-electronic and communications security (COMSEC) equipment.
- Planning for all matters concerning signal operations, automation, management, and information security for the MEB.

BRIGADE SUPPORT BATTALION

2-27. The BSB is the organic organization providing C2 of distribution, maintenance, and medical support for the MEB and consists of a headquarters and headquarters detachment (HHD), a distribution company, and an SMC. Like the NSC, it is an organization designed to meet the needs of all of the organic elements of the MEB and selected task-organized units. As the task organization of the MEB exceeds BSB capabilities, the BSB must be task-organized with commensurate sustainment structure, which is normally requested through the MEB to the sustainment brigade. An example of this would be the provision of a forward support company (FSC) when an engineer battalion is assigned to the MEB.

2-28. The HHD, BSB provides C2 support to the commander for units organic or attached to the BSB, which is normally located where it can best support the MEB based on METT-TC. As a general planning factor, the BSB has the capability to provide logistic C2 support to 5 to 8 battalions within the AO over unspecified distances, via a combination of throughput and supply point distribution methods from the BSB. The BSB may require additional capabilities based on the logistics estimate prepared to determine sustainment capabilities, anticipate support requirements, identify and resolve shortfalls, and develop support plans. It requires the BSB to coordinate local area support through the sustainment brigade when supported battalions cannot be reached due to excessive distance or heightened threat conditions. Additional medical support is provided on an area basis by U.S. Army Medical Command units.

2-29. The distribution company is employed in the brigade support area (BSA) providing logistics support to the brigade. It operates as part of the BSB with subordinate elements that operate throughout the brigade area.

2-30. The SMC headquarters provides command, control, administrative, and logistical support for an automotive/armament maintenance platoon, ground support equipment maintenance platoon, and electronic equipment maintenance platoon in support of the MEB. The number and type of modules attached to the SMC may fluctuate based on METT-TC.

2-31. The BSB has the following capabilities:
- HHD, BSB.
    - C2 of subordinate elements providing logistics support.
    - Support operation services to include critical coordination with gaining units/organizations receiving platoons and teams from MEB functional battalions.
    - Readiness oversight with linkages to organic distribution company class IX section.
    - Field feeding for the HHD, distribution company, signal network support company, and field feeding support for an additional 350 transient personnel. Maximum field feeding estimated to be for 599 personnel.
    - The combat service support automation management office (CSSAMO) section provides support of all logistics information automation system and Standard Army Management Information Systems (STAMIS) within the brigade. They provide complete customer-oriented assistance in using and operating logistics automated systems.
- Distribution company.
    - C2 of supply distribution points, transportation, fuel and water support to the MEB.
    - Daily receipt, temporary storage, and issuance of all classes of supply (less class VIII) to the MEB.
    - The transportation of up to 286 short tons of cargo daily.
    - Class III (B) retail fuel support to the brigade of up to 70,000 gallons per day.

- Water purification up to 30,000 gallons per day, and storage/distribution for the brigade of up to 22,000 gallons per day.
- Support maintenance company (SMC) (with assigned platoons).
  - C2 of subordinate elements performing field maintenance functions.
  - Consolidated unit administration, maintenance, supply, and field feeding support for up to 250 assigned personnel.
  - Maintenance control, shop stock, and wheeled vehicle recovery capability.
  - Field maintenance and technical inspection of small arms, artillery, fire control equipment, armament, tracked and wheeled vehicles.
  - Field maintenance and technical inspection of utilities equipment, power generators, construction equipment, quartermaster, and chemical equipment.
  - Field maintenance, operation, and technical inspection of microwave equipment, COMSEC/radio equipment, support electronics devices, and radar.

SUPPORTED COMMANDS

SUPPORT OF THE DIVISION AND ABOVE

2-32. The MEB is primarily designed to provide support to the division but is capable of being employed to provide support to EAD organizations as well. The division is the primary tactical warfighting headquarters for C2 of up to six BCTs, the five types of supporting brigades (to include the MEB), and other functional brigades conducting full spectrum operations. The division shapes the operation for subordinate brigades, resources them for assigned missions, coordinates, synchronizes, and sequences their operations. The MEB and its capabilities provide the division with the ability to shape operations and provide selected sustainment for other brigades (for example, I/R and general engineering). The division uses BCTs to fight battles and engagements and uses its attached support brigades primarily for shaping and sustaining operations and to complement or reinforce the BCTs. The MEB will normally be assigned an AO by the division that is focused on support area activities. This AO may contain all or part of a division's supporting sustainment brigade and other tenant units or headquarters positioned in support of the division. The MEB would conduct support area operations when given this role by the division. (See chapter 6.) (See FMI 3-0.1 for a discussion of modular force headquarters.)

2-33. Each MEB is uniquely tailored and task-organized for the role it is projected to perform for the echelon that it is supporting. The MEB will typically receive its missions from a division or other echelon headquarters it is supporting. Typical MEB support to the division (and potentially EAD organizations) would include the key tasks discussed on page 2-2. Of special note is the ability to conduct operations within a movement corridor (see chapter 5). As part of its support to a division, the MEB may simultaneously be supporting BCT offensive operations while conducting defensive operations in its assigned AO or division area. It may also be conducting stability operations in its own AO while it is supporting other units conducting stability operations in their AOs. These examples may be sequential or in some cases, occur simultaneously.

2-34. The key tasks associated with the MEB cover a broad range of potential support to the division or other echelon that is being supported. Depending on the types and numbers of elements assigned, the MEB can perform a significant portion of the functional or combined arms missions/tasks typically associated with CA, CBRN, engineer, EOD, and MP forces. The MEB is also capable of providing C2 to other forces, to include but not limited to, AMD elements and a TCF.

EXAMPLE

As an example of support to a division, the MEB is capable of providing the C2 headquarters for a division river crossing operation while conducting other minor operations. The MEB could do this one of two ways.

- The first is for the commander and DCO to each command different operations of the brigade and use the main CP for the largest operation.

- The second, with a more complex crossing, is for the division commander to position one deputy commanding general (DCG) and mobile command group with the MEB to perform as the crossing site commander using the staff of the MEB to facilitate C2.

Units are task-organized to the MEB to support this type of a gap crossing. A similar role could also be performed by the MEB in support of a complex passage of lines.

2-35. While capable of performing multiple simultaneous tasks, a higher headquarters must ensure that it does not exceed the span of control of the MEB with the number and types of missions that are given to the MEB. When the amount of functional missions challenge the ability of the MEB to perform its multifunctional role, functional brigades may need to be task-organized to the division. For example, an MEB responsible for a complex AO is not able to also perform as a headquarters supporting a major division gap-crossing operation within the division AO. In this example, another MEB or an engineer brigade would need to support the division to provide the necessary C2 headquarters for this mission. Multiple MEBs may be assigned to a division or higher echelon.

2-36. When assigned the mission of supporting EAD, joint, or multinational forces, the MEB could be task organized with other Service or national units and integrate staff augmentation to C2 a variety of elements necessary to support those forces. The MEB may or may not be assigned its own AO in such a role. The MEB could conduct operations to support the corps or joint command. When assigned to a joint command, the MEB may provide C2 of the joint security area (JSA). In this case, the MEB commander may be designated as the joint security coordinator by a joint force commander. The MEB may be required to establish or support a theater-level Joint Security Coordination Center. (FM 3-0 provides an example of the MEB being OPCON to a MEF that highlights the modular nature of Army forces and the role that the MEB plays in supporting Army modularity.)

SUPPORT OF OTHER BRIGADES

2-37. The MEB could be tasked to provide support to other divisional units to include BCTs, functional brigades, or other support brigades. The division could task the MEB to conduct certain operations in general support (GS) to the division with selected tasks requiring DS. When providing GS, the other brigades in the division would coordinate their requirements with the division staff and the MEB. Based on the division commander's intent, the MEB would recommend priorities, task organization, and provide directed support, refining specific details through collaboration with the BCTs and other support brigades to accomplish missions.

2-38. MEBs can support BCT operations in a variety of ways. In general, the division may task organize parts of the MEB to the BCTs for a specific mission or the MEB may complement or reinforce the BCT with forces under MEB control performing selected missions/tasks within the AO of the BCT. Examples include—

- Assisting in the construction of a BCT's initial detainee collection points.
- Assisting in construction of defensive positions.
- Building a bridge over a gap.
- Performing decontamination at a site within a BCT AO.
- Performing other tasks that are of a more temporary and specific nature.

2-39. Elements out of the MEB may also provide specific CBRN or engineer technical reconnaissance capability to a BCT AO. MPs may secure a sensitive site within a BCT AO. CBRN, engineer, EOD, and MP forces may provide a wide range of support to the BCT or other brigades within a division AO.

2-40. The MEB may also support mission staging operations (MSO) where a BCT rests, refits, and receives large quantities of supplies. This may occur with the MEB having been assigned the AO within which the MSO will occur or in another AO with the MEB providing support through MANSPT operations.

EMPLOYMENT EXAMPLES

2-41. Figure 2-3 is an example of a division task organization that contains a single MEB. This particular example does not provide the division with any functional brigades. Units that might otherwise be found in functional CBRN, engineer, MP, or other brigades would likely be task-organized to the MEB. Support that might otherwise be drawn from a functional brigade would likely come from the MEB if the necessary assets have been task-organized to the MEB.

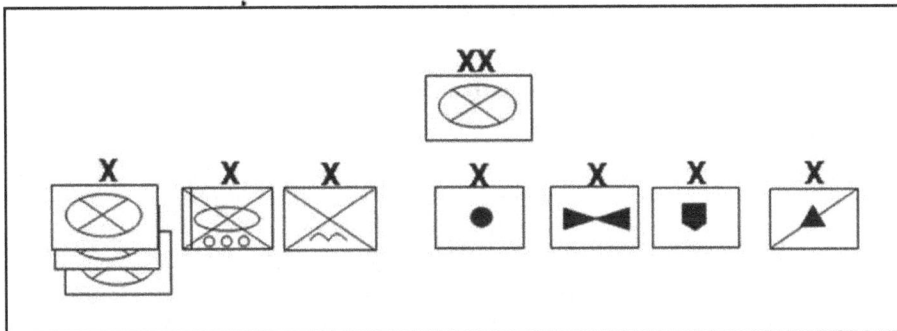

Figure 2-3. Example division organization

2-42. Figure 2-4 provides an example of the MEB organic units and of forces that may be assigned or attached to the MEB in support of a division. This is but one of many possible task organizations for the MEB. In special situations, the MEB may also have EOD, CA, and AMD units assigned or attached to it.

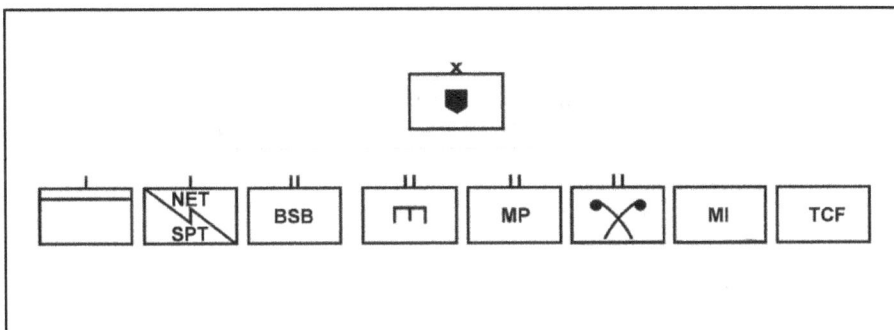

Figure 2-4. Example MEB organization

2-43. The effectiveness and success of the MEB depends on the synergy leveraged from integrating and synchronizing contributions from all attached or OPCON units. Depending on the METT-TC factors, MEB can task-organize assigned units into combined arms TFs and company teams. These combined arms elements can then perform both pure functional tasks and MANSPT collective tasks more effectively and efficiently. (See also chapters 5 and 7.) The MI unit reflected in this example (figure 2-4) would likely come from the BFSB and be task-organized to an MEB when the METT-TC factors associated with a particular AO require this augmentation of the MEB, similar to the organic MI companies that are found in all BCTs and the ACR. The TCF shown in this example could be made up of a variety of maneuver forces and its actual size and composition would be based on the level III threat it would be focused against. The MEB is not designed to C2 multiple maneuver battalions.

RELATIONSHIP TO FUNCTIONAL AND OTHER SUPPORT BRIGADES

2-44. The MEB bridges a capability gap between the limited functional units (CBRN/engineer/MP) of the BCTs and the more capable functional brigades. This headquarters provides more functional staff capability than BCTs but usually less than a functional brigade. The key difference between the MEB and the functional brigades is the breadth and depth of the MEB's multifunctional staff. The MEB provides complementary and reinforcing capabilities. Based on its task organization and mission, the MEB can detach functional modular units or combined arms elements (TFs or company teams) to support the BCTs and potentially other multifunctional brigades, providing both functional and combined arms support across the AO of the higher headquarters.

2-45. The MEB is normally employed when there is a requirement to C2 combined arms operations that are focused on the key tasks of conduct maneuver support operations, conduct support area operations, conduct consequence management operations, and conduct stability operations. When the situation changes to require a purely functional approach or exceeds the C2 focus of the MEB, selected functional missions should be transferred to functional brigades. Missions better performed by functional brigades could include counter-CBRNE weapons and threats in the operational area, major (several battalions) complex CBRNE operations, major focused combat and or general engineering operations, large scale interment/resettlement operations (brigade level), or major integrated MP operations. The presence of a CBRN, engineer, or MP brigade does not negate the need for an MEB to perform other functional-related missions within its own AO or potentially at other selected locations within the division AO.

2-46. The MEB may also provide C2 for assets moved into the AOR but not yet needed by other units during the current phase of operations. The MEB can C2 units in transition as they arrive in the division AO or are in between task organizations and detach these units to provide added support to BCTs or functional brigades when needed. The MEB capability to support reception, staging, onward movement, and integration enables our modular Army to employ assets when and where required.

2-47. The MEB may control the terrain where other support or functional brigades are located. They will synchronize their operations with all of the other tenant support brigades. The MEB may require capabilities in a command or support relationship from the other support brigades. The MEB will have some C2 authority over the tenant organizations within the MEB's AO to conduct security and defense; this may be TACON for security and defense. (See chapter 6.)

2-48. The MEB complements or reinforces the other support brigades. For example, the MEB can be expected to coordinate or provide protection of designated sustainment packages or convoys from the sustainment brigade to the BCTs or other brigades (functional or support) that are in support of the echelon that the MEB is supporting.

Chapter 3

Battle Command for the MEB

Each MEB headquarters begins with the same basic organization structure, staffing, and capabilities. The personality of the commander, the experience of the staff, the directed mission, task-organized units, and staff augmentation will require each MEB to exercise battle command with some variations. This chapter discusses principles and operational concepts of C2 for the MEB. Some procedures for the MEB must still be developed or refined by units in the field and shared with new MEBs as those units are formed and are prepared for employment. Battle command and mission command are applied as described in FM 3-0, FM 5-0, FM 6-0, and FMI 5-0.1. The MEB C2 system supports the commander as the MEB conducts operations.

COMMAND AND CONTROL

3-1. *Command* is the authority that a commander in the Armed Forces lawfully exercises over subordinates by virtue of rank or assignment. Command includes the authority and responsibility for effectively using available resources and for planning the employment, organizing, directing, coordinating, and controlling of military forces to accomplish assigned missions. It also includes responsibility for health, welfare, morale, and discipline of assigned personnel (the definition was shortened; the complete definition is printed in the glossary). The elements of command are authority, decisionmaking, and leadership. (See FM 6-0.) Commanders are responsible for applying the leadership element of combat power and training subordinate leaders to reinforce that element.

3-2. *Control* in the context of C2, is the regulation of forces and warfighting functions to accomplish the mission in accordance with the commander's intent (the definition was shortened; the complete definition is printed in the glossary). It includes collecting, processing, displaying, storing, and disseminating relevant information for creating the common operational picture, and using information, primarily by the staff, during the operations process. Control allows commanders to direct the execution of operations to conform to their commander's intent (FM 6-0).

3-3. *Command and control* is the exercise of authority and direction by a properly designated commander over assigned and attached forces in the accomplishment of the mission. Commanders perform C2 functions through a C2 system (the definition was shortened; the complete definition is printed in the glossary). C2 comprises the ability to envision activities over time and space necessary to achieve an end state, to translate and communicate that vision into a brief but clear intent, to formulate operational concepts, and to provide the force of will through the presence of leadership throughout the AO. These abilities enable the MEB to concentrate assets at the time and place necessary to accomplish all assigned and implied missions. Command is the art of war within the domain of the commander. Control is the science of war within the purview of the staff. C2 has two components—the commander and the C2 system. The MEB commander uses the C2 system to exercise C2 over forces to accomplish a mission.

3-4. *Battle command* is the art and science of understanding, visualizing, describing, directing, leading, and assessing forces to impose the commander's will on hostile, thinking, and adaptive enemy. Battle command applies leadership to translate decisions into actions—by synchronizing forces and warfighting functions in time, space, and purpose—to accomplish missions (FM 3-0).

ROLE OF THE COMMANDER

3-5. Commanders are the key to C2. (See FM 3-0.) Commanders assess the situation, make decisions, and direct actions. (See FM 6-0 for further discussion.) The MEB commanders' knowledge, experience, and personality determine how they interact with their units through C2. The commanders understand, visualize, describes, direct, lead, and assess. Battle command describes the commanders' role in the operations process. Commanders decide what they need to do and the best method to do it. They lead their units through the process in mission accomplishment. Commanders drive the process through mission command.

3-6. MEB commanders establish a command climate for units, prepare them for operations, command them during operations, and continually assess subordinates. Commanders use the warfighting functions to help them exercise battlefield command. They use Army procedural control and Army positive control. (See FM 3-0.) The MEB's C2 system will be operated based on doctrine and modified to meet the commanders' personality. Within the limitations of the current C2 systems architecture, commanders establish a system to meet the unique demands that they place on it, the abilities and personalities of subordinates, and the capabilities of the organizations assigned, attached, or OPCON to the MEB. Commanders visualize the nature and design of operations in terms of time, space, resources, purpose, and action using mission command, the C2 system, and the operation process to facilitate battle command. (See FM 3-0 for a discussion of leadership as an element of power, and FM 6-22 for a broader discussion of leadership.)

MISSION COMMAND

3-7. *Mission command* is the conduct of military operations through decentralized execution based on mission orders (this definition was shortened; the complete definition is printed in the glossary). Mission orders leave the *how* of mission accomplishment to the subordinates by allowing them maximum freedom of planning and action to accomplish missions. Successful mission command results from subordinate leaders exercising disciplined initiative to accomplish missions within the commander's intent. Mission command requires an environment of trust and mutual understanding.

Note: There are times when factors such as high risk or the technical nature of some operations will require the MEB commander to be more prescriptive in guidance. (See chapter 6.)

3-8. The four elements of mission command are as follows: (See FM 3-0.)

- Commander's Intent. The *commander's intent* is a clear, concise statement of what the force must do and the conditions the force must establish with respect to the enemy, terrain, and civil considerations that represent the desired end state (FM 3-0). MEB commanders formulate and communicate their intent to ensure unity of effort during operations, allowing subordinates to exercise disciplined initiative.

- Initiative (Individual). *Initiative (individual)* is the willingness to act in the absence of orders when existing orders no longer fit the situation, or when unforeseen opportunities or threats arise. (See FM 3-0.) MEB subordinates decide how to achieve their assigned missions within the delegated freedom of action and the exercise of disciplined initiative during execution; they have an absolute responsibility to fulfill the commander's intent.

- Mission Orders. A mission order is a technique for developing orders that emphasizes to subordinates the results to be attained, not how they are to achieve them. It provides maximum freedom of action in determining how to best accomplish the assigned missions. (See FM 3-0.) The MEB commander intervenes to direct coordination, restore operations, or exploit success. At a minimum, mission orders state the following:
  - Task organization.
  - Situation.
  - Commander's intent and concept of operations.
  - Unit mission.

■ Subordinate unit missions/important tasks for each unit.

■ Mission essential coordinating instructions and minimum necessary control measures.

● Resource Allocation. MEB commanders allocate appropriate resources to subordinates to enable them to accomplish their missions. When conditions change, commanders may change priorities, change tasks to subordinates, change task organization, and change the resource allocation accordingly. If commanders determine they lack sufficient resources, they request additional support. If additional resources are not available, commanders execute sequential operations. Commanders also must consider information as a resource and share it through all levels of their command using personal leadership and the unit's information systems (INFOSYS).

SYNCHRONIZING PLANS WITH OTHER HEADQUARTERS

3-9. The MEB routinely conducts planning with higher, lower, adjacent, supported, supporting headquarters, and interagency organizations. The commanders and staff ensure that the MEB plans are properly synchronized with the other organization.

3-10. Commanders should look for disconnects or disagreement between their staff and the other organization's staff. These frequently occur due to different situational understanding and perspectives. The executive officer should try to resolve these differences then the commander should discuss them with the other headquarters commander or leader as the two staffs work to develop their plans and orders.

RISK

3-11. Commanders may assess, evaluate, and decide when to accept prudent risk to create opportunities to achieve decisive results. Risk is an element of operational design. (See FM 3-0.) The MEB will often be required to accept operational or tactical risk somewhere to increase support elsewhere—to balance effort between support area operations and MANSPT operations. The MEB can mitigate this risk by developing branches and sequels and by providing subordinate commanders "be prepared" missions so that they are better prepared to react to planned and unplanned events and opportunities and changing mission priorities. The "be prepared" planning effort increases mental and organizational agility to respond to inevitable changes.

3-12. The MEB can mitigate some tactical risks by shifting resources, changing priorities, phasing or sequencing operations, reducing a subordinate units assigned tasks or size of AO, and deciding where to assume risk when required. (FM 3-90 and FM 6-0 discuss tactical risk. See FM 5-19 for discussion on risk management and composite risk management [CRM]).

3-13. Some high risk situations may require the MEB commander to exercise detailed command and less mission command. (See FM 6-0.) For example, an MEB commander may use detailed command where positive or central control is necessary to increase the probability of a specific effect occurring or when time and procedural discipline is critical to success. To use positive control, the MEB C2 system must be properly functioning.

COMMAND AND CONTROL SYSTEM

3-14. The MEB must be proficient on the GMET of conduct C2 and these supporting tasks that are part of the operations process discussed in chapter 4:

● Plan an operation.

● Prepare for an operation.

● Execute an operation.

● Assess an operation.

3-15. The *C2 system* is the arrangement of personnel, information management, procedures, and equipment and facilities essential for the commander to conduct operations (FM 6-0).

- **Personnel**. The C2 system in an MEB begins with people. No amount of technology can reduce the importance of the human dimension since combat involves Soldiers.
- **Information management is the science of using information systems (INFOSYSs) and methods**. Information management (IM) consists of the INFOSYS C2, information systems, and relevant information (RI). The C2 INFOSYS provides the commander with a major physical component of the C2 system. These computer and communication systems provide an accuracy and reliability of information that can accelerate decisionmaking in the MEB. The C2 INFOSYS also makes mission execution efficient and effective, allowing the commanders and staffs to spend more time and energy on the art and human dimension of C2.
- **Procedures**. Procedures are standard and detailed sequences of activities in the MEB to accomplish tasks. They govern actions in the C2 system to effectively and efficiently exercise C2. Adhering to procedures minimizes confusion, misunderstanding, and hesitance as commanders rapidly shift forces to meet contingencies.
- **Equipment and facilities**. The equipment and facilities provide sustainment and a work environment for the other elements of the C2 system.

3-16. The C2 system supports the commander by performing three functions—
- Creating and maintaining the common operational picture (COP).
- Supporting decisionmaking by improving its speed and accuracy.
- Supporting preparation and communication of execution information.

3-17. The MEB headquarters may be used as an additional division command post or to reinforce one. The breadth and depth of the MEB C2 system provides it with the capability to be collocated or linked with a division command group and C2 some division operations. An example would be a deliberate division gap (river) crossing operation under the C2 of a DCG using the mobile command group and the MEB main CP. A similar example would be a complex passage of lines. Depending on the complexity of the operation, this may be the only mission the MEB could support during that timeframe.

3-18. The commander decides how to use the MEB DCO and XO. Considerations include the personalities, individual strengths and weaknesses, and the unit's mission. The commander uses the DCO to help command; this gives the MEB the ability to have the commander continuously available in the main CP or to command a separate operation. The commander may use the DCO to C2 specific areas within the MEB so that the commander may focus elsewhere. The XO normally performs the role of chief of staff in the main CP.

PERSONNEL

3-19. This section includes organization of the staff for C2. (See appendix A, appendix B, and chapter 2.) The staff operates the commander's C2 system. (See FM 6-0 for further discussion of staff functions.) The MEB's staff sections normally are distributed among three C2 organizations—the command groups, tactical (TAC) CP, and main CP. The MEB commander organizes the staff within each CP to perform essential staff functions to aid him or her with planning and in controlling operations. Enhanced CP capabilities allow the commander to maintain CP functionality regardless of the spatial positioning of the staff. The modularized design of each function (for example, maneuver and MANSPT, protection, and ISR) provides commanders with the flexibility to tailor their CPs based on their assessment of the current and future situation.

3-20. These C2 organizations are normally positioned within the MEB's AO to maintain flexibility, redundancy, survivability, and mobility. The CP of the BSB, while not a MEB-level CP, performs functions that have significant impact on MEB operations. Accordingly, the BSB staff is often closely involved in parallel or collaborative planning with the MEB CPs.

Command Post Organizations

3-21. The MEB commander may organize command groups, TAC CPs, and a main CP.

- The *command group* consists of the commander and selected staff members who accompany commanders to enable them to exercise C2 away from a command post. (FMI 5-0.1)
- A *command post* is a unit's or subunit's headquarters where the commander and the staff perform their activities (JP 1-02). CPs are the principal facilities commanders use to control operations; it is a CP regardless of whether the commander is present.

3-22. The MEB may use command groups to observe critical events and direct C2 of MEB operations. They are not permanent organizations and are organized based on the mission.

Command Group

3-23. Command group 1 is for the commander and command group 2 is for the DCO C2 organization. The command groups are formed any time the MEB commander or deputy commander relocates to control the operation. They will be equipped to operate separately from a CP whenever commanders or their deputy commander must locate to influence operations with rapid decisions and orders. The commander will determine the location of the command group.

3-24. The commander chooses how often to control operations from the command group and positions it at the decisive point to observe, influence, sense, and ensure communications. The DCO's command group complements the commander's command group in the direction of C2 of the MEB. Command group 2 is organized when the MEB commander requires it to control an operation or the commander needs an additional senior leader presence to influence the operations with rapid decisions and orders. The DCO uses the same considerations as commanders in positioning their command groups in the AO.

- The commander may control operations from the command group and locates near the most critical event, normally with the main effort CP. From this location, the commander is better able to observe critical events, maintain communications, and sense operations. Despite the increased capability provided by the C2 INFOSYS, command remains a personal endeavor and often requires a commander's on-site assessment and leadership. Commanders should leverage the C2 INFOSYS to allow adequate capabilities within the CP physical view of subordinates and the terrain without affecting their decision-making ability.
- Commanders consider the following in determining their location in the AO:
  - Linkage of the ABCS network to make timely decisions, including the ability to judge the progress, condition, and morale of their forces. Within technical limitations, communications systems adapt to the needs of the commander, not vice versa.
  - Time and location of critical events and/or decision points that have the greatest impact on mission accomplishment. Ideally, commanders select a location where they can observe the conditions that aid in making a critical decision.
  - Security for the command group, including the commander's personal protection.

Tactical Command Post

3-25. The tactical command post (TAC CP) contains a tailored portion of the MEB's headquarters to control current operations. The TAC CP is established when the commander must be positioned away from the main CP location for an extended period, when METT-TC factors do not permit the commander access to the main CP, and when the main CP is moving. The TAC CP focuses on assisting the commander with C2 of current operations. It is commander focused and execution centric. Usually, or in accordance with the commander's guidance, the MEB S-3 is responsible for the TAC CP.

3-26. While desirable, a 24/7 capability is not an overriding consideration in forming the TAC CP. TAC CP functions depend on connectivity to the main CP. The organization of the TAC CP is smaller and more austere than the main CP. Its connectivity to the more robust main CP by way of the ABCS suite of systems allows for efficient collaboration to ensure that it gets the required information necessary for the commander's decision-making process. The TAC CP can execute collaborative, distributed, and simultaneous decisionmaking to translate the decision to action. This allows rapid decisionmaking focused on current operations.

Main Command Post

3-27. The main command post contains the portion of the MEB's headquarters in which the majority of planning, analysis, and coordination occurs. The main CP is the commander's primary C2 facility. The MEB XO normally supervises the staff activities and functions of the main CP. It operates from a relatively secure location and moves as required to maintain C2 of the operation. The main CP integrates and synchronizes the conduct of MEB operations and the staff mission functions of ISR; planning; sustainment; and command, control, communications, and computers.

3-28. The main CP monitors all operations, coordinates with higher and adjacent units, and provides in-depth analysis of information and intelligence to provide recommendations to the commander. If the TAC CP is not employed, the main CP controls tactical operations. The main CP is the focal point for intelligence operations in the MEB and provides SU to the commander. The main CP monitors and anticipates the commander's decision points and commander's critical information requirement (CCIR).

Early-Entry Command Post

3-29. An early-entry command post contains tailored portions of the MEB's headquarters for a specific mission over a specific time. It normally includes members of the TAC CP and additional planners, intelligence analysts, liaison officers, and others as required. The MEB's modified table of organization and equipment (MTOE) does not provide the unit with a stand-alone early-entry command post (EECP). Since the brigade may be one of the first to deploy into an AO, it should consider establishing an EECP.

3-30. The EECP allows a small part of the headquarters to deploy early into the AO, establish an initial C2 presence, link up with other organizations, assess the situation on the ground to refine plans, and prepare for the arrival of the brigade. The EECP would allow continuous C2 of the MEB mission as the brigade deployed into the AO. The EECP could accept C2 of other early entry units that will be part of the MEB as they enter the AO. The EECP is typically an ad hoc and temporary C2 arrangement.

BSB CP

3-31. The BSB CP has a special role in controlling and coordinating the administrative and logistical support for the MEB. The improvements in communications and INFOSYS means the MEB does not have to operate a rear CP collocated with the BSB CP. If necessary, MEB sustainment staff (S-1, S-4, and surgeon), may locate portions of their sections with the BSB CP.

3-32. The BSB CP performs the following functions for the MEB:
- Tracking the current battle so it may anticipate support requirements before units request them.
- Serving as the entry point for units entering the MEB AO.
- Monitoring main supply routes (MSR) and controlling sustainment vehicle traffic.
- Coordinating the evacuation of casualties, equipment, and detainees.
- Coordinating movement of personnel killed in action.
- Coordinating with the sustainment brigade for resupply requirements.
- Assisting in operation of a detainee facility or a dislocated civilian (DC) point.
- Providing ad hoc representation to the main CP to support the logistics section.

LIAISON OFFICER TEAM

3-33. The MEB LNO team is designed to go to the controlling or supported headquarters, especially if the controlling headquarters is other than the U.S. Army. The LNO team cannot provide liaison to all of the other types of units that might be in the MEB AO. Those other units should send LNOs to the MEB.

3-34. The MEB LNO team provides liaison, when required, to designated division, corps, SOF, joint, interagency, multinational, multinational units in the AO to ensure effective coordination between the designated unit and the MEB. The LNOs convey information and its meaning and context by interpreting and explaining it. It is essential to have an LNO at the immediate higher headquarters during development of plans and orders to help their staff fully understand the MEB capabilities and limitations and how to best employ it. After the higher headquarters is more familiar with the MEB, the LNO can be reassigned. The LNO team may need to be augmented to effectively link the brigade with multiple headquarters in a complex operation. For example, due to the lack of organic ISR capability, the MEB may need to provide a LNO to the BFSB to ensure the flow of information needed for MEB operations. At times, the MEB may need to provide an LNO to a unit that receives significant assets from the MEB in a command or support relationship. Other units in the MEB AO may need to provide LNOs to the MEB to coordinate their operations.

SUCCESSION OF COMMAND

3-35. Succession of command occurs automatically on the death, capture, or evacuation of the brigade commander. It also occurs when communications are lost with the commander for an extended period of time. The brigade must treat succession of command as a type of drill. The MEB should establish an SOP and consider METT-TC factors and other relevant considerations when determining succession of command.

3-36. All leaders must understand the procedures required for a quick, smooth succession. The following is one logical succession of command:

- Brigade commander.
- DCO.
- BSB commander.
- Brigade XO.
- Brigade S-3.

INFORMATION SUPERIORITY (INCLUDES INFORMATION MANAGEMENT)

3-37. *Information superiority* (IS) is the operational advantage derived from the ability to collect, process, and disseminate an uninterrupted flow of information while exploiting or denying an adversary's ability to do the same (JP 3-13). The Army integrates IS in the C2 warfighting function. (See FM 3-0.)

3-38. To counter threats and focus on various audiences, commanders understand, visualize, describe, and direct efforts that contribute to IS. These contributors (see FM 3-0) fall into four primary areas:

- Army information tasks—tasks used to shape the OE.
- Intelligence, surveillance, and reconnaissance—activities conducted to develop knowledge about the OE.
- Knowledge management—the art of using information to increase knowledge.
- Information management—the science of using information systems and methods.

3-39. The Army conducts five information tasks to shape the OE. These are information engagement, C2 warfare, information protection, operations security, and military deception. The Army integrates the IS contributors in the C2 warfighting function. (See FM 3-0.) The MEB may conduct or support these information tasks.

3-40. IM is a continuing activity that the MEB must perform. It uses procedures and information systems to collect, process, store, display, and disseminate information. (FM 3-0). Information management includes RI and INFOSYS. (See FM 6-0 and appendix C.)

3-41. Proper information management ensures MEB commanders receives the information they need to make timely decisions. It consists of relevant information and INFOSYS. The commander and staff must understand how to avoid potential information overload while developing SU within the MEB; well structured SOPs assist them by rapidly conveying necessary information within the MEB.

3-42. The XO is responsible for IM within the MEB. The XO outlines responsibilities and supervises the staff's performance in collecting and processing relevant information. During operations, the XO ensures that all staff members understand and support the CCIR. The XO ensures all staff members understand the requirements, review incoming and outgoing information traffic, and understand procedures for informing the commander and other designated staff officers of critical or exceptional information.

PROCEDURES

3-43. The MEB uses the Army operations process and military decision-making process (MDMP) to plan and conduct operations. (See chapters 4 through 8 for more information.)

3-44. The MEB typically develops standardized battle drills to respond to episodic events during the conduct of operations in the CP. One technique is to use the Combined Arms Center's "Tactical Operations Center (TOC) Battle Drills" as a basis of developing unit standing operating procedures (SOPs) and CP procedures. The MEB develops SOPs for integrating task-organized units and staff augmentees, and highlighting those tasks that are associated with MANSPT, support area, consequence management, and stability operations.

EQUIPMENT AND FACILITIES

3-45. The MEB uses the ABCS. (See appendix C.) The CP is established using organic equipment either in a field environment or within fixed facilities if available. (See appendix B for further MEB CP discussion.)

EXERCISING COMMAND AND CONTROL

3-46. The MEB commander must place the C2 system into action. Exercising C2 is dynamic throughout the operations process, as exampled below—

- Although planning, preparing, executing, and assessing C2 occur continuously in operations, they need not occur sequentially. The MEB must prepare to perform all four actions simultaneously, with the commander at the center of the process.
- The operations process is execution focused rather than planning focused. The C2 INFOSYS compress planning to allow more time to focus on execution. The INFOSYS do this in two ways.
  - The INFOSYS allows better collaborative and parallel planning among echelons within the MEB.
  - The INFOSYS provides a more accurate COP, allowing forces to execute faster with less detailed planning.

Chapter 4

MEB Operations

This chapter discusses how the MEB conducts operations and some of the considerations that may be more important to the MEB than other organizations as the operations process are conducted. The MEB must be prepared to support the simultaneous combinations used during full spectrum operations whether they are conducted overseas or within the United States and its territories. Changes in the scope and focus of each operation are likely to occur during the execution of a mission and the MEB must be prepared to transition to support the needs of the unit to which it is attached or OPCON. The operations process supports the requirement for the MEB to balance efforts across what will likely be multiple missions, some conducted sequentially, and others simultaneously as part of the role of this unique organization.

OVERVIEW

4-1. The MEB uses Army planning processes. The MEB should understand joint planning processes when their controlling headquarters is a JTF and the national planning processes when conducting civil support operations. (See chapter 8.) The standard Army planning processes and staff functions are contained in FM 5-0, FMI 5-0.1, and FM 6-0, and they apply to all operations. MEB operations demand an integrated combined arms approach. The key tasks that the MEB trains to conduct are unique and include MANSPT operations, support area operations, consequence management operations, and stability operations. These operations are each discussed in chapters 5 through 8 respectively.

4-2. The MEB will require tailoring or task organization for every mission that it performs since its organic organization only includes the brigade's HHC, an NSC, and a BSB. Capability requirements should be identified early in the planning process and constantly reevaluated to ensure the MEB is able to perform all of the specified and implied tasks that are necessary to achieve mission success. Some of the shortfalls in the organic structure of the MEB are also discussed in this chapter.

Notes: For additional information to support the planning process for the MEB, see FM 3-0, FM 5-0, FMI 5-0.1, and FM 6-0. For additional information on the capabilities of the CBRN, engineer, and MP organizations that will typically make up the majority of MEB assets, see FM 3-11, FM 3-19.1, and FM 3-34.

SIMULTANEOUS COMBINATIONS

4-3. The Army conducts full spectrum operations with few significant pauses, creating a relentless tempo that overwhelms the enemy's capability to respond effectively. A tactical pause allows an enemy to reorganize, reconstitute, prepare for our next action, or potentially seize the initiative. Not only does this provide an enemy with an advantage, it prolongs the duration of operation leading to unnecessary additional operations. High operational tempo and continuous pressure can seriously hinder the enemy's ability to reconstitute capabilities or reconfigure forces to prepare for subsequent operations. Simultaneous and continuous operations combine defeat and stability mechanisms to achieve decisive results. The MEB operations must also be simultaneous and continuous to facilitate the actions and the desired operational tempo of the supported commander. Proper task organization of the necessary MEB assets must occur early in the process and provide the necessary flexibility of employment and the necessary transitions that will occur in operations. Effective multifunctional and functional C2 of MEB capabilities are essential to achieving this.

4-4. Each element of full spectrum operations—offense, defense, and stability or civil support—is necessary in most the campaigns. There are exceptions in that during most domestic operations Army forces will only conduct civil support operations. Offensive and defensive operations may be required within the continental United States (CONUS) in support of Homeland Security (HLS). Stability operations may predominate in foreign humanitarian assistance (FHA) with minor defensive operations, and with little or no offensive component.

GENERAL MEB CONSIDERATIONS

4-5. This manual uses the term conduct as defined in FM 6-0—to perform the activities of the operations process: planning, preparing, executing, and continuously assessing. Full spectrum operations follow a cycle of planning, preparation, execution, and continuous assessment with the commander driving the operations process through battle command.

4-6. The following are general operations process considerations that apply to all MEB operations.

PLANNING

4-7. The MEB must conduct its operations in collaboration with higher, lower, and adjacent units. It conducts a broad range of tasks in full spectrum operations, with a broad range of task-organized units and capabilities. This requires it to conduct integrated (this includes "synchronized") planning and balance effort across several operations. It must integrate several major simultaneous operations. It must integrate the functions, activities, processes, staffs, and the units, tasks, systems and capabilities of numerous Army branches and joint, interagency, and multinational forces, often into combined arms teams, to conduct complex operations. It must integrate planning with its higher headquarters, planning processes, staff sections, warfighting functions, directorates, centers, and boards. It must integrate with supported units. It must integrate plans, measures, actions, and activities. The MEB commander, staff, and LNOs all contribute to this integrated planning effort.

4-8. FM 5-0 and FM 6-0 discuss integration in its various forms and the many things that must be integrated during planning. FM 3-0 discusses the use of integrating processes to synchronize operations during all operations process activities. They must be synchronized with each other and integrated into the overall operation—

- Intelligence preparation of the battlefield. (See FM 34-130 [to be revised as FM 2-01.3].)
- Targeting. (See FM 6-20-10.)
- ISR synchronization. (See FM 34-2.)
- CRM. (See FM 5-19.)
- Knowledge management. (See FM 3-0.)

4-9. The MEB uses the operations process to synchronize across all of the warfighting functions within the brigade and with its supported higher headquarters. The MEB commander uses the warfighting functions to assist in exercising battle command. Some of the key tasks within each warfighting function, or related to the warfighting functions that the MEB focuses on for planning include—

- Movement and maneuver.
    - Deploy.
    - Move.
    - Maneuver.
    - Employ direct fires (typically, when task-organized with a TCF).
    - Occupy an area.
    - Conduct mobility and countermobility operations.
    - Employ battlefield obscuration.

- Intelligence.
  - Support to situational understanding.
  - Conduct ISR.
- Fires.
  - Decide which surface targets within MEB AO that should be attacked.
  - Detect and allocate surface targets.
  - Provide fires support (if task-organized, TCF has artillery or mortar systems).
  - Assess effectiveness of fires delivered.
  - Integrate C2 warfare, including nonlethal fires, into MEB operations.
- Sustainment.
  - Provide general engineering support.
  - Conduct I/R.
  - Support of distribution (within an assigned AO).
  - Coordinate for Army Health System health service support (HSS).
- C2.
  - Execute the operations process.
  - Conduct CP operations.
  - Integrate the IS contributors.
  - Conduct information engagement.
  - Conduct terrain management.
  - Provide C2 to a support AOs.
  - Conduct CA activities.
  - Integrate AC2 (within an assigned AO).
  - Execute command programs.
- Protection.
  - AMD (within an assigned AO).
  - Personnel recovery (within an assigned AO).
  - Information protection.
  - Fratricide avoidance.
  - Operational area security.
  - AT.
  - Survivability.
  - Force health protection.
  - CBRN operations.
  - Safety.
  - Operations security.
  - EOD.

4-10. Commanders use integrating processes and continuing activities to synchronize operations during all operations process activities. They are synchronized with one another and integrated into the overall operation. (See FM 3-0 for additional information.)

4-11. Maintaining balance is critical for the MEB staff and commander. The MEB must continually maintain a balance of effort across the elements of full spectrum operations to ensure the success of the supported headquarters. The MEB must initially allocate resources against all required tasks. The MEB can request additional capabilities to meet identified shortfalls. When the brigade's assets will not allow the simultaneous conduct of all tasks, the MEB must sequence or phase tasks or operations or assume risk on some tasks by executing them with less than ideal resources or not at all. Through continuous assessment, the MEB adjusts the balance of effort across operations by changes in task organization, resource allocation, and priorities. The MEB can use uncommitted resources to add combat power as necessary. One tool the MEB can use to maintain balance is a synchronization matrix that tracks all MEB resources against the warfighting functions, operations, tasks, or similar categories. Any tool or process used by the brigade to maintain balance must be very flexible and adaptive to continually identify emerging requirements, and then weigh them against ongoing efforts and make changes. The MEB must be very responsive in the conduct of tasks, assessing risk, and shifting effort between competing requirements. Contingency plans, branches and sequels, and be prepared missions help provide responsiveness. MEBs must develop other techniques or processes to maintain balance and share these lessons learned.

GENERAL PLANNING CONSIDERATIONS

4-12. The MEB will normally conduct MANSPT operations and support area operations in support of full spectrum operations. The MEB performs tactical level planning even when attached or OPCON to an operational level headquarters. The MEB conducts assessment during planning to include—

- Monitoring the OE.
- Monitoring the measures of performance (MOPs) and measures of effectiveness (MOEs).
- Evaluating courses of action (COAs) for their operations and supported and supporting headquarters planning.

4-13. The commander and staff visualize how to creatively arrange forces and group missions to provide MANSPT operations in the most effective fashion. MANSPT operations are a combined arms activity. (See chapter 5.) The MEB may use lines of effort to help visualize stability and civil support operations. (See example in chapter 8.)

4-14. The MEB must balance support across conflicting mission areas. (See chapter 2.) The MEB must balance between detailed and mission command orders. The support area operations orders may be more detailed while MANSPT operations orders may be more mission command. (See chapter 6.)

4-15. The MEB uses mission variables (as discussed in chapter 1 and later in this chapter) to support analysis of the OE and conditions in their designated AO. (See FM 3-07 for more complete discussion of the relevance of each of these variables to stability operations.) The initial assessment conducted by the MEB is continuously updated and supported by running estimates maintained by each staff section.

4-16. The MEB commander considers mutual support when task organizing forces and assigning areas of operations and positioning units. *Mutual support* is that support which units render each other against an enemy because of their assigned tasks, their position relative to each other and to the enemy, and their inherent capabilities (JP 3-31). In Army, doctrine mutual support is a planning consideration related to force disposition, not a command relationship. The concept of mutual support is useful to plan MANSPT operations and support area operations. Mutual support can be between MEB units, between units in the echelon support area, or between MEB units and supported units. (See FM 3-0.) The MEB uses mutual support between bases to conduct base cluster security and defense when assigned responsibility for an echelon support area. (See chapter 6.)

4-17. The continuum of operations helps understand the context and purpose of MEB operations. While conducting its current operations or missions, the MEB affects the OE to establish conditions for conducting subsequent operations. The operations of the supported headquarters are generally conducted to move conditions to a lower level of violence and ideally establish a stable peace. A stable peace may include any or all of the following:

- A safe and secure populace.
- A legitimate central government.
- A viable market economy.
- Effective rule of law.

4-18. A *major operation* is a series of tactical actions (battles, engagements, strikes) conducted by combat forces of a single or several Services, coordinated in time and place, to achieve strategic or operational objectives in an operational area. These actions are conducted simultaneously or sequentially according to a common plan and are controlled by a single commander. See JP 3-0 for noncombat operations to the relative size and scope of a military operation. Major operations have varying levels of violence over time and location within the AO. The operational theme for a major operation may change with phases or changes in the OE.

4-19. The development of task organization may be a more significant effort for the MEB than most units. This is due to the large number and range of specified and implied tasks for the MEB, the lack of organic units and the wide range of assigned, attached, or OPCON units, and the variety of operations it must conduct. (See FM 5-0 for general considerations.)

4-20. Some considerations for task organizing versus employing function units:

- Although based on METT-TC, the MEB may form battalion TFs and company teams. (See chapter 5.)
- A mission with a broad range of tasks (multifunctional), uncertain or quickly changing requirements, and geographically spread out with a desire to minimize unit travel to mission sites may be better performed by a battalion TF or company team.
- A mission with mostly functional task requirements, with a long duration, conducted within a smaller area and where other capabilities may be integrated without changing the task organization may be better performed by functional units rather than a battalion TF or company team. (See FM 3-0 for further discussion on supporting range and supporting distance.)

4-21. Some other considerations for developing the task organization (see paragraph 1-37, page 1-8) for the MEB include:

- Decide what to retain under MEB control and what to allocate to each subordinate based on METT-TC.
- Forces under brigade control give the commander flexibility to shift or mass resources without affecting forces task-organized to subordinates.
- The assigned command and support relationships either increase responsiveness to subordinate or supported units or limit the MEB commander's flexibility or agility in shifting resources.
- Consider how to weight the MEB decisive operation and support the higher headquarters decisive operation.
- When directing the execution of "be prepared" task organization changes to subordinates, consider their response time to detach and attach forces and prepare them for new tasks.
- It is much easier to change task organization upon immediate mission completion or changes in phases of an operation.
- The MEB should expect to change task organization frequently and rapidly to meet changes in the METT-TC factors.

MILITARY DECISION-MAKING PROCESS

4-22. The MEB uses the operations process to critically think about how to conduct its operations. The MEB routinely conducts parallel and collaborative planning with subordinates and higher headquarters. (See FM 5-0 and FMI 5-0.1.) Throughout the planning process, the MEB staff may need to advise supported commanders and their staffs about MEB capabilities, methods of employment, and possible capabilities shortfalls. The MEB may also need to provide planning support to those units without embedded functional staff capabilities, such as construction engineering, that are resident in the MEB staff that might otherwise only be available through reachback. The MEB staff will use the automated tools and systems of their functional areas such as Joint Warning and Reporting Network (JWARN) and Joint Engineer Planning and Execution System.

4-23. The large number of essential tasks developed during MDMP for the MEB may be grouped into larger doctrinally approved tasks in the restated mission. Any nondoctrinal terms used must be defined to reduce confusion. The commander's intent and concept of the operation can provide details. (See FM 5-0.)

4-24. Intelligence preparation of the battlefield (IPB) remains the same for all types of military operations; however, its focus may change depending on the predominant type of operation or the unit's primary focus. Products required to portray the information may also change based on the type of operation or unit focus. Doctrinal and situation templates used to portray the various threats will differ. In addition, civil considerations have assumed an importance on a par with the enemy and environment for all types of operations. IPB products must provide enough detail for commanders and staffs to make informed decisions.

4-25. Because of the current limited organic ISR capabilities of the MEB, the staff must carefully develop the ISR plan and set priorities to gain critical information first. Additional assets may be attached or otherwise provided to the MEB to accomplish the ISR mission when the MEB is responsible for an echelon support area. In most cases, UAS support would come from the BFSB or combat aviation brigade.

4-26. The MEB may use the rapid decision-making and synchronization process (RDSP) as a tool to make decisions, and rapidly resynchronize forces and warfighting functions when presented with opportunities or threats during execution. (See FMI 5-0.1.) One of the significant differences between the RDSP and the MDMP is that RDSP is based on an existing order. A second difference between the RDSP and the MDMP is that RDSP seeks an acceptable solution, while the MDMP seeks the optimal (most desirable) one.

4-27. The MEB staff balances the time to plan at brigade level and allows subordinates time to plan and prepare. Parallel planning, collaborative planning, and warning orders (WARNOs) help subordinate units and staffs prepare for new missions by providing them with maximum time. MEB subordinate units without staffs use troop leading procedures (TLPs) to prepare for a mission.

MISSION VARIABLES

4-28. This section discusses in more detail the mission variables METT-TC introduced in chapter 1. The information from the operational variables analysis is used during MEB mission analysis using six mission variables—mission, enemy, terrain and weather, troops and support available, time available and civil considerations. (See chapter 1.) (FM 3-0, FM 3-90, and FM 6-0 discuss METT-TC in more detail.) This section will discuss the OE in terms of the tactical tool of METT-TC.

4-29. The tactical level is the level at which the MEB headquarters typically operates as it narrows the focus to the mission variables of METT-TC. The MEB staff will use METT-TC to synthesize operational and tactical level information with local knowledge relevant to its missions.

4-30. Incorporating the analysis of the operational variables into METT-TC emphasizes the OE's human aspects, most obviously in civil considerations, but in the other factors as well. This requires critical thinking, collaboration, continuous learning, and adaptation. It also requires analyzing local and regional perceptions. Many factors affect perceptions of the enemy, adversaries, supporters, and neutrals. These include—

- Language.
- Culture.
- Geography.
- History.
- Education.
- Beliefs.
- Perceived objective and motivation.
- Communications media.
- Personal experience.

Mission

4-31. The *mission* is the task, together with the purpose, that clearly indicates the action to be taken and the reason therefore (this definition was shortened; the complete definition is printed in the glossary). Mission is always the first factor commanders consider during decisionmaking. Commanders and staff view all other METT-TC factors in terms of their impact on mission accomplishment. A thorough understanding of why the unit is conducting an operation provides the focus for planning. Under mission command, the staff determines the minimum control measures necessary to ensure coordination. (See FM 6-0.)

4-32. The MEB assigns a mission to each subordinate commander. The commander allocates resources between subordinates and the often competing mission requirements to best support the decisive operation and the higher commander's intent. Consider the mission of adjacent units and support AO tenant units to ensure complementary and reinforcing efforts. The missions of support AO tenant units are also considered in locating units within the support area.

Enemy

4-33. The second factor to consider is the enemy—disposition (strength, location, and tactical mobility), doctrine, equipment, vulnerabilities, and probable COAs. (See FM 34-130.) Commanders look for enemy weaknesses and strengths in order to deny options to enemy commanders and keep them reacting to friendly maneuvers. They also analyze their forces for weaknesses and vulnerabilities that enemies might exploit and act to counter them. (See FM 6-0.)

4-34. The MEB is optimized with the capability to enhance friendly or inhibit enemy maneuver and movement options and to conduct selected protection and sustainment tasks. These capabilities facilitate retaining the initiative while maximizing combat power potential at the operational and tactical levels of war. The IPB helps the staff identify opportunities to shape the OE. The staff must analyze the enemy across their higher headquarters AO, the AOs of supported units, the assigned support AO, and unassigned areas. The MEB depends on supported units sharing their COP, higher headquarters assistant chief of staff, intelligence (G-2), and the BSFB information, and ISR support.

4-35. The MEB staff assists in the operational analysis of the enemy's ability to deny United States access to the region itself—to ports and airfields along with maritime zones. Future adversaries will use all means possible to prevent U.S. forces from establishing a foothold in the region and seek to disrupt the flow of organizations and supplies. These likely enemy operational goals drive the requirement for the MEB to support rapid entry through unimproved or expedient ports, austere forward airfields, and across all environmental domains—air, ground, maritime, space, and information.

Terrain and Weather

Terrain

4-36. Terrain is not neutral. Terrain includes natural conditions and manmade structures. The staff analyzes how the terrain affects trafficability, wind patterns, drainage, operations, weapons and other systems, selecting objectives, movement and maneuver, protective measures, locating bases and facilities, and Soldiers. (See FM 6-0.) OEs feature a wide range of terrain characteristics that include various soils, topographies, elevations, and densities of vegetation and populations.

4-37. The MEB has the capability to conduct and leverage engineer topographic teams to provide a detailed topographical analysis of the five military aspects of terrain—observation and fields of fire, avenues of approach, key and decisive terrain, obstacles, and cover and concealment. This analysis is especially critical to conduct both MANSPT and support area operations. The MEB also provides the supported commander with the ability to influence terrain and use the effects of weather to friendly forces' advantage especially with engineer and CBRN capabilities. Terrain analysis and effective use of terrain is important to position bases and facilities within an assigned MEB AO. This is especially important within an echelon support area where positioning bases add to their inherent defensive capabilities and reduces demand on other resources to defend them. (See chapter 6.)

4-38. Complex terrain describes areas that feature jungles, dense forests, mountains, and urban areas. Steep slopes and high elevations found in mountainous environments will challenge MEB Soldiers, aviation, and ISR support. All terrain, open, jungle, mountain, and urban must be analyzed in relation to three disparate dimensions: elevated, surface, and subsurface. Complex terrain can often provide an opponent with the opportunity to offset the advantages of a superior force. Adaptive opponents will leverage jungles, tunnel complexes, high ground, and other aspects of complex terrain to minimize friendly forces advantages and to create conditions for close combat. The enemy may use highly restricted and urban terrain to hide and shield themselves from our precision fires. They may also use cultural, religious, and civilian structures to hide and shield themselves, to stockpile weapons, to limit line of sight, and to constrain weapon trajectories and effects.

4-39. Complex terrain in general and urban terrain in particular can restrict and canalize forces along a finite number of predictable routes where they can be destroyed or attacked by a prepared and patient enemy. The MEB deliberately shapes designated or critical routes through a series of developed tactics, techniques, and procedures (TTPs) to ensure protected access to a specific route or to retain maneuver options among a number of different routes.

Weather

4-40. Planners consider climate with longer-range plans, while most tactical planners consider weather for shorter-range plans. Weather effects are classified as direct and indirect. Weather can create opportunities or difficulties for each side. (See FM 6-0.)

4-41. Weather affects the operational performance of troops, equipment, and technology and when not properly anticipated and considered, can result in mission failure. The MEB analyzes weather effects in the OE by assessing all phases of the concept of operations in relation to the five military aspects of weather—temperature and humidity, visibility, precipitation, winds, and clouds.

4-42. Land forces must be capable of conducting operations anywhere that our national interests are at issue. Historically and geographically, these locations have typically been environments that experience extreme variations in many of the military aspects of weather. These extremes will challenge the endurance and performance of MEB troops and even the most hardened high-technological systems. When operating in environments with extreme weather variations, the MEB emphasizes responsive and layered protective postures for troops and equipment. Sensor, communication, and situational awareness technologies are susceptible to extreme weather degradation and the MEB insulates and arrays them, using TTPs that are redundant, integrated, and overlapping.

Troops and Support Available

4-43. This includes number, type, capabilities, and condition of friendly troops and support from Army, HN, contractor, joint, interagency, and multinational sources. Commanders maintain an understanding of friendly information two echelons down. They track subordinate readiness—including training, maintenance, logistics, strengths and weaknesses, and morale. Commander and staffs visit subordinates to confirm data and reports and gain insights into the intangibles that data and reports cannot capture. (See FM 6-0.)

4-44. Since many organizations will join the MEB during deployment or even in theater, the MEB commander considers the level of trust and confidence that exist between himself or herself, the staff, and subordinate commanders when deciding mission assignment, and how best to C2 them (mission command versus detailed command).

4-45. The MEB staff identifies shortfalls, requests task organization or staff augmentation, and makes recommendations to the commander about how to allocate resources. It is probable that the MEB will routinely need task organization of MI assets, an area support medical company, and a geospatial staff that is similar to that which is organic to BCTs. This task organization would be essential when the MEB is assigned an AO. The MEB will require CA units/staff to perform CA operations. MP battalions task organized to the MEB should be augmented with aid stations. Selected units of the MEB may require fire support teams. The MEB staff may require an Air Force tactical air control party (to include a joint terminal attack controller). Staff augmentation may also require (or require additional) medical plans and operations, ammunition planning, mortuary affairs, logistics planning, public affairs, finance operations, contracting, EOD, and information engagement operations personnel augmentation.

Time Available

4-46. Effective commanders and staff know how much time and space their units need to plan, prepare, and execute operations. They also consider time with respect to the enemy ability to plan, prepare, and execute. (See FM 6-0.)

4-47. The MEB must consider the time needed to effect task organization changes, move to supported units locations, link up, rehearse, and integrate forces. Parallel and collaborative planning maximizes use of available time. SOPs to conduct routine tasks, especially in the support area, also reduce planning and orders preparation time.

Civil Considerations

4-48. Civil considerations comprise the influence of manmade infrastructure, civilian institutions, and attitudes and activities of the civilian leaders, populations, and organizations within an AO on the conduct of military operations. If the military's mission is to support civil authorities, civil considerations define the mission. (See FM 6-0.)

4-49. The staff analysis of civil considerations improves SU and lends directly to mission accomplishment. Civil considerations are essential to developing effective plans for all operations—not just those dominated by stability or civil support. Full spectrum operations often involve stabilizing the situation, securing the peace, and transitioning authority to civilian control. Combat operations directly affect the populace, infrastructure, and the force's ability to transition to HN authority. The degree of the populace's expected support or resistance to Army forces affects nearly all operations.

4-50. At the tactical level, commanders and staffs analyze civil considerations in terms of the six categories expressed in this memory aid (ASCOPE: areas, structures, capabilities, organizations, people, and events). MEB operations require the consideration of many of the items identified here and others that are not represented in this example. Figure 4-1, page 4-10, provides a graphical depiction and an example of the use of the memory aid ASCOPE. The ASCOPE characteristics further expand into 29 subcategories to provide a framework for greater fidelity and a more detailed analysis of the civil dimension as needed. The ASCOPE structure and categories can form the basis for the development of evaluation criteria, MOP, or MOE.

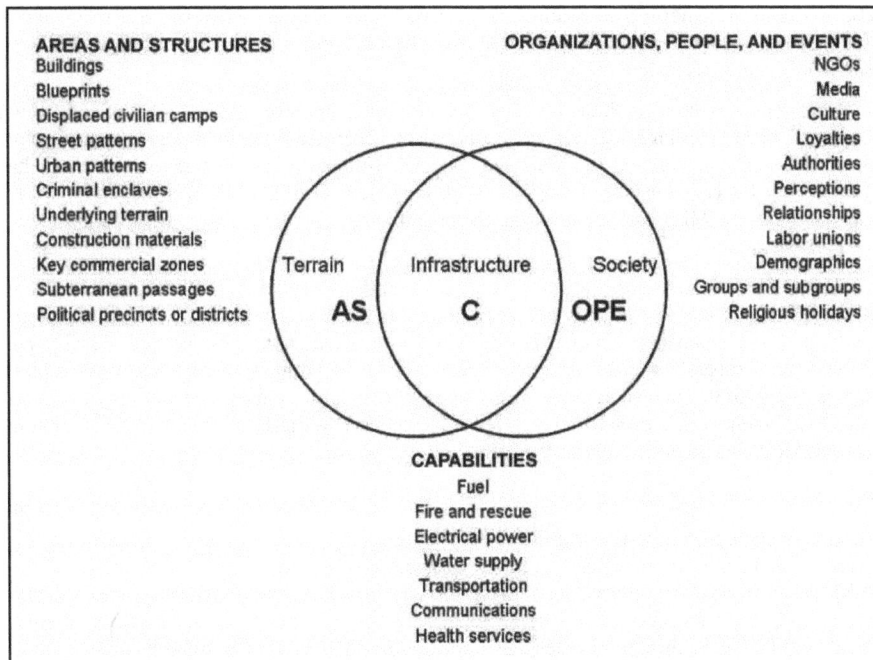

AREAS AND STRUCTURES
Buildings
Blueprints
Displaced civilian camps
Street patterns
Urban patterns
Criminal enclaves
Underlying terrain
Construction materials
Key commercial zones
Subterranean passages
Political precincts or districts

ORGANIZATIONS, PEOPLE, AND EVENTS
NGOs
Media
Culture
Loyalties
Authorities
Perceptions
Relationships
Labor unions
Demographics
Groups and subgroups
Religious holidays

Terrain   Infrastructure   Society
AS   C   OPE

CAPABILITIES
Fuel
Fire and rescue
Electrical power
Water supply
Transportation
Communications
Health services

Figure 4-1. ASCOPE construct with examples

4-51. The MEB may encounter a multitude of difficult political, economic, religious, social, and technological variables when conducting operations. During stability and civil support operations, the MEB may assist in performing functions that would otherwise fall to local governmental agencies. The MEB may also control populations or restore humanitarian infrastructure while supporting a division or corps or while directly engaged in combat operations. The MEB must prepare for operations in areas and environments where the fabric of society is in tremendous disarray.

4-52. Full spectrum operations recognize that military land power formations must defeat enemy forces and capabilities while effectively shaping the civil environment in which they operate. This is often done simultaneously and should be accomplished in a way that gives all elements of national power the greatest chance of lasting success. When a mission is specified, civil considerations must be included in the planning process and during the METT-TC analysis as associated with a particular operation or mission. To do this, the MEB draws upon information and analysis already developed and derived from a thorough understanding of the operational variables characteristics of the OE.

4-53. The conduct of military operations and Soldiers are often essential to popular support. Populations that accept the presence and behavior of intervening or occupying military forces may be the greatest source of information and the best protection against insurgencies and unconventional warfare. An understanding of the civil and human dimensions of the operating environment is necessary to prevent the unintended consequences of deliberate military action and to effective decisionmaking.

TRANSITION OPERATIONS

4-54. Transitions between missions and operations have the potential to be challenging. The design of the MEB optimizes its ability to deal with transitions. The design of the staff and the typical augmentation received by the MEB are those elements that are critical to performing MANSPT operations and the tasks associated with stability or civil support operations.

4-55. The MEB may hand over all or some of its AO to other military forces, governmental agencies, NGOs, or the local authorities as stability is achieved. This transfer is similar to a relief and must be carefully planned, coordinated, and executed with the relieving force or agency. The MEB may also transition only some sectors to local authorities.

4-56. Transitions may be a continuation of an ongoing operation, execution of a completely new tactical mission, or conducting logistical resupply operations. Increased flexibility and agility afforded by improved SA and collaborative C2 tools facilitates transitions to the next mission without halting to conduct extended decision-making processes. With increased capability to affect the enemy over a larger area of influence, the MEB can begin setting the conditions for the next engagement during the transition from the last mission.

4-57. The MEB facilitates rapid transition between operations for the unit it is supporting. Its ability to rapidly transition denies the enemy an opportunity to recover, regroup, and conduct preparations. Similarly, it allows commanders to quickly deal with consequences arising out of tactical action precluding its growth into a separate operational requirement. The MEB normally conducts combat replenishment operations as part of transitional activities. This series of tactical sustainment operations will continue until the supported commander's cycle of operations accommodates a transition to a mission staging operation and a subsequent change in mission for the MEB.

PREPARE

4-58. Back briefs and rehearsals occur during preparation. They are essential to ensure those responsible for execution have a clear understanding of the mission, commander's intent, and concept of operations. Most MEB operations are executed at the battalion level and below. However, some operations may require a MEB level rehearsal. The MEB conducts the brigade combined arms rehearsal, sustainment rehearsal, and ISR and fire support rehearsals (when assigned an AO) after subordinate battalions or base and base cluster commanders have had an opportunity to issue their OPORDs. These rehearsals ensure that subordinate plans are synchronized with those of other units and that subordinate commanders understand the intent of the higher headquarters. Usually, the MEB commander, DCO, XO, primary staff, and subordinate battalion commanders and their S-3s attend the rehearsals. Based upon the type of operation, the commander can modify the audience such as the brigade attachments. (See FM 6-0 for a detailed discussion on rehearsals.)

4-59. The MEB must establish and disseminate clear, concise rules of engagement (ROE) and rules of interaction (ROI) before deploying to the AO. Back briefs and rehearsals help ensure everyone understands the ROE since small-unit leaders and individual Soldiers must make ROE decisions promptly and independently. For a discussion of the rules in ROE, see FM 3-07.

4-60. The ROI embody the human dimension of stability operations. They lay the foundation for successful relationships with the numerous factions and individuals that play critical roles in these operations. The ROI encompass an array of interpersonal communication skills such as persuasion and negotiation. These skills are the tools the individual Soldier needs to deal with the nontraditional threats that are prevalent in stability operations. Examples of such threats are political friction, unfamiliar cultures, and conflicting ideologies. In turn, ROI enhance the Soldier's survivability in such situations. The ROI are based on the applicable ROE for a certain operation. The ROI must be tailored to the specific regions, cultures, and populations affected by the operation. Like ROE, the ROI can be effective only if they are thoroughly rehearsed and understood by every Soldier in the unit.

4-61. Key preparation activities (see FM 6-0) include—
- Assessment—monitor and evaluate preparations.
- Reconnaissance operations.
- Security operations.
- Protection.
- Revising and refining the plan.
- Coordination and liaison.
- Rehearsals.
- Task organizing.
- Training.
- Movement.
- Preoperations checks and inspections.
- Logistic preparations.
- Integrating new Soldiers and units.

EXECUTE

4-62. Execution is putting a plan into action by applying combat power to accomplish the mission and using situational understanding to assess progress and make execution and adjustment decisions. It focuses on concerted action to seize, retain, and exploit the initiative. The Army's operational concept emphasizes executing operations at a tempo enemies cannot match by acting or reacting faster than they can adapt. To achieve this type of flexibility, commanders use mission command to focus subordinate commanders' initiative. Subordinates exercising initiative within the commander's intent can significantly increase tempo; however, they also may desynchronize the unit's warfighting functions. This may reduce commanders' ability to mass the effects of combat power. Even relatively minor, planned actions by command post cells affect other cells' areas of expertise, affecting the operation's overall synchronization.

4-63. Collaborative synchronization—enabled and expected by mission command—uses individual initiative to achieve resynchronization continuously. Subordinates' successes may offer opportunities within the concept or develop advantages that make a new concept practical. In either case, the commander's intent keeps the force acceptably focused and synchronized. Subordinates need not wait for top-down synchronization. Mission command is especially appropriate for operations in which stability operations predominate. It allows subordinates to exploit information about enemies, adversaries, events, and trends without direction from higher echelons.

4-64. During execution, the current operations cell strives to keep the warfighting functions synchronized and balanced between individual initiative and synchronized activities as the situation changes. The current operations cell follows and provides its own level of collaborative synchronization. To assist commanders in massing the effects of combat power at decisive times and places, the current operations cell considers the following outcomes when making synchronization decisions or allowing others' collaborative synchronization to proceed:
- Combined arms integration.

- Responsiveness—both proactive and reactive.
- Timeliness.

4-65. Execution involves monitoring the situation, assessing the operation, and adjusting the order as needed. Throughout execution, commanders continuously assess the operation's progress based on information from the COP, running estimates, and assessments from subordinate commanders. When the situation varies from the assumptions the order was based on, commanders direct adjustments to exploit opportunities and counter threats.

4-66. Both the MEB unit commander's staff and the subordinate commander's staff, assist the commander in execution through the integrating processes and continuing activities during execution. (See FM 3-0.) In addition, commanders assisted by the staff perform the following activities that are specific to execution:

- Focus assets on the decisive operation.
- Adjust CCIR based on the situation.
- Adjust control measures.
- Manage movement and positioning of supporting units.
- Adjust unit missions and task as necessary.
- Modify the concept of operations as required.
- Position or relocate committed, supporting, and reserve units.
- Determine commitment of the MEB reserve (becomes the main effort and decisive point of the brigade).

4-67. Key execute activities (see FM 6-0) include—

- Assessing the current situation and forecasting progress of the operation—monitor operations and evaluate progress.
- Making execution and adjustment decisions to exploit opportunities or counter threats.
- Directing actions to apply combat power at decisive points and times—synchronize and maintain continuity.
- Balancing effort and risk among competing tasks.

4-68. Entry operations encompass those actions necessary to move from home station or forward locations into the TO for further employment. The MEB conducts entry operations from points of embarkation into designated points of entry using a full range of transportation modes. Employing air movement, ground movement, or intratheater sealift, the MEB provides the force commander with a flexible tailored force capability package for entry and shaping operations to prepare for follow-on forces.

4-69. Employing embedded en route mission planning, rehearsal, and training capability may allow commanders and their staff to refine plans, rehearse with leaders at all levels, and update plans as new intelligence becomes available. Necessary task organization of assets occurs before departure to optimize the combined arms performance of the MEB.

4-70. During entry operations, the MEB is involved in the deployment process. While en route, the MEB conducts en route mission planning with the echelon above brigade headquarters it will support to shape the OE before the brigade's arrival. In a nonpermissive OE, a BCT may precede the MEB entry. Echelons above brigade assets provide the lethal and nonlethal effects that set the conditions for BCT entry operations that may be needed to set the conditions for MEB entry operations. Upon arrival, the MEB integrates into the operations of the higher headquarters, continues mission planning, and prepares for operations. In a permissive environment, the MEB may be one of the first deployed headquarters.

ASSESS

4-71. Assessment is the continuous monitoring and evaluation of the current situation, particularly about the enemy and progress of an operation. Assessment occurs during planning, preparation, and execution. Initial assessments are made during planning and continually updated. Assessment involves monitoring and evaluating the OE and the progress of operations using MOEs and MOPs. Continuous assessment involves situational understanding, monitoring, and evaluating. (See FM 6-0.) (See FMI 5-01 for TTPs to assess operations and for a discussion of monitoring and evaluation.)

4-72. The *running estimate* is a staff section's continuous assessment of current and future operations to determine if the current operation is proceeding according to the commander's intent and if future operations are supportable (FM 3-0). The running estimate format parallels the steps of the MDMP and serves as the primary tool for recording a staff section's assessments, analyses, and recommendations.

4-73. The commander and staff assess the progress of the operation, new information, and changes in conditions to revise plans. On-site assessments are essential to validate IPB, assess subordinates understanding of orders, progress, preparations, and combat readiness. The MEB anticipated branches and sequels, initially formulated during the planning stage, are assessed and updated for possible execution. The staff can make adjustment of the plan within their area of expertise.

4-74. Assessment precedes and guides every activity in the operations process and concludes each operation or phase of an operation. It involves a comparison of forecasted outcomes to actual events, using MOPs and MOEs to judge progress toward success. It entails two distinct tasks—continuously monitoring the situation and progress of the operation towards the commander's desired end state, and evaluating the operation against measures of effectiveness and performance as defined below:

- A *measure of performance* is a criterion used to assess friendly actions that is tied to measuring task accomplishment (JP 3-0). MOPs answer the question, "Was the task or action performed as the commander intended?" MOPs confirm or deny that we have done things right.
- A *measure of effectiveness* is a criterion used to assess changes in system behavior, capability, or OE that is tied to measuring the attainment of an end state, achievement of an objective, or creation of an effect (JP 3-0). MOEs focus on the results or consequences of friendly actions taken. They answer the question, "Are we doing the right things, or are additional or alternative actions required?"

OFFENSIVE OPERATIONS

PLAN

4-75. The MEB plans to support division and BCT offensive operations; routine support may include MANSPT operations and support area operations. They also may plan limited MEB controlled offensive operations (such as counter or spoiling attacks) as part of defending while conducting support area operations. (See chapter 6.)

4-76. The MEB follows the doctrine in FM 3-90 when conducting limited offensive tasks within their assigned AO and is familiar with how the BCT conducts offensive operations to plan MEB support. The MEB never attacks or conducts offensive operations as a brigade.

PREPARE

4-77. During offensive operations, the initial focus of the MEB is typically on movement and maneuver and then on support to protection and selected sustainment based on the intent and priorities of the supported forces. The MEB may conduct reconnaissance with their task-organized units or capabilities as part of MANSPT operations to support the BCTs offensive actions. The MEB may also conduct or support movement corridor operations to support troop movement and logistics preparations.

4-78. The MEB can form TFs or company teams to support the offensive operations of its supported headquarters. These organizations may be attached or placed OPCON to BCTs, or employed by the MEB to complement or reinforce all maneuver forces across the higher headquarters' AO. The units under MEB control can be more easily reallocated or massed where and when needed to meet higher headquarters directed requirements than units attached to BCTs. Deciding the best command and support relationships for the specific situation can be a challenge. The fluid nature of offensive operations may require adjustments to the initial task organization. Due to the difficulty of linkup and integration, any changes in task organization are best made at conclusion of a battle or at the end of a phase of an operation.

4-79. Detached elements from the MEB must link up and integrate into supported maneuver forces combat formations. The MEB conducts preoperations checks inspections to ensure readiness before the detachment of these elements. These detached MEB forces participate in the supported forces' rehearsals.

4-80. The MEB apportions its resources across the various operations to best meet the supported commander's intent. The MEB also allocates resources across the warfighting functions within an operation. For example, the MEB will—

- Allocate resources to provide protection during movement.
- Enhance the supported BCT's mobility within the movement and maneuver warfighting function.

EXECUTE

4-81. The MEB executes MANSPT operations to support the maneuver commander's intent. The MEB conducts support area operations in the division/EAD support area. When required, the MEB conducts consequence management operations or stability operations in support of forces conducting the offense.

4-82. The MEB assesses the offensive operations and anticipates changes in task organization, priorities, and balances resource allocation between its operations to support the decisive operation.

ASSESS

4-83. The MEB continually assesses these areas—the balance of effort between mobility and survivability; if shaping operations are setting the intended conditions; and the balance between supporting division and corps offensive operations and its responsibilities within the MEB's AO

DEFENSIVE OPERATIONS

PLAN

4-84. The MEB plans to support division and BCT defensive operations. Routine support may include MANSPT operations, support area operations, and consequence management operations. They also may plan limited MEB controlled defensive operations as part of the conduct of support area operations or when defending themselves. (See chapter 6.)

4-85. The MEB follows the doctrine in FM 3-90 when conducting defensive tasks and is familiar with how BCTs conduct defensive operations to plan MEB support.

PREPARE

4-86. If the MEB is supporting a division-level defense, the MEB's focus is on defensive operations within its AO as discussed in chapter 6 of this manual. It is also prepared to provide task-organized assets to support BCTs in their defensive preparations.

4-87. During defensive operations, the initial focus of the MEB is typically on protection and then on support to movement and maneuver and selected sustainment based on the intent and priorities of the supported forces. The MEB may conduct reconnaissance operations to support the defense. The MEB prepares to execute consequence management and ADC. Depending on the situation, the MEB will continually improve defensive positions within its AO or relocate some or all of its activities if required by the higher headquarters defensive plans.

EXECUTE

4-88. The MEB executes defensive operations to achieve the supported commander's intent. The MEB provides support to the division/EAD defensive operations and conducts support area operations when assigned an AO.

4-89. When required, the MEB executes consequence management operations and ADC in support of the supported division or corps conducting the defense.

ASSESS

4-90. The MEB continually assesses its effort to support the defensive efforts of its supported division or corps. This includes these areas:

- When to commit the MEB reserve.
- The balance of effort between support to movement and maneuver, protection, and sustainment.
- The balance of effort between self-defense and mission support.

4-91. Each staff section updates the running estimate to ensure the latest information is available for the commander to support decisionmaking.

CIVIL SUPPORT OPERATIONS

PLAN

4-92. Army civil support operations fall under defense support of civil authorities (DSCA). *Defense support of civil authorities* is defined as civil support provided under the auspices of the National Response Plan (now known as the National Response Framework [JP 3-28]). When published, DODD 3025 is expected to define DSCA as support provided by U.S. military forces. The Army's roles and responsibilities for civil support operations fall under the following three primary tasks:

- Task 1: Provide support in response to a disaster or terrorist attack.
- Task 2: Support civil law enforcement.
- Task 3: Provide other support as required.

4-93. These tasks of civil support can overlap. For example, providing Army support to civil law enforcement can occur during a response to a disaster or its aftermath. In most cases, an MEB may provide support for tasks 1 and 2. The MEB may provide that assistance as a unit or as part of a joint TF in support of a lead civil authority for civil support operations. (See JP 3-28.) U.S. laws carefully circumscribe the actions military forces conduct within the United States, its territories, and possessions. The MEB complies with these laws while assisting citizens affected by a disaster.

- Task 1 involves providing essential services support to civil authority in response to a disaster or terrorist attack. It encompasses the full range of natural and manmade events, whether labeled as emergencies, incidents, hazards, natural or manmade disasters, or domestic acts of terrorism. Essential service categories are medical; water, food, and everyday essentials; transportation network; police and fire; electricity; schools; and sanitation. Army forces assist civil authority for restoration or protection of essential services.
- Task 2 refers to restricted use of military assets for support to civil law enforcement personnel conducting civil law enforcement operations within the United States and its territories. These operations are significantly different from operations in other nations. MEB forces may support civil law enforcement under U.S. Constitutional and statutory restrictions and corresponding directives and regulations.
- Task 3 denotes planned, routine, and periodic support not related to a disaster. Examples include providing military support for parades, funeral details, and community relations. National policy directs the military and other organizations to use National Incident Management System (NIMS) and National Response Framework (NRF) policies and procedures, where applicable, for conducting other support as required.

4-94. There is one primary case where the MEB is well suited to provide support to civil authorities; consequence management. (See chapter 7.) Consequence management pertains to the civil support tasks 1 and 2. The MEBs in the ARNG could be among the first military forces to respond on behalf of state authorities. Planning civil support operations is similar to planning stability operations (See chapter 8.); they both interact with the populace and civil authorities to provide essential services. The MEB tasks are similar but the environment is different (domestic versus foreign). The specialized capabilities of the MEB to conduct stability operations apply to civil support operations, primarily for tasks 1 and 2. (See chapter 8.) However, the MEB supports the lead civil authority for civil support operations. A civil authority is in the lead for civil support operations while the TF or joint task for (hence MEB) supports the lead civil authority.

4-95. The MEB uses Army or joint planning procedures for civil support but must be able to participate and integrate its planning with other U.S. national, state, or local organization's planning procedures as discussed in the next section. Soldiers receive their orders in an Army format, but they must be consistent with the overall shared objectives for the response. They are aligned with the specific guidance other on-the-ground responders of other civilian and military organizations are receiving. Soldiers exercise individual initiative to establish and maintain communication at all levels. Based upon the type of support provided, MEB leaders, staff and Soldiers need to be familiar (to varying degrees) with the terminology, doctrine, and procedures used by first responders to ensure effective integration of Army personnel and equipment to ensure that citizens affected by the disaster receive the best care and service possible.

4-96. When the MEB conducts civil support operations, a lead federal or state governmental agency has the overall responsibility depending on the MEB's status as a Title 10 or Title 32 organization.

- If the MEB is a state asset, it reports to its state National Guard chain of command.
- If the MEB is a Federal title 10 asset (Regular Army), it reports to its federal chain of command.

Note: The military chain of command is not violated while the MEB supports the lead federal agency in order to assist citizens affected by a disaster.

4-97. MEB leaders and staff may help support the emergency preparedness planning conducted at the national, state, or local level. The MEB may conduct contingency planning, crisis response planning, or deliberate planning. MEB leaders and staff must understand two documents from the Department of Homeland Security (DHS):

- The National level civil disaster and emergency response doctrine contained within the NIMS.
- NRF documents located at the following web sites:
    - www.nimsonline.com
    - www.dhs.gov/nrp

Note: All military, civil agencies, and organizations are directed to follow this doctrine. MEB leaders must understand the doctrine in JP 3-28.

4-98. The NRF organizational structure includes emergency support function annexes. There are currently fifteen emergency support function annexes. (See www.fema.gov/nrf for list, scope, and coordinators.) The emergency support functions are used to help identify who has what type of resources to provide as part of a disaster response.

4-99. Joint doctrine states that disaster response is conducted in five phases: shaping, staging, deployment, conducting civil support operations, and transition. The role of the military is most intense in the shaping by conducting civil support operations phases, decreasing steadily as the operation moves into the recovery and restoration stages. Although each civil support mission is different, the visualization process, military decision-making process, and troop leading procedures still apply and correlate with those contained within joint doctrine, the NIMS, and the NRF. Army MOPs and MOEs can be used to help develop NIMS objectives.

4-100. Possible considerations for MEB civil support planning include—

- Assistance with interorganizational planning.
- Assistance with initial needs assessment.
- Logistics support for civil authorities.
- Sustainment in a damaged austere environment.

4-101. Other possible considerations include—
- Assist the lead civil agency to define and share courses of action.
- Solicit agency understanding of roles.
- Develop measurable objectives.
- Assist in coordination of actions with other agencies to avoid duplicating effort.
- Plan to handover to civilian agencies as soon as feasible; end state and transition based on—
  - The ability of civilian organizations to carry out their responsibilities without military assistance.
  - The need to commit Army forces to other operations or preparation for other operations.
- Provide essential support to the largest possible number of people.
- Know the legal restrictions and rule for the use of force.
- Establish funding and document expenditures. (See NIMS procedures.)
- Identify and overcome obstacles.
  - Plan media operation and coordinate with local officials.
  - Maintain information assurance.
  - Establish liaison with the lead federal government agency.

PREPARE

4-102. Commanders should prepare for civil support operations by understanding the appropriate laws, policies, and directives that govern the military during response and planning and preparing with the agencies and organizations they will support before an incident. There may be little or no time to prepare for a specific civil support mission. When possible, the commander helps develop contingency plans and SOPs for potential natural and manmade disasters. The MEB may plan, receive units, and deploy within hours. It is possible that the MEB would link up with units on site during execution as they arrive from across a state or region.

4-103. Based on METT-TC factors, training before deployment in support of civil operations aids in preparing for and executing the necessary tasks. Many stability operations tasks correlate with civil support tasks. When possible, the MEB leaders and staff train with civil authorities.

4-104. Notification for civil support operations employment usually requires rapid reaction to an emergency, but sometimes may allow for deliberate preparation. After notification, the MEB commander and staff leverage the C2 system to coordinate and synchronize their operations with civilian authorities.

4-105. The deployment may be within a state or anywhere within the United States or its territories. The MEB should develop SOPs for the various methods and locations of deployment. Based on METT-TC, the MEB task organizes to conduct civil support operations. The MEB may deploy its TAC CP with additional staff augmentation as an EECP to provide on-site assessment and an immediate C2 presence. Whether the civil support mission warrants the entire MEB or one or more TFs from the MEB, affects deployment. The MEB task organization may change periodically as the need for particular services and support changes. MEB involved in civil support operations normally will be task-organized with CBRN, engineer, medical, MP, PA, and potentially units from other Services as well. Throughout the coordination effort, it is important for the commander and staff to understand and inform interagency personnel of the MEB's capabilities and limitations.

4-106. Due to nonhabitual supporting relationships and dissimilar equipment, the MEB and the lead governmental organization must ensure that there is close coordination in all areas. The MEB may collocate its headquarters with the lead agency to improve coordination. The MEB's headquarters may be established in tactical equipment or fixed facilities. By using liaison teams, the commander and staff work closely with interagency and other military elements.

4-107. A defense coordinating officer and assigned staff may not suffice for a complex disaster. When required, the MEB headquarters can control capabilities that the lead authority requires from the Department of Defense (DOD). Depending on the complexity of the operation, some staff augmentation may be required. The previously existing task organization of the MEB may require reinforcement with additional functional units to accomplish assigned missions. The MEB commander task organizes available assets for the mission and requests reinforcement as necessary.

4-108.   The MEB C2 headquarters can employ most capabilities that the lead agency requires from the DOD. Depending on the complexity of the operation, some staff augmentation may be required.

4-109.   All MEB leaders must understand the complex environment in which the brigade conducts its mission. The MEB must integrate its activities into the planning effort of the supported civilian agency, understand support requirements, and be aware of the supported agency's capabilities and limitations. This leader understanding creates an atmosphere that permits shared communications and forges a unified effort between elements. Integrating the MEB C2 system into the C2 systems of the lead governmental agency and local first responders may be a challenge. The extent to which the MEB C2 system is able to integrate into the supported agency C2 system depends upon the communications/network compatibility/capability of the supported agency.

4-110.   Often times an agency possesses data that, in its present form, creates compatibility issues with the MEB's format and the COP. It is incumbent upon the MEB to facilitate the exchange of information with the lead agency. During planning and execution, the MEB can deploy LNOs to the lead agency. The network centric environment of the MEB serves as the conduit for rapidly communicating information, while either stationary or while moving en route to the geographical site for support operations.

4-111.   When the MEB works closely with an agency, the problem sets can be complex and diverse. Both the MEB and the agency must leverage their skill sets and resources to better inform leaders and maximize its greatest potential when preparing to conduct a civil support operation. By eliminating redundancies and identifying shortfalls in corresponding capabilities, the MEB creates the conditions for a unified effort. The MEB must always protect its information, leverage its ISR capabilities and the communications network to enhance situational awareness, and verify the lead governmental agencies capability to fuse data. There are several key points preparing for civil support operations.

EXECUTE

4-112.   The MEB will do what is required to accomplish its mission during the conduct of civil support operations even though task organizations may need to be changed. The MEB will execute support area operations for the brigade and may do so for others. The MEB may not be assigned an AO. The brigade will execute consequence management in addition to other required civil support.

4-113.   Executing civil support operations must occur within the guidelines laid out by the lead civil agency. When requested and within the legal limits of federal and state law, the MEB may leverage attached/OPCON ISR assets and network by positioning sensors, robotics, or forces in a manner that provides rapid and accurate data flow to lead governmental agencies, which enables them to assess the situation and the status of objectives. The civil agency may require an adjustment to the plan and the MEB must be ready to modify its ongoing operations. The information processes the MEB has in place, because of its communication network, will allow for rapid dissemination of potential issues to the lead agency for resolution.

4-114.   When executing civil support operations, MEB leaders and staff must—

- Be familiar with the incident command system (ICS) and be able to follow unified command system procedures for the integration and implementation of each system.
- Know how the systems integrate and support the incident.
- Be familiar with the overall operation of the two command systems and be able to assist in implementing the unified command system if needed.
- Know how to develop an Incident Action Plan and identify assets available for controlling weapons of mass destruction (WMD) and hazardous material events.
- Coordinate these activities with the on-scene incident commander.
- Be familiar with steps to take to assist in planning operational goals and objectives that are to be followed on site in cooperation with the on-scene incident commander.

- Know how to interface with and integrate requisite emergency support services and resources among the emergency operations center (EOC) management and the incident or unified command on-scene incident management team.
- Be familiar with the coordination functions and procedures that are to be conducted by and with the EOC in support of on-scene emergency response activities.

4-115. The tasks of Soldiers are similar to many of the tasks in stability operations. In most cases, they do not need to have as much knowledge of the ICS.

4-116. While civil support operations vary greatly in every mission, the MEB can expect events to follow a pattern of planning, preparation, response, and recovery. If civil support is provided concurrently with homeland defense, then the MEB must be prepared to transition to support the offensive and defensive operations of other military forces. Planning was discussed above. Transition is the last phase in joint doctrine and is discussed below.

PREPARATION

4-117. MEB preparation for disaster response depends upon priority of other missions. If the MEB is a regular Army Title 10 unit, then mission priorities may dictate minimal planning and preparation for civil support operations. On the other hand, a National Guard MEB may have enough time to plan and prepare for civil support operation with other civil and military organizations.

4-118. Preparation implements approved plans and relevant agreements to increase readiness through a variety of tasks. Such tasks may include, but are not limited to—

- Develop common SOPs and TTP with expected supported and supporting elements.
- Task organize to fill any gaps in duties and responsibilities.
- Train personnel and leaders on nonmilitary terminology and procedures used in support of civil authorities (such as the incident command system).
- Obtain (through training) the proper credentials for key personnel.
- Exercise and refine plans with military and civilian counterparts.
- Obtain the proper equipment to provide the required capability.
- Develop, request, and maintain logistics packages for follow-on resupply and maintenance of all classes of supplies in support of extended operations.
- Prepare and maintain medical records for all personnel to ensure that they are up to date.
- Ensure that all communications equipment, communications security, and controlled cryptographic items are serviceable and ready to deploy.

RESPONSE

4-119. As part of a response, the MEB's subordinate units and/or liaison teams enter the affected area and make contact with relief organizations. They relay pertinent information about the effort of these organizations up through their military chain of command. The military chain of command relays this information to the lead civil authority. Planning for the operation, staging command posts into the area, establishing security, deploying the MEB's subordinate units, and initiating contact with supported activities and other parts of the relief force occur during this phase of operations.

4-120. The commander considers leading with liaison teams and urgent relief assets, such as debris clearance, law enforcement, search and rescue, food, and water. The lead unit's C2 system gives the MEB units robust early ability to communicate and coordinate with each other and those organization with which the C2 INFOSYSs are compatible. Further, MEB units' ability to reconnoiter and gather information makes them useful in the initial efforts by civil and other authorities to establish SA and control of the area and oversee critical actions.

RECOVERY

4-121. Once the MEB civil support operation is underway, recovery begins. With initial working relationship between all organizations in place, the MEB maintains steady progress in relieving the situation throughout this phase of operations. The MEB's work includes coordination with its higher headquarters, supported groups, and other relief forces and daily allocation of its own assets to recovery tasks.

4-122. The MEB task organization is likely to change periodically as the need for particular services and support changes. Security, maintenance, effective employment of resources, and Soldier support all need continuing attention. The brigade surgeon advises and assists the MEB commander in counteracting the psychological effects of disaster relief work and exposure to human suffering on the MEB's Soldiers throughout the operation.

RESTORATION

4-123. Restoration is the return of normality to the area. In most cases, the MEB disengages before restoration begins. The Federal Emergency Management Agency is in charge of restoration operations for civil support.

4-124. Civil support operations end in different ways. Crises may be resolved or the MEB may hand off a continuing civil support operation to a replacement unit, a relief agency, a police force, or other civil authority. Missions of short duration or narrow scope may end with the completion of the assigned task.

ASSESS

4-125. The MEB C2 system is essential to support the interagency overall assessment. The MEB's network centric environment provides for a robust exchange of information. A common problem that both the MEB and a nonmilitary agency may encounter is information overload or a different perception on how an operation is progressing. Commanders share the COP with their civil agency counterpart and their interpretation of the situation in order to ensure a unified effort. Liaison should occur to demonstrate this capability and verify the method in which information sharing will occur.

4-126. The MEB leverages its C2 system capabilities and supports a degraded or destroyed civilian C2/communications system. The MEB brings its mobile network and augments and/or replaces a devastated civil infrastructure. Most first responders' communications are wireless using tower-based repeating which are powered by the grid. In the case of hurricane Katrina in 2005, the storm rendered all municipal communications inoperative. In such a case, the MEB augments local law enforcement, emergency medical, fire services, and other first responder's communications with the Battle Command Network to restore vital services to the AO.

JOINT AND FORCE PROJECTION CONSIDERATIONS

JOINT PLANNING PROCESS

4-127. When an MEB is directly subordinate to a JTF it may participate in joint operations planning and receives joint-formatted orders. The MEB could also support joint planning under a division or corps supporting a JTF but would use the Army planning process and the five-paragraph field order format for its internal orders. (See FM 3-0.) The MEB staff may participate in joint contingency or crisis action planning. MEB leaders should understand the joint planning process and be familiar with the joint format for plans and orders. (See CJCSM 3122.03A and JP 5-0 for additional guidance on joint operations planning and preparation of joint plans and orders.)

4-128. MEB systems are joint interdependent and the brigade routinely employs joint capabilities. The MEB integrates joint capabilities that complement Army assigned capabilities to accomplish tactical objectives. Joint capabilities include fires, layered ISR sensors to fill in voids in brigade coverage, protection, communications, and sustainment capabilities.

FORCE PROJECTION PROCESS

4-129. *Force projection* is the ability to project the military instrument of national power from the United States or another theater in response to requirements for military operations (JP 5-0). Force projection operations extend from mobilization and deployment of forces to redeployment to CONUS or home theater. (See JP 3-35.) Force projection also applies to rapidly deploying forces to respond to a HLS requirement or national emergency or disaster (civil support operations).

4-130. The MEB could participate in or may be required to provide support to any of the five processes of force projection: mobilization, deployment, employment, sustainment, and redeployment. The operations discussed in this manual focus on employment and sustainment. When required, the MEB may conduct operations to support deployment or redeployment. (See figure 4-2, page 4-22.)

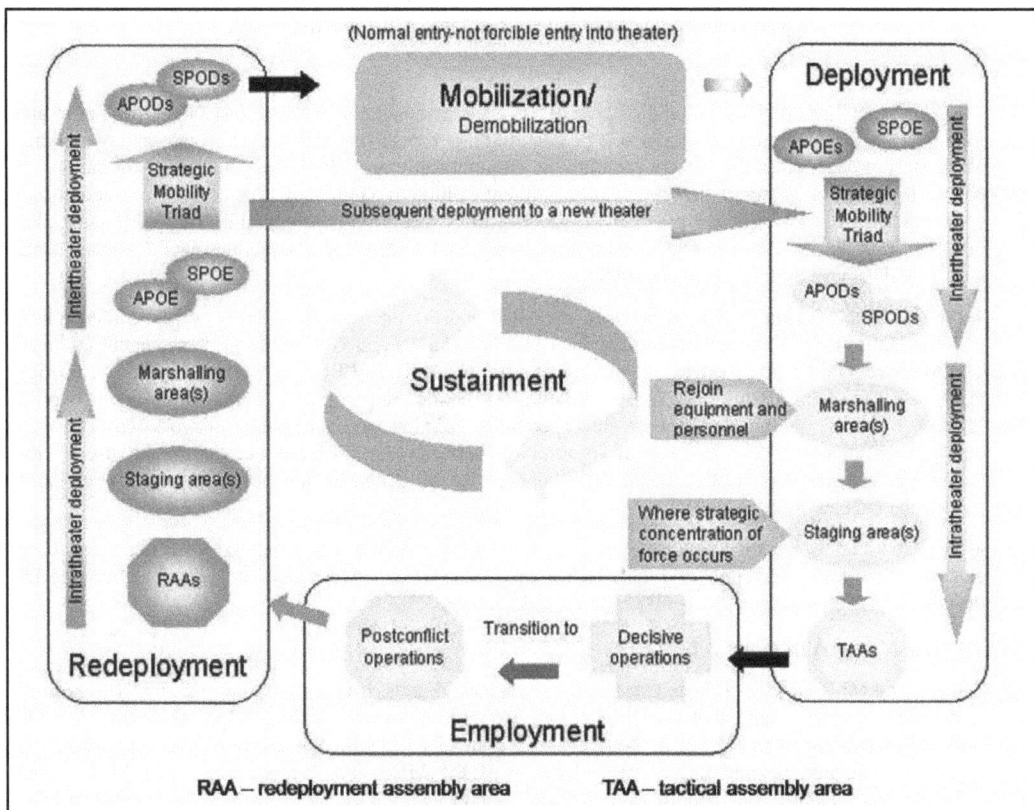

Figure 4-2. Force projection process

TASK ORGANIZATION AND STAFF AUGMENTATION

4-131. The MEB both receives and provides units and capabilities as a part of task organization. The MEB staff requires augmentation to perform some tasks and will provide C2 for some units until they are needed to be attached to other units for a mission, and then receive them back or assist them in moving to another area or command.

4-132. The MEB commander is responsible for ensuring that the brigade's organic and task-organized forces are combat ready and properly integrated into existing MEB formations. The MEB should develop SOPs for attaching and detaching units and small teams.

TRAINING ATTACHMENTS

4-133. Because the MEB has few organic units, there is a high-frequency requirement to train attached units and small teams and occasionally augmentation of staff expertise to understand the units or capabilities it will be receiving, plan for their integration, and C2 their use and sustainment within the MEB. The MEB staff must also be trained to properly conduct operations employing the capabilities provided by these attachments. The MEB staff may also require augmentation to accomplish nonstandard missions. Successful MANSPT operations depend on the ability of the MEB to integrate functionally organized units, task organizes them as needed, and employ them during the conduct of full spectrum operations. The MEB must train to request and leverage pooled Army and joint capabilities as necessary.

4-134. The MEB provides training to assigned, attached, and OPCON units on the MEB SOPs, MANSPT operations, and security and defense TTPs. Units within the MEB's AO that are attached or TACON for security will be trained on security TTPs and incorporated into MEB defensive plans.

PLANNING

4-135. The MEB optimizes the employment of assigned, attached, OPCON, or TACON Army forces and joint, interagency, and multinational assets by ensuring the respective staffs integrate plans and operations. MEB staff procedures must include continuous communications with the augmentation formations to ensure that they understand the commander's intent. Unity of command, planning, and standardized communications procedures are essential to successfully execute battle command. The MEB must plan how it will integrate Army forces and joint, interagency, and multinational assets into its C2 system, share a COP, and achieve high levels of shared SA.

4-136. The networking interfaces between the MEB and the integration of Army or joint, interagency, and multinational units requires coordination with gaining units and configuration management controls. The MEB requires established legacy waveforms SINCGARS, EPLRS, high frequency and ultra high frequency, COMSEC keying, and signal operating instructions requirements to maintain voice networks. Internet protocol routing and server interoperability requires a coordinated network configuration management to ensure the passage of information between the different networks. The use of the communication elements must be coordinated between the MEB and its attached, OPCON, TACON, and supported elements.

4-137. In addition, logistical and personnel issues must be coordinated between the MEB and its attached elements. Sources of personnel and materiel resupply must be understood and considered in planning for the conduct of MEB operations by all elements under its control.

SUSTAINMENT OF ATTACHED UNITS

4-138. The MEB provides selected sustainment to attached units. It is not required doctrinally to provide sustainment support to units that are OPCON or TACON to the brigade although special arrangement can be made. As discussed in chapter 2, the MEB BSB generally lacks the capability to provide sustainment support to anything beyond the organic elements of the MEB—the brigade HHC, the MEB signal company, and the BSB HHD, and distribution and support maintenance companies. While it may provide limited and selected support to some attachments, as a rule attachments must bring their own sustainment support with them. For example, a combat engineer battalion attached to a MEB should have a supporting FSC that will be attached to the MEB BSB. Joint, interagency, and multinational elements likewise should bring their own support capabilities with them when they are attached to the MEB. Otherwise, the headquarters directing the attachment of joint, interagency, and multinational elements to the MEB, or their support by the MEB, will have to provide additional Army sustainment assets to the MEB. The MEB staff will integrate its organic and attached sustainment assets to support brigade operations.

4-139. In any MEB operational plan, sources of sustainment must be determined for and understood by the MEB and all attached, OPCON, or TACON elements in order to ensure successful MEB operations.

4-140. If properly resourced, the MEB could provide support for—
- Other U.S. joint forces.
- Multinational or HN government agencies.

- Other U.S. government agencies.
- Multinational or HN civilians.
- Multinational or HN military forces.
- Authorized international organizations and nongovernmental organizations.

OTHER TASK ORGANIZATION CONSIDERATION

4-141. Joint, interagency, and multinational resources supporting the MEB will all have different organizational and operational cultures and procedures. Care should be taken by the MEB commander, staff, and units to be aware of these differences to ensure successful operations. With U.S. joint and interagency assets, the differences between the MEB commander and staff culture and procedures and the culture and procedures of these assets may not be as great as with multinational participants but those differences still require consideration. Other services and civilian agencies may have different definitions of similar-seeming terms. Common operational expectations and understandings must be ensured before planning and operations begin.

4-142. With multinational augmentation, the need for ensuring common operational expectations and understanding increases. MEB leaders and Soldiers should respect the culture, religions, customs, and principles of multinational forces, combined with an understanding and consideration of their ideas, to solidify the working relationship. Respect builds confidence while lack of respect leads to friction that may jeopardize mission accomplishment. MEB personnel must be proactive in building a mutually beneficial relationship.

4-143. If the MEB is part of a multinational force, the MEB commander must immediately establish rapport with the senior commanders of the multinational force. Effective liaison is essential to overcome misunderstandings and misconceptions. Using liaison teams, both horizontally and vertically, eliminates confusion and cannot be overemphasized. Commanders and staffs must learn and understand the capabilities of multinational forces. Differences in languages and customs may create barriers and tension leading to fractures in a multinational force.

4-144. The MEB must develop procedures to share COP information with multinational forces. While some multinational or multinational members may possess the technology to digitally share information, others may not. Disseminating classified COP information to multinational partners requires detailed coordination to establish proper protocols. Before sharing information, the MEB must establish procedures for processing and sharing data. Units must anticipate what information and intelligence can be exchanged and then obtain the necessary authorizations. When necessary, intelligence should be sanitized to facilitate dissemination. (See FM 100-8 for additional information on working with multinational forces. See JP 3-08 for additional information on working with international organizations.)

This page intentionally left blank.

Chapter 5

Maneuver Support Operations

This chapter introduces the Army definitions for maneuver support operations and movement corridor. It discusses the integration of key protection, movement and maneuver, and sustainment tasks and the continuous integration of these major areas of MANSPT operations. It discusses how to think differently about combined arms operations to support movement and maneuver and apply key aspects of protection to movement as part of maneuver support operations. The MEB was designed with a staff that is optimized to conduct MANSPT operations. The integration of MANSPT operations is typically a continuous process. This chapter discusses the fundamentals of MANSPT operations and looks at the typical tasks associated with MANSPT operations. See FM 3-90 and other appropriate manuals for further discussion of tasks associated with movement and maneuver. For further discussion of selected sustainment tasks, see FM 3-19.1, FM 3-34, and, and FM 3-34.400.

FUNDAMENTALS

FRAMEWORK

5-1. *Maneuver support operations* **integrate the complementary and reinforcing capabilities of key protection, movement and maneuver, and sustainment functions, tasks, and systems to enhance freedom of action.** An overview of MANSPT operations was provided in chapter 1 and its primary subordinate tasks were identified in chapter 2. This chapter further develops the discussion of what maneuver support operations are and how they may be implemented. The following is a framework to think systematically about MANSPT operations.

5-2. MANSPT operations integrate the complementary and reinforcing capabilities of key functions, tasks, organizations, and systems organic to and task organized to the MEB within the primary warfighting functions included in the definition above and synchronizes them across all of the Army warfighting functions. A lesser focus is applied to sustainment and intelligence warfighting functions with selected application within the fires and C2 warfighting functions. MANSPT actions occur throughout the operations process (plan, prepare, execute, and assess).

5-3. Rather than the independent performance of functional tasks, MANSPT operations are usually combined arms activities. *Combined arms* is the synchronized and simultaneous application of units to achieve an effect greater than if each was used separately or sequentially. Many units may conduct specific tasks that complement or reinforce protection, movement and maneuver, or sustainment. However, when MEB units perform these tasks in an integrated fashion, it is viewed as MANSPT operations rather than a branch function operation or task. It is often more efficient and more effective when all members of the supporting units provide the creative thinking to identify tasks best performed by task-organized subordinate headquarters to increase the teamwork, synergy, and efficient use of forces. For example, a similar task common for many units is conduct reconnaissance. When multiple task-organized MEB units perform these similar reconnaissance tasks as a team to complement protection, movement and maneuver, or sustainment, they may be conducting MANSPT operations. This teamwork reduces security requirements, economizes use of manpower and equipment, improves operational security (OPSEC), improves ISR integration, and increases the combat power of the formation performing the tasks.

5-4. The MEB integrates task-organized organizations and units, capabilities, tasks, and systems to conduct MANSPT operations. CBRN, engineer, and MP units constitute the core body of MEB units that contribute to MANSPT operations. If required support can be performed by a single branch pure unit, then the MEB would assign a pure functional battalion or company a branch task and purpose rather than a MANSPT task and purpose. To view the nested efforts; the MEB would conduct MANSPT operations while a subordinate functional pure battalion or company would conduct a branch task. If METT-TC determines that required support can be performed better by integrating branch pure units, then the MEB may create a battalion TF or company team and assign them a MANSPT operations task and purpose. The TF or company team may still perform some purely functional tasks.

5-5. MANSPT operations can shape the OE and help protect the force. MEB mobility and countermobility support can modify the physical environment, and help dominate terrain. MEB protection support can protect the force and physical assets. The MEB conducts MANSPT operations to support the higher headquarters and its assigned units.

PROTECTION

5-6. An overview of protection was provided in chapter 1. Joint doctrine defines protection as preventive measures taken to mitigate hostile actions against DOD personnel (to include family members), resources, facilities, and critical information. Protection does not include actions to defeat the enemy or protect against accidents, weather, or disease (JP 5-0). Protection is an overarching concept that is inherent to command within all military operations. The Army includes protecting personnel (combatants and noncombatants) within the protection warfighting function. (See FM 3-0.)

5-7. Unable to challenge the United States in conventional combat, adversaries seek to frustrate operations by resorting to asymmetric means, weapons, or tactics. Protection counters these threats. The MEB uses counterintelligence and threat assessments to decrease the vulnerability of friendly forces. Dispersion during movement helps reduce losses from enemy fires and asymmetric actors. Camouflage discipline, local security, and field fortifications do the same. Protection of electronic links and nodes is vital to protecting information, information systems, and Soldiers.

5-8. All support and functional brigades provide needed protection support. Although it does take a unit with a robust staff to integrate all the protection efforts, no single brigade can best integrate or own protection. Protection may a significant commitment of resources that can limit a formation's freedom of action if not integrated deliberately.

5-9. Some protection tasks are GMETs for all units. Units normally do not need augmentation to perform these GMET tasks. For unit self-protection, the MEB must be proficient on the GMET of Protect the Force and these supporting tasks:

- Conduct Area Security.
- Employ Survivability Measures.
- Employ CBRNE Protection Measures.
- Employ Air Defense Measures.
- Conduct Personnel Recovery Operations.

5-10. When resourced and tasked, the MEB can best integrate, provide combined arms augmentation, or support these tasks included in the protection warfighting function:

- AMD (coordination).
- Operational area security.
- Antiterrorism.
- Survivability.
- CBRN operations.
- EOD.

5-11. The MEB will provide some support of the protection warfighting function tasks to forces located within the MEB's assigned AO:

- AMD.
- Fratricide avoidance.
- Operational area security.
- Survivability.
- CBRN operations.
- EOD.

5-12. Most units can generally conduct the other tasks included in the protection warfighting function with minimal support:

- Personnel recovery.
- Information protection.
- Fratricide avoidance.
- Antiterrorism.
- Force health protection (FHP).
- Safety.
- Operations security.

5-13. Some protection warfighting function tasks frequently require support or augmentation from the MEB or another support or functional brigade. The MEB coordinates the integration of key protection tasks with the higher headquarters protection staff, cells, or directorates. The MEB may conduct all protection tasks for themselves. Table 5-1 shows the protection tasks that may be performed or coordinated by the MEB for others during MANSPT operations or support area operations.

Table 5-1. MEB protection support

Protection tasks	During MANSPT operations	During support area operations
AMD	Coordination	Coordination
Personnel recovery		X
Information protection		
Fratricide avoidance		Coordination
Operational area security	X	X
Antiterrorism	X	X
Survivability	X	X
Force health protection		Coordination
CBRN operations	X	X
Safety		
Operations security		
EOD	X	X

Air and Missile Defense

5-14. The MEB staff includes an air space management section and an air operations section to coordinate actions during support area operations or when the MEB is assigned an AO. The MEB may include AMD units. (See chapter 6.)

Personnel Recovery

5-15. The MEB staff has no unique capabilities to conduct this protection task but could support a unit personnel recovery mission with the MEB's assigned, attached, or OPCON units. Personnel recovery is one task the MEB performs when assigned an AO. (See FMI 3-0.1.) The Army defines *personnel recovery* as the sum of military, diplomatic, and civil efforts to prepare for and execute the recovery and reintegration of isolated personnel (JP 3-50).

Operational Area Security

5-16. Many parts of the MEB staff contribute to the MEB's capability to conduct operational area security, typically performed when the MEB is assigned an AO. (See chapter 6.) At the operational level, survivability, area and base security contribute to protection and preserves combat power. (See JP 3-10.1.) Commanders should consider—

- **Sites, accommodations, and defensive positions.** Precautions should be taken to protect positions, headquarters, support facilities, and accommodations. These may include obstacles and shelters. Units must also practice alert procedures and develop drills to rapidly occupy positions. A robust engineer force can provide support to meet survivability needs. Units should maintain proper camouflage and concealment based on METT-TC. Additional information on precautions is provided in FM 3-06 and FM 5-103.
- **Roadblocks.** MP forces may establish and maintain roadblocks. If MP forces are unavailable, other forces may assume this responsibility. Roadblocks can be used not only to restrict traffic for security purposes but also to control the movement of critical cargo in support of humanitarian operations. As a minimum, the area should be highly visible and defensible with an armed over watch.
- **Personnel vulnerabilities.** Forces are always vulnerable to personnel security risks from local employees and other personnel subject to bribes, threats, or compromise. The threat from local criminal elements is also a constant threat and protection consideration.
- **Personal awareness.** An effective measure for survivability is individual awareness by Soldiers in all circumstances. Soldiers must look for things out of place and patterns preceding aggression. Commanders should ensure that Soldiers remain alert and do not establish a routine.
- **Sniper threats.** In stability operations and civil support operations, the sniper can pose a significant threat. Counters include rehearsed responses, reconnaissance and surveillance, battlefield obscuration, and cover and concealment. ROE should provide specific instructions on how to react to sniper fire, to include restrictions on weapons to be used. Units can use specific weapons, such as sniper rifles, to eliminate a sniper and reduce collateral damage.
- **Security measures.** Security measures are METT-TC dependent and may include the full range of active and passive measures such as patrolling, reconnaissance and surveillance, and use of reaction forces. Every Army leader has the inherent responsibility to secure their formation or position and must do so with the organic capabilities and the means at hand.
- **Coordination.** Commanders should coordinate security with local military and civil agencies and humanitarian organizations when possible.
- **Evacuation.** Commanders must have a plan to evacuate the force should conditions warrant, such as war erupting during the conduct of a peacekeeping operations or a host nation withdrawing support for humanitarian and civic assistance. This plan should include appropriate routes for ground, sea, or air evacuation. All units should rehearse their evacuation plan and develop contingency plans that cover such tasks as the breakout from an encirclement or the fighting of a delaying action. OPSEC is critical as public knowledge of such plans or witnessing of a rehearsal could erode the confidence of the local population and thus the legitimacy of the mission.

Security During Movement

5-17. The MEB has several capabilities that can be used to apply additional protection to movement. One method may be to use movement corridors to provide protection and enable movement. (See the example at paragraph 5-75.) When controlling movement, the MEB determines the most effective means and mode of transporting, moving, maneuvering, or repositioning organic, attached, OPCON, and TACON units and capabilities in concert with the environment, the commander's intent, and available assets. The MEB considers several factors to determine or to provide guidance on the arrangement of force capabilities, movement planning and preparation requirements, combat loads, movement techniques and formations, and on using HN or civilian support. Some of those factors include—

- Likelihood of threat interference or contact.
- Weapons and munitions mix and configuration.
- Proximity to field trains or resupply capability.
- Terrain and weather effects.
- Access to other route or maneuver options.
- Specific characteristics of the transported capability or cargo.
- Movement control measures.
- Civil considerations.

Antiterrorism

5-18. *Antiterrorism* is the defensive measures used to reduce the vulnerability of individuals and property to terrorist acts, to include limited response and containment by local military and civilian forces. (JP 3-07.2) (See JP 1-02 and FM 3-07.) Terrorism may well be the most likely threat that Army forces will face when conducting stability operations and civil support operations. Commanders have an inherent responsibility for conducting antiterrorism measures to provide for the security of the command.

5-19. Antiterrorism support from the MEB could include assisting in unit and installation threat and vulnerability assessments, establishing special reaction teams and protective services, establishing civil-military partnerships for WMD crisis and consequence management, supporting survivability operations, ADC, and security of key locations and personnel.

Survivability Operations

5-20. *Survivability operations* are the development and construction of protective positions, such as earth berms, dug-in positions, overhead protection, and countersurveillance means, to reduce the effectiveness of enemy weapons systems. (FM 3-34.) Key tasks also include protecting against enemy hazards in the AO conducting related security operations, and conducting actions to control pollution and hazardous materials. The MEB engineer operations cell and engineer units may conduct survivability operations in their AO or as part of MANSPT operations. Other cells and units (to include the CBRNE cell and CBRN units) may also participate in survivability operations. (See FM 5-103.)

Chemical, Biological, Radiological, Nuclear, and High Yield Explosives Operations

5-21. CBRNE operations include integrated CBRN and EOD operations that may also require collaborative coordination with engineers. The MEB staff includes a CBRNE cell to integrate CBRN and EOD tasks and units into CBRNE operations. EOD actions are often also integrated with engineer operations.

MOVEMENT AND MANEUVER

5-22. Movement is necessary to disperse and displace the force as a whole when maneuvering. (See FM 3-0.) Movement helps provide/enhance protection. Most units move without a combat force to provide added security. This is normally an economy of force measure. The movement of units not conducting maneuver does not have this inherent level of protection. The opposite is true; they become more vulnerable and need added protection. Protection must often be applied to units that are conducting movement and are not capable of maneuver. Most units that conduct only movement do not have the combat power that a maneuver unit does and therefore are less secure during movement. MANSPT operations apply protection to movement and are initially integrated though the operation process. Units apply protection to movement by the combined arms application of its assigned units, capabilities, and systems. Effective movement also requires MANSPT operations planning and resources.

5-23. Maneuver is the employment of forces in the operational area through movement in combination with fires to achieve a position of advantage in respect to the enemy in order to accomplish the mission (JP

3-0). Maneuver is the means by which commanders mass the effects of combat power to achieve surprise, shock, and momentum. (See FM 3-0.) When a unit maneuvers, it moves and fires which provides an inherent level of protection. Any other move may be referred to as movement, categorized as tactical ground movement, air movement, and administrative movement. These movements require deliberate effort to apply protection.

5-24. As highlighted in chapter 1, movement and maneuver is an Army element of combat power and a warfighting function. The movement and maneuver warfighting function is the related tasks and systems that move forces to achieve a position of advantage in relation to the enemy. Direct fire is inherent in maneuver, as in close combat. (See FM 3-0.) The integration and synchronization of MANSPT-related tasks shape the environment to provide mobility and countermobility, provide or enhance other movement and maneuver tasks, and expand the freedom of action of friendly forces while denying it to the enemy. MANSPT operations directly enable the movement and maneuver warfighting function. The movement and maneuver warfighting function does not include administrative movements of personnel and materiel. These movements fall under the sustainment warfighting function.

SUSTAINMENT

5-25. Sustainment is an Army element of combat power and a warfighting function (FM 3-0 and FM 4-0). Several key tasks performed by the MEB are aligned under sustainment in FM 7-15. The support to the sustainment warfighting function provided by the MEB is primarily through its focus on tasks associated with general engineering support and internment and resettlement operations.

MANEUVER SUPPORT INTEGRATION

5-26. MANSPT operations represent combined arms operations that typically require the MEB to integrate key capabilities within and across the warfighting functions in a complementary or reinforcing manner to achieve the effect of enhancing freedom of action within the division or higher echelons. The MEB conducts MANSPT operations to complement or reinforce primarily the protection, movement and maneuver, and sustainment related capabilities in a scalable manner necessary to extend and maintain tactical momentum and operational reach. For example, the MEB reinforces the movement and maneuver function with mobility, countermobility, and obscuration capabilities to enable an operational tempo that threat forces cannot maintain. (See figure 5-1.) Similarly, the MEB complements the sustainment function when it applies protection to transportation through the conduct of convoy escort. However, movement corridor operations reflect an expansion of security tasks within the protection function and therefore are considered reinforcing capabilities to route and area security operations.

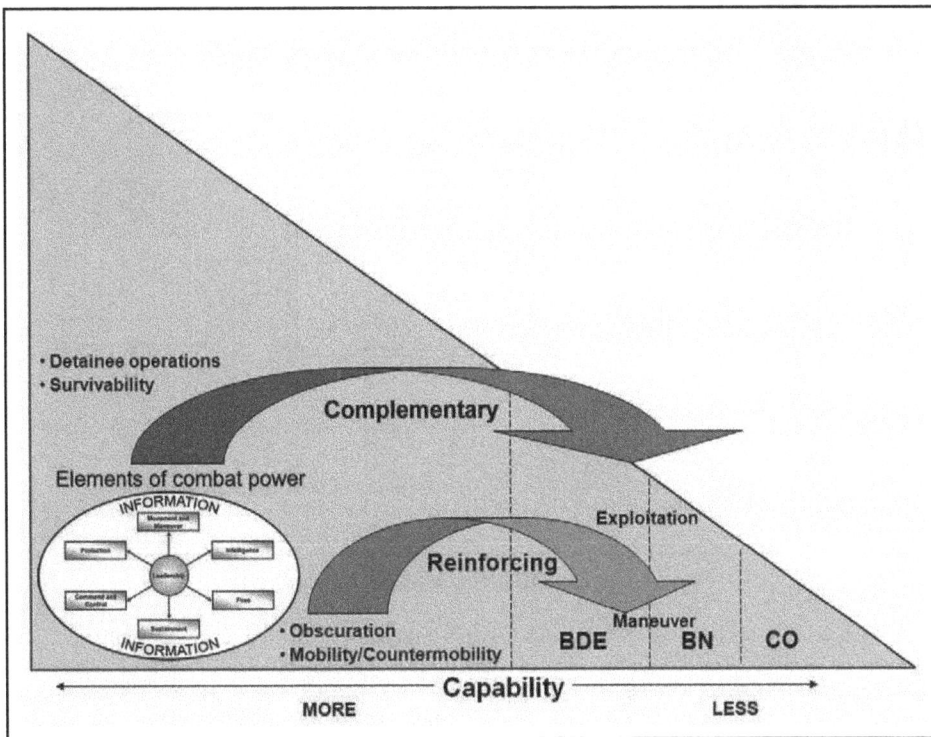

Figure 5-1. Complementary and reinforcing capabilities

5-27. The MEB is in essence a C2 organization that represents the C2 function. For this reason, when functional brigades, such as MP or engineer, provide functional forces to the MEB, we can say that they are providing complementary capabilities because they are supporting the C2 warfighting function represented by the MEB headquarters. (See figure 5-2, page 5-8.)

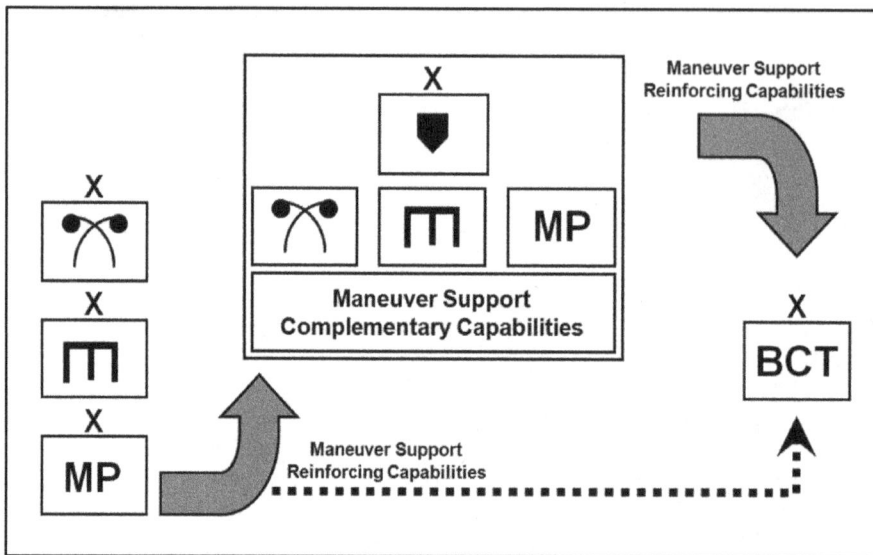

Figure 5-2. The MEB and MANSPT operations

5-28. The composition of the MEB headquarters staffed with CBRN, engineer, MP, fire support, intelligence, and aviation expertise makes it uniquely capable among other support or functional brigades when integrating these capabilities. The significant level of expertise resident in the CBRN, engineer, and MP functional areas enable a level of detail and precision in all facets of the operations process (prepare, plan, execute, assess) not possible in the BCTs or the functional brigades without augmentation. The MEB staff is trained and organized to facilitate MANSPT operations.

5-29. Typically, MANSPT operations at division and above are best conducted by the MEB rather than other potential headquarters because the MEB has the highest concentration of staff capabilities required for its integration and synchronization. Another formation may be tasked with conducting MANSPT operations if deliberately augmented with functional expertise from across the required functional units required for the specific purpose of providing freedom of action for a supported force.

5-30. Determining whether the MEB will provide complementary or reinforcing capabilities to the force supports decisionmaking and serves as a point of departure when task-organizing formations or recommending command and support relationships. The complementary and reinforcing character of the capabilities that the MEB typically provides permits the scalable expansion of key tasks and functions along a range or continuum of functional capability. (See figure 5-3.) This is significant because some warfighting functions do not maintain the same character as operations transition along the full spectrum operations among the levels of military action (strategic, operational, tactical) or as resources are applied to solve the tactical problem. The protection and movement and maneuver warfighting functions provide good examples of this.

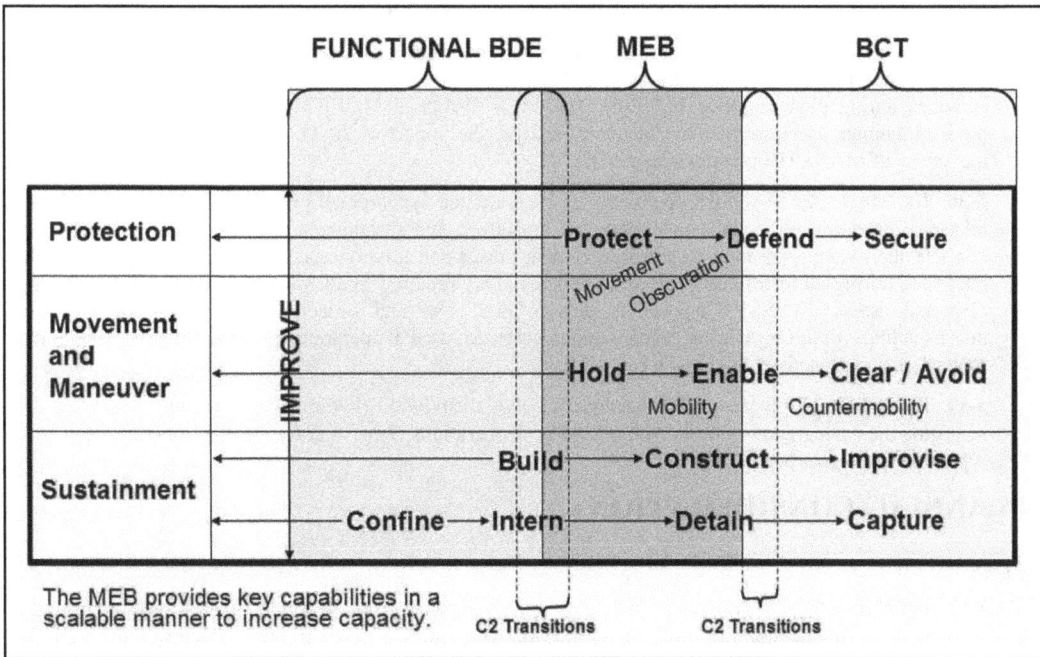

Figure 5-3. Increasing functional capabilities

5-31. Typically, the MEB simultaneously reinforces maneuver with mobility operations or tasks while complementing the movement with protection coordination. The MEB staff continually analyzes and examines how specific functions are affected as they expand along a capability scale to meet the changing requirements of the OE. Consequently, the MEB adjusts it mission profile, task organization, and C2 arrangement to accommodate those scalable effects.

FREEDOM OF ACTION

5-32. An overview of freedom of action is provided in chapter 1. Freedom of action allows the commander to seize, retain, and exploit operational initiative. Army forces gain and preserve freedom of action, reduce vulnerability, and exploit success through maneuver. (See FM 3-0.) Freedom of action includes the ability of commanders to exercise their wills to complete the mission, achieve the objective, affect movement, or to protect the force. MANSPT operations enhance maneuver and help protect forces that typically do not conduct maneuver. This contributes to enhancing freedom of action for the force.

5-33. The MEB increases freedom of action by shaping the OE, providing protection, and reducing impediments to operations. MANSPT operations deny the enemy freedom of action. Some MANSPT efforts set conditions, some are preemptive, and some are in response to the OE. Regardless of when they occur, MANSPT operations enhance the freedom of action of the commander.

5-34. MANSPT operations enhance freedom of action for the supported commander similarly to the sustainment warfighting function that provides support and services to ensure freedom of action. MANSPT operations are multifunctional and typically performed throughout all types of operations. The MEB primarily conducts mobility and countermobility operations to enhance freedom of maneuver. The brigade also primarily performs protection support coordination, movement corridor operations, and selected sustainment operations to enhance freedom of movement.

MANEUVER SUPPORT OPERATIONS AND THE OPERATIONS PROCESS

5-35. Commanders and staff use continuing activities to synchronize operations throughout the operations process (plan, prepare, execute, and assess). They use MDMP and troop leading procedures to integrate activities during planning (See FM 3-0). The MEB also uses METT-TC to continually consider the physical, human, and informational factors to analyze the impact of the OE on MANSPT operations and the impact of MANSPT operations on the OE.

5-36. The MEB uses MANSPT operations to integrate and synchronize primarily the selected key tasks related to primarily protection, movement and maneuver, and sustainment with the continuing activities and into the overall operation to generate combat power and mission success. MANSPT operations are integrated during all operations process activities and are required in all full spectrum operations. During plan and assess, MANSPT operations provide predictive and proactive capabilities and a better understanding of the OE. During prepare and execute, MANSPT operations provide initiative, flexibility, protection, and proactive OE shaping capabilities.

5-37. The MEB and other selected headquarters use their battle rhythm as a key control measure for managing their integration of tasks within MANSPT operations, across the warfighting functions, and with supported and higher headquarters.

PLANNING CONSIDERATIONS

PLAN

5-38. The integration of MANSPT operations is continuous and must be included in offense, defense, stability, or civil support operations. Using the operation process and MDMP, the MEB staff conducts mission analysis to determine the company level (two levels down) tasks. The staff then continuously integrates the tasks to plan combined arms MANSPT operations. The staff determines how these tasks can best be grouped. The staff may determine that some tasks are best performed by functionally pure units. The staff would then propose TF or company team formations and assign tasks to them or to functional unit headquarters. The TFs or company teams would execute most grouped tasks using combined arms formations but may also perform some functionally pure tasks. The staff may be asked to recommend the command or support relationship between the MEB forces or functional units and the supported headquarters. The staff continually assesses to update required tasks, integration, and changes to the task organization. The staff also synchronizes the MANSPT effort within all the warfighting functions at the brigade and with higher and supported headquarters. MANPST operations synchronization matrix can be used to integrate complementary and reinforcing efforts within and across the warfighting functions.

5-39. The MEB normally conducts combined arms shaping and sustaining operations or tasks. Occasionally the MEB may conduct the decisive operation or task for a higher headquarters. The purpose of the operation or task would define whether to think of the effort as shaping or sustaining. For example emplacing an obstacle to deny an enemy freedom of maneuver against a BCT conducting an attack would be a shaping operation. Emplacing the same obstacle as part of a base entry control point to protect a guard tower would be viewed as a protection task. The building of the same obstacle may be a general engineering and considered as a sustainment task.

5-40. Planners should use these maneuver support planning considerations:

- Integrate operations, task, and new units.
- Integrate with supported headquarters.
- Analyze when to transfer efforts to functional organizations.
- Analyze when to form combined arms TFs and company teams.
- Phase task organization of attachments and detachments; ensure sustainment.
- Deliberately apply protection to movement.
- Balance support area operations efforts and MANSPT operations.
- Reach back to augment expertise.
- Mitigate the effects of the complex environment.

5-41. Planners also—

- Analyze tasks where a combined arms MANSPT operations approach is a better way to conduct tasks than a pure functional effort. Some examples may include gap (river) crossing, reconnaissance, route clearance, convoy protection/security, consequence management, and movement corridors.
- Keep the tasks under brigade control that it takes a brigade staff to C2.
- Give the TF and company team the tasks they are resourced to perform.
- Give other tasks to subordinate pure functional units.
- Provide MEB units and capabilities to others with a command or support relationship if they are best done by one unit or capability under the supported units C2.

5-42. The MEB has a multifunctional staff to plan, prepare, execute, and assess the efforts of organic, attached, and OPCON units and capabilities so that the supported headquarters staff does not need to. TF and company team headquarters also alleviate the need for supported headquarters to integrate multiple supporting units. This is valid for most operations but especially valid for MANSPT operations.

5-43. A supported unit may receive support from the MEB and other pure functional units at the same time. The supported unit could use the attached or OPCON MEB unit headquarters to C2 or integrate the other functional support. When the MEB and one or more functional brigades support a BCT the brigade headquarters coordinates the efforts. If no MEB is available a functional (CBRN, engineer, or MP brigade (or battalion) may be required to integrate efforts to conduct MANSPT operations.

PREPARE

5-44. Once a task organization has been approved, the staff can issue a warning order to the subordinate MEB units to allow them to reorganize and synchronize movement and rehearsals with supported headquarters.

5-45. The MEB must orient assigned units to understand how they contribute to MANSPT operations and how they operate as part of MANSPT combined arms teams. There will be cases where MEB units provide purely functional support.

5-46. The MEB forms TFs and company teams as necessary to accomplish its missions. The MEB must build mutual trust quickly with units that have been task-organized to them and verify that all formations are combat ready.

5-47. When units from the MEB are required to support other units, the MEB may provide battalion TFs, company teams, or functional units to the BCT. The gaining unit integrates and synchronizes task organization of these resources (if the command and support relationship allows that) until the mission is completed. The provided resources will then be returned to the MEB or tasked to provide mission support in another AO.

5-48. The MEB will conduct key rehearsals. When assigned an AO or conducting the tasks associated with a movement corridor, rehearsals may include—fires, commitment of the MEB reserve, or commitment of a TCF.

EXECUTE

5-49. The MEB is a multifunctional combined arms headquarters that accepts and provides C2 to units that conduct MANSPT operations across the higher headquarters AO in support of other units or within its assigned AO, and in support of the higher headquarters. It assists its higher headquarters to conduct the integration of MANSPT operations. It also supports operational movement and maneuver of units during deployment.

5-50. Although the MEB may frequently attach and detach more units than other support brigades, it must also continually provides integrated and synchronized services like the other support brigades. The MEB must not be viewed as an intermediate force pool/force provider.

5-51. The MEB provides C2 over key mobility areas within its AO or as tasked to support within a BCT's AO. Based on reconnaissance, topographical, and terrain analysis, the MEB validates and further develops the supported headquarters modified combined obstacle overlay in its assigned AO. When necessary to ensure the mobility of the force, the MEB directs necessary actions to eliminate, neutralize, or reduce physical and potential inhibitors to friendly movement and maneuver. The MEB develops information requirements essential to maintaining a maneuver-focused situational awareness that contributes to the commander's COP. This focused awareness enables the acceleration of friendly maneuver decisions and the prevention of enemy countermobility efforts.

5-52. Based on an analysis of METT-TC and commander's guidance from the higher headquarters, the MEB will tailor forces for MANSPT operations, structure support assignments and forces, and provide support from within its task organization to the remainder of the force. The MEB has a wide array of capabilities with which to defeat enemy threats in its assigned AO. These capabilities consist of direct fires of assigned, attached, OPCON, or TACON forces and the ability to leverage Army and joint lethal and nonlethal precision fire assets, Army and joint aviation assets. (See FM 3-90.)

ASSESS

5-53. The MEB must continually assess the OE to predict and detect impediment to operations and adjust MANSPT operations to mitigate impediments. It must assess the progress and effectiveness all MEB operations to shift resources across those operations as required. It must assess the effects of MANSPT operations on enemy freedom of action and the freedom of action provided for the echelon headquarters that it is supporting.

5-54. The staff can use the measures from FM 7-15 where tasks exist. Other MANSPT operations tasks are still being developed at this time and units may need to initially develop specific MOPs or MOEs to address some of the MANSPT operations tasks.

PROTECTION

5-55. The MEB performs key supporting tasks as a part of the task-perform protection. These key supporting tasks are highlighted below.

CONDUCT SURVIVABILITY OPERATIONS

5-56. The MEB is optimized to conduct a host of survivability related tasks and operations across the full spectrum operations. Plans and procedures are developed by the MEB to provide immediate protection to the units residing in the brigade AO based on postulated threat assessments, intelligence summaries, and unit reporting. Individuals, equipment, facilities, communications, infrastructure and other mission essential materials will be safeguarded, prepared, or hardened to prevent damage, casualties, or mission failure. The MEB area security section considers the dispersal of tenant units within the brigade AO while conducting terrain management and allocating terrain. Most units attached, OPCON, or TACON to the MEB conduct operations that contribute to the survivability of the force as they protect information and execute security operations. The MEB can be configured to contain and control hazardous material incidents or to defend against CBRN attacks in the brigade AO. Key survivability tasks may include direct survivability construction, construct earthen walls and berms, and construct vehicle protective positions. (See FM 5-103.)

CONDUCT CHEMICAL, BIOLOGICAL, RADIOLOGICAL, AND NUCLEAR OPERATIONS

5-57. The MEB can integrate or conduct most CBRN operations using the principles of CBRN defense (contamination avoidance, protection, and decontamination), CBRN information management (CBRNE Warning and Reporting System, and hazard modeling and prediction), and CBRN consequence management (CM) in support of full spectrum operations. CBRN operations may include offensive operations (for example, raids to secure sensitive sites), active defense measures (for example, active air defense), and passive defense measures to prevent and defend against attack by CBRN weapons and their effects; and to survive and sustain combat operations in a CBRN environment. CBRN passive defense measures predominate for the MEB and include the following principles: avoidance of CBRN hazards; protection of personnel and equipment from unavoidable CBRN hazards; and decontamination. An effective CBRN defense deters belligerent threats and attacks by minimizing vulnerabilities, protecting friendly forces, and maintaining an operational tempo that complicates targeting. By denying or countering any advantages that the enemy may accrue from using CBRN weapons, Army forces and their multinational partners significantly deter their use. (See FM 3-11.)

5-58. CBRN passive defense measures include: CBRN reconnaissance and surveillance, CBRN asset support to WMD-elimination operations as required, CBRN warning and reporting, CBRN hazard modeling and prediction, CBRN protection for personnel, equipment, and installations, and CBRN decontamination. CBRN CM includes activities to plan, prepare, respond, and recover from intentional or accidental incidents involving CBRN hazards. The MEB also may have CBRN units capable of providing large area obscuration in its task organization to support friendly forces.

PROVIDE EXPLOSIVE ORDNANCE DISPOSAL PROTECTION SUPPORT

5-59. The MEB will coordinate with the higher headquarters protection staff and any EOD unit in a command or support relationship to the MEB to provide EOD support, within the MEB AO. Key EOD tasks may include develop EOD disposal support plan, coordinate EOD disposal support, supervise EOD operations, and respond to IED incidents. As an example, an EOD battalion may be attached to an Army division and the division may further establish a command or support relationship with the particular subunits of a division. An EOD company may be allocated to those subordinate headquarters within a division that are assigned an AO (BCTs and MEBs). EOD elements in the division that are not allocated to a headquarters assigned an AO typically receive their planning and execution guidance from the division through their EOD battalion or TF headquarters. The MEB only exercises control over EOD operations within their AO while BCTs control their own EOD assets.

CONDUCT LAW AND ORDER OPERATIONS

5-60. The MEB can conduct law and order (L&O) operations primarily with task-organized MP units. Law and order operations include measures necessary to enforce laws, restore order, reconstitute indigenous police forces, conduct investigations, control populations, and provide customs support. The conduct of law and order operations specifically supports protection, as do police intelligence operations (PIO) (discussed below as part of the movement corridor discussion). Key tasks may include conduct, coordinate, and perform L&O operations, and coordinate law enforcement patrols. (See FM 3-19.1.)

MOBILITY AND MANEUVER

5-61. The MEB performs key supporting tasks as a part of the task-perform mobility. These key supporting tasks are highlighted below.

CONDUCT MOBILITY OPERATIONS

5-62. Mobility operations are defined as obstacle reduction by maneuver and engineer units to reduce or negate the effects of existing or reinforcing obstacles. The objective is to maintain freedom of movement for maneuver units, weapons systems, and critical supplies. (See FM 3-34.) The MEB directs, integrates, and controls the capabilities necessary to clear an area, location, or LOC of obstacles or impediments that could hazard or hinder friendly movement and maneuver or the occupation of a location. The MEB may conduct this operation in its own AO to support movement corridors, rapid runway repair, and horizontal construction. The MEB may support combat operations of a BCT such as breaching operations, and gap crossings. Key mobility tasks may include: plan engineer mobility operations, plan gap (river) crossing operations, conduct maneuver and mobility support (MMS) operations, plan breaching operations, direct, overcome barriers, obstacles, and mines; enhance movement and maneuver; and negotiate a tactical AO. (See FM 7-15.) (See FM 3-19.1 and FM 3-34 and for detailed discussion of these operations.)

CONDUCT COUNTERMOBILITY OPERATIONS

5-63. Countermobility operations are the construction of obstacles and emplacements of minefields to delay, disrupt, and destroy the enemy by reinforcement of the terrain. (See FM 3-34.) The MEB direct, integrates, and controls the capabilities necessary to alter the mobility of adversaries. The MEB may conduct this operation in its own AO as part of security and defense. The MEB may support combat operations of a BCT such as defense and use terrain reinforcement or directed targets. Key countermobility tasks may include plan engineer countermobility operations, prepare an obstacle plan, site obstacles; construct, emplace, or detonate obstacles; mark, report, and record obstacles; and maintain obstacle integration. (See FM 90-7.)

PROVIDE BATTLEFIELD OBSCURATION

5-64. The MEB may employ its CBRN units to provide battlefield obscuration effects to include large area or long duration effects. Military applications include protection, marking, and deception. The CBRN staff and units conduct the planning, coordination, and synchronization and use tactical and technical considerations to provide battlefield obscuration. They select and employ smoke and obscurants to achieve and maintain spectrum superiority, denying adversaries' access to select portions of the spectrum while leaving other portions open for U.S. forces to attack and suppress or destroy adversaries, contributing to the protection of forces while enhancing maneuver and firepower. Key tasks may include plan smoke operations and conduct smoke operations.

SUPPORT SITE EXPLOITATION

5-65. Multifunctional capabilities enable the MEB to exploit sites for information, intelligence, and consequence management. Site exploitation (SE) is primarily a reconnaissance effort but could result in an incident that requires consequence management. The MEB conducts consequence management to prevent, neutralize, or mitigate the effects of threat activity, natural and manmade disasters, or criminal incidents with the goal of restoring and recovering essential capabilities, information, and combat power potential. Using attached or OPCON units, the MEB may form a TF or company team to conduct SE; CBRN unit capabilities provide detection, reconnaissance, identification, hazard prediction and assessment capability for CBRN related sites or incidents; MP assets can assist by isolating and securing the site by establishing a restricted perimeter, restrict access to prevent evidence destruction, conduct detainee operations, evidence collection, provide military working dog teams with explosive detection, narcotic detection, or specialized search dog capabilities, and provide investigators (MP/criminal investigation division) who can assist with site evaluation and collection of forensic evidence. (See FM 3-19.17.) Engineers conduct military searches and may conduct operations to isolate, protect, or demolish sensitive sites as necessary; and EOD integrate with both CBRN units and engineers to facilitate the render safe and disposal of explosive ordnance and IEDs.

ESTABLISH A MOVEMENT CORRIDOR

5-66. A *movement corridor* **is a designated area established to protect and enable ground movement along a route.** Units establish a movement corridor to set the conditions to protect and enable movement of traffic along a designated surface route. Units conduct synchronized operations within the movement corridor such as reconnaissance, security, mobility, and information engagement for forces that require additional C2, protection and support to enable their movement. A movement corridor may be established to facilitate the movement of a single element or be established for a longer period of time to facilitate the movement of a number of elements along a given route. The owner of an AO may establish a movement corridor within their AO along an established MSR or a route designated for a unit's movement. The movement corridor would typically include the airspace above it to allow the establishing unit to conduct aerial reconnaissance and fires.

5-67. One way to apply protection to movement is by planning for MANSPT operations during the operations process. The unit commander or convoy commander is responsible for a base level of security during movement. Most support brigades and functional units have a need for more security that they can organically provide during their movement and receive little support from maneuver units to provide additional required security. Units owning an AO may provide additional security support to units moving through or present in their AOs to include the ability to provide fires. Several tasks and TTPs can be integrated within an AO to set conditions to help secure individual unit movement, to include—

- Support to situational understanding.
- Conduct tactical maneuver (performed by the AO owner or maneuver security forces).
- Conduct route and convoy security operations.
- Conduct antiterrorism activities.
- Conduct CBRNE operations.
- Conduct survivability operations.
- Hand off security responsibility when crossing AO borders or at nearest secure area/facility/base.
- Integrate fires.
- Coordinate logistics support.
- Conduct tactical troop movement.
- Employ combat patrols.
- Conduct counter ambush actions.
- Employ obscurants.
- Provide tactical overwatch.

5-68. The MEB routinely controls the enablers and has the staff necessary to establish a movement corridor and integrate operations within it. Chapter 6 discusses MEB support to movement within the assigned support AO. This paragraph discusses support to movement beyond the MEB's initially assigned support area by using the technique of movement corridors. There are several techniques the MEB may use to support movement beyond their assigned support area. Where an MSR passes from the MEB support area AO through division controlled unassigned area directly into a BCT AO the division could designate an AO around the MSR and assign it to the MEB as part of the support area. The MEB could create a movement corridor from the MEB's original AO to the BCT AO. In this case, the MEB would be responsible for all actions within the movement corridor. The division would provide the required ISR and fires support. The MEB would coordinate with the higher headquarters and unit conducting the movement to provide the required MANSPT operations. The MEB would transfer responsibility for units moving along the corridor to the BCT at their boundary. The BCT could extend the movement corridor within their AO to their BSA or to their other boundary if the MSR passes through the AO. MEB support to movement that does not move on an MSR could also be provided within a movement corridor. A movement corridor that does not use an established MSR may require additional ISR and other MANSPT effort to set conditions. The MEB can perform the key supporting tasks discussed below to conduct movement corridor operations.

Perform Intelligence, Surveillance, and Reconnaissance

5-69. ISR conducted within the movement corridor provides support to targeting and IS. This may include complementary route and area reconnaissance and ground and aerial reconnaissance. These actions may help identify and target the threats to the other's operations within the movement corridor. The MEB employs the ISR capabilities of assigned, attached, or OPCON units and produces a COP for the movement corridor.

Conduct Operational Area Security

5-70. Operational area security may include route security operations, observation posts, check points, antiterrorism activities, security of convoy support facilities, and convoy security operations. Convoy security operations protect convoys. Units conduct convoy security operations any time there are not enough friendly forces to continuously secure lines of communications in an AO and there is a danger of enemy ground action against the convoy. Convoy security operations are defensive in nature and orient on the protected force. (See FM 3-90.) The MEB may be tasked to enhance convoy security operations through the technique of creating and supporting a movement corridor.

5-71. Route (including highway, pipeline, rail, and water) security operations protect lines of communications and friendly forces moving along them. Units conduct route security missions to prevent enemy ground forces from moving into direct fire range of the protected route. Route security operations are defensive in nature and terrain-oriented. (See FM 3-90.)

CONDUCT MOBILITY AND COUNTERMOBILITY OPERATIONS

5-72. Mobility operations may include aspects of movement control, route maintenance, and clearance operations (to include potential EOD participation). These operations tend to focus on combat and supporting general engineering tasks and MP tasks associated with MMS operations. See FM 3-19.1, FM 3-34.2, and FM 3-34.210 for more information.

5-73. Countermobility operations may include actions required to limit threat movements. The result of these operations is to provide added security to the movement corridor. (See FM 3-34, FM 3-90.12, and FM 90-7, for additional information.)

Conduct Police Intelligence Operations (PIO)

5-74. PIO is an MP function that capitalizes on the capability to analyze criminal information and intelligence through the integration and employment of MP assets and other police organizations, networks, forums, and relationships. PIO supports, enhances, and contributes to commanders' situational understanding and battlefield visualization and protection programs by portraying the relevant criminal threat and friendly information, which may affect their operational and tactical environment. These operations ultimately assist the commander in focusing and applying combat power. PIO establishes and supports networks that can be used to leverage HN police, security organizations, and the local population in support of operations in movement corridors. PIO is integrated with all other MP functions and activities to gather police information, increase situational awareness, and help mitigate the threats associated with the criminal environment that can influence the success of operations within the movement corridor. The MEB integrates the police intelligence activities and products within, or as an adjunct to, the overall intelligence process to support the operations and targeting processes. (See FM 3-19.50.)

EMPLOYMENT EXAMPLE

5-75. One example of an MEB establishing and conducting operations in a movement corridor is shown in figure 5-4. In this example, the MEB AO and the BCT AO are connected by MSR BLACK. Based on METT-TC, the division needs to secure movement between the brigade AOs and has tasked the MEB to expand its existing AO to include an area that runs about 4 kilometers on each side of the MSR and establish a movement corridor. The MEB is required to conduct reconnaissance, clear, and secure the new area; support the sustainment brigade to establish the convoy support center (CSC) and conduct movement regulation and traffic control; and to maintain the MSR in its expanded AO. Due to the complexity of the requirement, the MEB has assigned the mission to an MP TF (shown with its headquarters in the CSC), but retained control of the movement corridor as part of its AO. The MEB has developed an initial ISR plan. The TF MP conduct police engagement to leverage HN or multinational police assets to enhance security. The brigade has also established traffic control points along the MSR, an air corridor, and air control points (ACPs) in conjunction with the division headquarters and the BCT to regulate ground traffic and control rotary wing and UAS traffic between the MEB and BCT airfields. The ACP near the CSC supports air traffic to and from the CSC and respond to the named area of interest (NAI) in the built up area. The MEB develops an initial fires plan for convoy and CSC security and defense with target reference points (TRPs) as shown in figure 5-4.

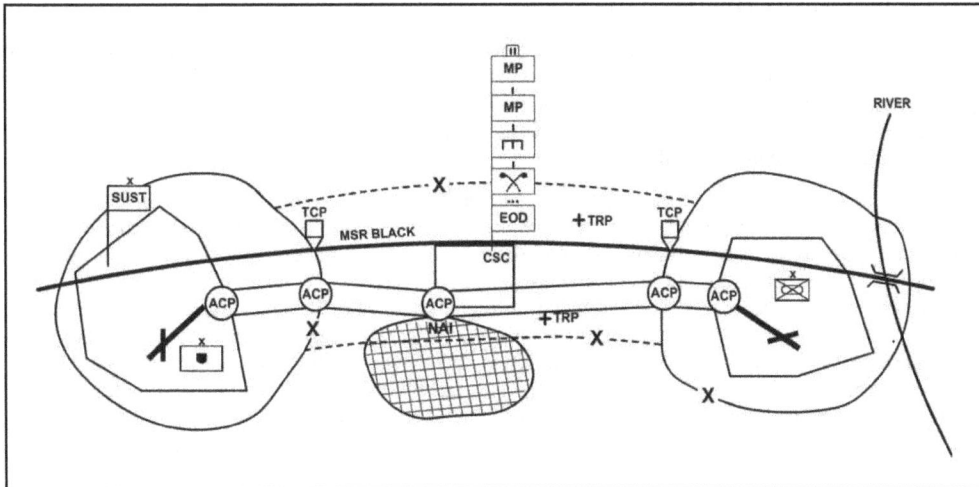

Figure 5-4. Example of an MEB supporting a movement corridor

SUSTAINMENT

5-76. The MEB performs supporting tasks as a part of the task of conduct sustainment. These supporting tasks are reflected in the internment/resettlement and engineer construction support tasks.

CONDUCT INTERNMENT/RESETTLEMENT OPERATIONS

5-77. This is primarily an MP task that could require combined arms. The conduct of I/R operations may require operations to collect, move, secure, and care for various groups of people. The general engineering construction support may be required to construct or modify facilities. MI and CA staff augmentation or task-organized capabilities are integrated as required.

5-78. I/R operations include detainee operations, U.S. military prisoner operations, and dislocated civilian operations. I/R operations are a complex set of activities with diverse requirements that require clear and concise guidelines, policies, and procedures to ensure success. MP leaders and Soldiers conducting I/R operations must maintain task proficiency for every category of detainee, U.S. military prisoner, and dislocated civilian operations to ensure adherence to relevant standards for each.

5-79. The MEB can facilitate the development and the C2 of I/R operations to support the onward momentum of combat forces or to control the dispersion of displaced populations. Organic legal personnel and assigned MP can operate temporary detainee holding areas (DHAs) until dedicated functional, theater, or joint capabilities can expedite the evacuation of detainees to a theater internment facility (TIF) or strategic internment facility (SIF). Assigned engineer assets are capable of modifying, preparing, or constructing facilities for internment and they can develop the life support infrastructure necessary for resettled groups. The MEB may also provide support for the construction or security of a theater internment facility reconciliation center (TIFRC) positioned within a division AO to facilitate the release of detainees back into the civilian population.

5-80. The MEB may conduct operations to control the influence of populations and resources on friendly operations and freedom of movement while preventing the enemy from leveraging human and material resources. These operations may include the enforcement of curfews, martial law measures, movement restrictions, or identity registration and resource/commodity controls, inspections and amnesty programs, and checkpoints. Resettlement operations for dislocated civilians may also require the wholesale movement, resettlement, and subsequent sustainment of populations for their protection or to increase the combat power potential of the force.

PROVIDE ENGINEER CONSTRUCTION SUPPORT

5-81. This is primarily an engineer effort and is focused general engineering. The capability of the MEB to conduct engineer construction support may require staff augmentation and will primarily depend on task-organized unit capabilities. The construction support could include assessments, estimates, project management, and vertical and horizontal construction. Project site security may be provided by non-engineer units to maximize the engineer effort.

5-82. The MEB integrates engineer C2 augmentation to provide a wide array of engineer construction capability and support applicable across the full spectrum of operations. The MEB staff can integrate the tasks necessary to repair infrastructure; restore, repair; and maintain lines of communications; provide base camp sustainment, site preparation, ongoing operational and recovery support: or restore areas damaged by environmental hazards, natural and manmade disasters, or threat action. Fire fighting, facilities, vertical construction and repair are included in this capability. Using task-organized units, the MEB is capable of developing and maintaining electric power generation, distribution, and management in a tactical environment. The MEB engineer section is also capable of conducting engineer assessments and inspections of routes, structures, facilities, or other infrastructure. (See FM 3-34 and FM 3-34.170.)

EMPLOYMENT EXAMPLE

5-83. One example of an MEB performing sustainment is shown in figure 5-5. In this example the tactical assembly area (TAA) from the division support area was included in the AO assigned to an MEB is shown in detail. (See figure 6-1, page 6-19, for a broader discussion of the MEB AO.) The example includes primarily examples of general engineering and I/R support. In this example, the MEB is required to construct and C2 the DHA within the TAA. This includes the internal structure of the DHA, the security fence and measures, the road connecting it to MSR ORANGE, and an improved rotary wing landing zone (LZ). The MEB creates an MP TF that is task-organized with an MP team (that includes an MP I/R company and a transportation section to allow for initial movement of personnel to the DHA) and an engineer construction company. The MEB has assigned the TAA to the MP TF and they have designated subordinate areas for their subordinate elements to occupy while the DHA is being constructed. Once the DHA is constructed, the MEB will change the task organization and the MP battalion will assign the DHA mission to the MP I/R company. The task organization may then change to include MI and/or CA capabilities.

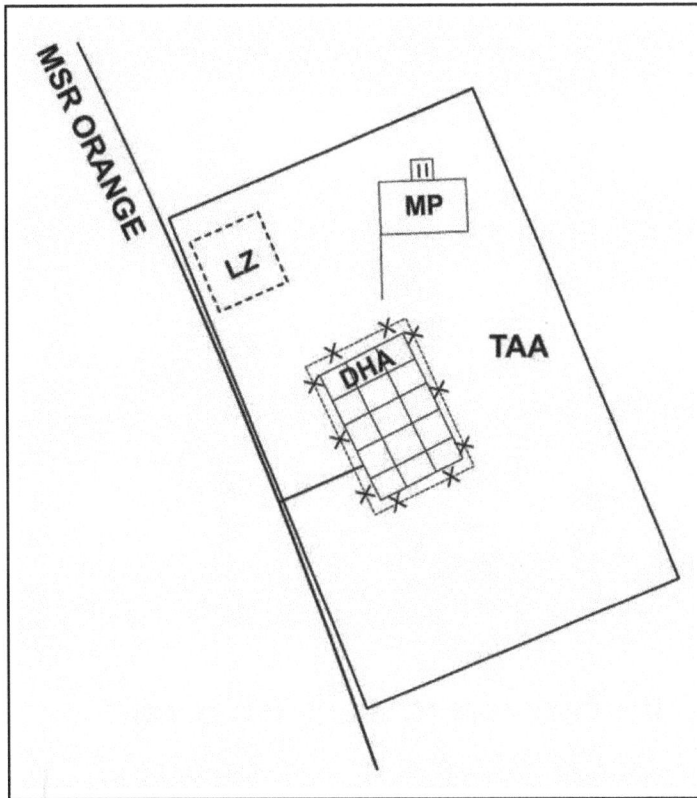

Figure 5-5. Example of an MEB performing sustainment

This page intentionally left blank.

Chapter 6

Support Area Operations

The MEB must plan, prepare, execute, and assess support area operations. This chapter includes a discussion of base security and defense operations within the higher headquarters support area assigned to the MEB as an AO. The other units operating with the MEB AO must understand this doctrine to protect, secure, and defend themselves; to support other units when needed; and to operate within the support area. This FM will not discuss the detailed procedures for base security and defense or the detailed standards for base construction. (See FM 3-34.400 and the Joint Contingency Operations Base [JCOB] Protection Handbook.) Further information on defense within an AO can be found in FM 3-90. Information on defensive operations conducted by the MEB and its subordinate elements can be found in FM 3-90. Further information on movement and base/base cluster defense can be found in FM 63-2 and FMI 4-93.41.

FUNDAMENTALS

6-1.   The MEB is staffed to control terrain and should be assigned an AO. The MEB conducts support area operations within the echelon support area to assist the supported headquarters to retain freedom of action within areas not assigned to maneuver units. When conducting support area operations, the MEB is in the defense regardless of the form of maneuver or the major operation of the higher echelon. Defensive doctrine, tasks, and TTPs provide a clear framework to conduct area security and defense. The MEB uses the defensive tactics in FM 3-90 as a construct on how to think about, structure and conduct defensive operations in the support area. The challenge for the MEB is integrating the actions of and providing for units of varying defensive capabilities operating under multiple chains of command and focused on their primary missions as they occupy terrain inside the echelon support area assigned to the MEB.

DEFINITIONS

6-2.   To understand the fundamentals of support area operations, the staff of the MEB must first understand the terms and their definitions, and the fundamental principles common to support areas—

- *Area damage control* is the measures taken before, during, or after hostile action or natural or manmade disasters to reduce the probability of damage and minimize its effects. (JP 3-10)
- *Base* is locality from which operations are projected or supported; an area or locality containing installations which provide logistic or other support; home airfield or home carrier. (JP 1-02) See FM 3-90 for guidance on protecting military bases.
- *Base camp* is an evolving military facility that supports military operations of a deployed unit and provides the necessary support and services for sustained operations. Base camps consist of intermediate staging bases and forward operating bases.
- *Base cluster*, in base defense operations, is a collection of bases, geographically grouped for mutual protection and ease of C2. (JP 3-10) See FM 3-90.
- *Base cluster operations center* is a C2 facility that serves as the base cluster commander's focal point for defense and security of the base cluster. (JP 3-10) See FM 3-90.
- *Base defense* is the local military measures, both normal and emergency, required to nullify or reduce the effectiveness of enemy attacks on, or sabotage of, a base, to ensure that the maximum capacity of its facilities is available to U.S. forces. (JP 1-02). See FM 3-90.

- *Base defense operations center* is a C2 facility established by the base commander to serve as the focal point for base security and defense. It plans, directs, integrates, coordinates, and controls all base defense efforts. (JP 3-10.) See FM 3-90.

- Base defense force (BDF) is a security element established to provide local security to a base. It normally consists of the combined security assets provided by each unit on the base toward the ongoing security requirement of the base. The mission is to deter, resist, or destroy enemy level I force attacking the base. (See FM 3-90.) It may include a quick reaction force to reinforce the guard force in the event of a level I or level II attack.

- *Mobile security force* is a dedicated security force designed to defeat level I and II threats on a base and/or base cluster. (JP 3-10) The mobile security force "shapes" the fight with level III threats until a TCF arrives.

- *Base cluster defense force* is all of the BDFs within the base cluster or a designated response force. The base cluster commander directs the employment of BDFs or response force to counter level II threats. See FM 3-90.

- *Base defense reaction forces* are forces comprised of personnel or elements of units assigned to a specific base with the responsibility to rapidly bolster base defenses or react to an unforeseen threat. (See FM 3-90)

- *Response force* is a mobile force with appropriate fire support designated, usually by the area commander, to deal with level II threats in the rear area. (JP 3-10). It usually consists of MP forces supported by available fire support and Army aviation assets. Other possible response force options include engineer units, chemical units, transiting combat elements, elements of the reserve, or host nation assets. See FM 3-90.

- *Reserve* is a portion of a body of troops which is kept to the rear or withheld from action at the beginning of an engagement, in order to be available for a decisive movement; (See FM 3-90.) members of the military services who are not in active service but who are subject to call to active duty; portion of an appropriation or contract authorization held or set aside for future operations or contingencies and, in respect to which, administrative authorization to incur commitments or obligations has been withheld. (JP 1-02)

- *Support area* specific surface area designated by the echelon commander to facilitate the positioning, employment, and protection of resources required to sustain, enable, and control tactical forces. (FM 3-0.1)

- *Tactical combat force* is a combat unit, with appropriate supporting assets that is assigned the mission of defeating level III threats. (JP 3-10) See FM 3-90.

PRINCIPLES

6-3.   There are fundamental principles that are common to all support areas. Support areas may be designated by any Army echelon or by operational necessity but are usually associated with organizations that are capable of synchronizing and integrating continuing activities necessary to control terrain. A joint force would designate a JSA. See JP 3-10 for discussion of joint security area, joint security coordinator, and joint security coordination center. For each echelon, the support area is annotated with the echelon size, such as a brigade support area or a division support area. The use of the Army term AO applies when an Army unit is assigned responsibility for the JSA.

6-4.   Support area operations are conducted by the MEB and tenants to prevent or minimize interference with C2 and support operations, provide unimpeded movement of friendly forces, to provide protection, operations to find, fix, and destroy enemy forces or defeat threats, and provide ADC. Key functions performed in the support area include terrain management, movement, protection (security and defense), and sustainment. The support area may provide critical infrastructure and secondary C2 nodes. In this chapter, sustainment will only be discussed with respect to sustaining the MEB. Support area operations as discussed in this chapter do not include the mission support operations conducted by tenants within the support area.

6-5.   Support areas achieve economy of force by having properly staffed headquarters control terrain so combat forces can conduct battles and engagements in other AOs. The MEB conducts battles and engagements within the support area when needed to defend. At division level, the assigned support area headquarters perform similarly to the previous Army division level organization, the rear operations center (ROC). However, the previous ROC supply/logistics/sustainment functions are the responsibility of the sustainment brigade. ROCs or rear area operations centers will continue to be used at EAD.

6-6.   When a division support area is designated, the MEB may be given responsibility for it. In this case the division support area becomes the MEB's AO. The MEB commander conducts operations within the AO for the echelon headquarters it is supporting in a similar fashion to what a BCT does within its AO. The higher headquarters/echelon remains responsible for all unassigned areas within its AO that are not assigned to subordinate units. If the supported echelon has more than one MEB assigned, then the support area may be split into two or more AOs, one for each MEB. At times, a single MEB may be required to C2 two noncontiguous AOs and conduct split-based operations for a short period of time, but this is not the desired situation. The MEB designates and controls its own BSA.

6-7.   All units in the support area will be assigned to an established base, will be directed to establish a base, command a base/base cluster, or will establish their own perimeter security and provide mutual support to a base cluster. The assignment or direction may be by the higher headquarters or the MEB.

RESPONSIBILITIES

6-8.   Assignment of an AO (see FM 3-0) includes the authority to perform the following:

- Terrain management.
- Intelligence collection.
- CA activities.
- Air and ground movement control.
- Clearance of fires.
- Security.

6-9.   The following tasks must also be performed by commanders assigned AOs for units located in or transiting their AO:

- Integrate ISR.
- Protection.
- Base/base cluster defense.
- Liaison and coordination.
- Information engagement.
- Infrastructure development.
- Integrate HN support.
- ADC.

6-10.   Support area operations include ADC. The higher headquarters is responsible for ADC and delegates this responsibility to the AO commander. (See chapter 7.) Incident response, consequence management, and ADC follow established battle drills and SOP. These drills allow effective action against fear, panic, and confusion that follows an attack.

6-11.   Units within an AO have responsibility for unit self defense and should be integrated into the area security plan, base defense plan, and base cluster defense plan. See FM 3-90.

6-12.   The MEB commander may designate subordinate AOs and base and base cluster commanders. Units may establish their own defensive perimeters or be assigned to operate within an established base. The MEB commander can group units with their own defensive perimeters or established bases into a base cluster for mutual support. The higher headquarter or the MEB commander will designate the senior commander as the base or base cluster commander who will establish a base defense operation center (BDOC) or base cluster operations center (BCOC) to C2 the operations among the bases close to each other. The BDOC or BCOC will be staffed and equipped from units within the base or cluster. Unless the AO or base/base cluster commander has assets to secure and defend the AO or base, and staff and equip the BDOC or BCOC, the AO or base/base cluster commander may task other tenant units to support these collective tasks. The base/base cluster commanders will submit requests for other support to conduct support area operations to the MEB commander. The MEB commander provides the support or coordinates for it.

6-13. When a higher headquarters assigns the MEB an AO it also may assign them the authority to C2 or task units operating within the AO. This is essential for unity of command and effort. The higher headquarters or the MEB commander may designate base/base cluster commanders. The MEB commander, normally by order of the echelon commander, will typically have TACON of all units within the AO for security and defense and specified broader TACON over base/base cluster commanders within the AO (this could include aspect of protection, security, defense, movement control or terrain management). The base/base cluster commanders have TACON over their tenant and transient units unless the higher headquarters orders otherwise. The tenant or transient units may be tasked to support security, AT/FP, defense, guard, and response force requirements within the limits of their capability. The conduct of these operations will challenge all units to closely assess the troops-to-tasks, and other mission priorities. Each unit commander in the support area will have to decide on acceptable risk as they apportion effort between security and defensive tasks and conduct their primary mission. The MEB commander will designate a minimum level of effort that each unit must provide to security and defensive tasks. The higher headquarter may establish a TACON relationship of other forces to the MEB. The AO commanders, subordinate AO commanders, base cluster commanders, or base commanders ensure unity of effort regardless of C2 relationships. This requires coordinated, integrated, and synchronized planning, preparation, execution, and assessment.

6-14. The MEB commander's operations center establishes communications and coordinates directly with higher headquarters, the subordinate AO commanders, base cluster commanders and base commanders. The AO commander will provide C2 for AO collective efforts and support individual unit's tactical operations in the AO.

6-15. The MEB commander determines the support mission, commander's intent, task and responsibilities, and issues the order(s) for movement, protection, area security, and defense, as does each individual base commander. If the MEB is responsible for a base located outside the support area, it may need to conduct split-based operations for a short period of time.

6-16. Each base has a BDOC to maintain SA and make timely decisions, coordinate base defense, C2 counter strikes, and coordinate incident and consequence management. The AO commander and base/base cluster commanders designate base defense force, base cluster defense force, base defense reaction forces, mobile security force, response force, TCF, and a reserve as needed. Depending on the threat assessment, the MEB may form a TCF from assigned, attached, or OPCON units to handle a less mobile threat level III. If the threat assessment indicates a continually present more mobile or armored force, then the MEB should be assigned a maneuver TCF to defeat this threat. The AO, base/base cluster commanders should use liaison teams to coordinate operations. The higher level commander may direct the base cluster, base or tenant unit provide a liaison member.

6-17. Following an attack, the AO commander and his headquarters may assist the higher echelon commander to C2 the mission support of the units in the support area if their chain of command or C2 assets are disrupted. This assistance would be temporary until the higher headquarters reestablishes the chain of command or C2 assets or the unit completes reorganization.

CONSIDERATIONS

PLAN

6-18. The MEB plans for support area operations within an assigned support area or within the MEB support area. The AO responsibilities of the MEB require it to plan decisive, shaping, and sustaining operations within the AO. It must integrate numerous units and headquarters elements to conduct support area operations. Even if the MEB is not assigned an AO, it still must plan support area operations to operate its own BSA.

6-19. The higher headquarters order should define the C2 and support requirements within the AO and give the MEB commander clear authority to alleviate the MEB commander from having to request or negotiate with units for their compliance/adherence/support. Within this authority and that inherent in being assigned the AO, the MEB commander directs, tasks, provides oversight of tenants and transient units within the AO. The MEB must be able to have positive control of all tactical actions and movements within the AO. Other support and functional brigades within the support AO provide necessary support to the MEB for the conduct of support area operations within the support AO. The rest of this chapter will focus on the MEB designated as the support area commander.

6-20. When the OE or particular missions require a high degree of certainty and order, compliance, or centralization, the MEB may exercise detailed command. Examples are in terrain management with the positioning and design of bases. This is often needed for base inherent defensibility and clustering of bases for mutual support and employment of base and base cluster response forces and the MEB reserve. Detailed fire plans, security plans, defense plans, and ADC plans require a more prescriptive OPORD. Some units that are tenants within the MEB's AO will not have the staff to conduct detailed IPB and defense planning and preparation needed to execute a decentralized mission command type operation. This requires the MEB to conduct operations in a level of detail not normally done by other brigades.

6-21. The MEB develops plans to support its operations. When it has been given an AO it must also integrate the actions of tenant units to include base/base cluster commanders. Responsibilities may include protection, ISR, security, defense, movement control, fires, air support, AMD, CM, incident response, and ADC. The brigade coordinates decentralized execution by its assigned units and base/base cluster commanders. It integrates the actions of tenant units to include base/base cluster commander. The MEB may also need to coordinate ADC support to functional brigades, the sustainment brigade and/or the theater sustainment command. The brigade reviews and coordinates the supporting base/base cluster defense plans and develops plans to employ the TCF and/or reserve, fires, and coordinates for HN, joint, interagency, and multinational assets.

6-22. The MEB coordinates with the higher headquarters to establish priorities, develop plans, and decide when and where to accept risk in the AO. The MEB can use several levels of vulnerability assessments and the composite risk management process discussed in FM 5-19. Plan for contractor and HN worker security.

6-23. During fluid offensive operations with advancing BCT AOs, the higher headquarters may be tempted to assign a support area to the MEB that exceeds their ability to see/control/secure/defend it. The higher headquarters would need to provide the MEB with additional task organization to include ISR support, additional security forces, or additional fires and other forces. The increased span of control might be excessive for the MEB and require the higher headquarters to deal with more unassigned area within its larger AO, commit a second MEB or another unit that is capable of providing C2 for another portion of those unassigned areas if that is feasible, or accept risk in another fashion.

6-24. The MEB usually will command one of the bases within the support area and may designate the BSB commander or an assigned battalion size unit as the base commander. The MEB may assign subordinate unit boundaries within the AO.

6-25. The MEB may use several boards or working groups during planning and execution. For example, the protection working group's multifunctional members ensures all aspects of protection are considered, assessed, and incorporated.

6-26. The MEB may perform CA activities within their AO. Commanders use CA activities to mitigate how the military presence affects the populace and vice versa. *Conduct CA activities* is a task under the C2 warfighting function (FM 3-0). The MEB CA staff works with assigned CA forces, higher headquarter CA staff, the division CA battalion and if required the corps level CA brigade to develop civil considerations assessments and plan CA operations. CA units can establish liaison with civilian organization to enhance relationships and integrate their efforts as much as possible with MEB operations.

6-27. Although the MEB was not designed to be a maneuver headquarters, some of its subunits must be capable of maneuver and enabled with capabilities to enhance their freedom of maneuver when required. The MEB may be assigned a maneuver unit as a TCF (designed to combat level III threats) or may potentially form a response force short of a TCF from other attached or OPCON units such as combat engineers or MP units. The MEB would control the maneuver of the TCF or response force as they employ maneuver and fires to defeat threats. The discussion of maneuver in this chapter is within this limited context. The MEB will initially fight any size threat operating in the AO and must plan to employ all fires, Army aviation, and close air support (CAS). The MEB select targets and plans where to locate and use counterfire radars to determine points of origin and predicted impact location of enemy indirect fires. The MEB develops the intelligence requirements to commit the base response force, MEB AO response force, TCF, and/or MEB reserve.

PREPARE

6-28. During initial entry, the designated base commanders may prepare their individual bases according to standards directed by the MEB. If the support area is established in an initially secure area, then contractors alone or assisted by military units may construct the bases. A technique may be to have the MEB construct "turn-key" bases within their AO. "Turn-key" would include planning, designing, siting, constructing, and securing against level II or III threats as required. This is similar to the effort performed to construct Camp Bondsteel in Kosovo. This required the efforts of the 94th Engineer Battalion (Combat Heavy), 1st Engineer Brigade of the 1st Armored Division, United States Army Corps of Engineers (USACE) and contractors to accomplish the mission. There may be situations in which the MEB takes control of bases that are not constructed to acceptable standards and must redesign and renovate them.

6-29. The MEB can conduct MANSPT operations to prepare the support AO defensive plan and prepare for ADC. This includes mobility, countermobility, and survivability; obstacles; structures; and antiterrorism. The MEB will conduct initial reconnaissance of their AO to verify intelligence preparation of the battlefield (IBP). The proper location selection, design, construction, and manning of bases/base clusters can help to reduce the need for a maneuver TCF.

6-30. The MEB will establish SOPs to ensure protection, security, defense, and the ability to perform ADC within their AO. These SOPs allow the MEB to use more mission command orders. The MEB will ensure the base security and defense forces are trained, rehearsed, and ready. Important rehearsals include commitment of base response forces, commitment of cluster response forces, commitment of the MEB reserve, and fire plan rehearsals.

EXECUTE

6-31. The MEB conducts support area operations within the assigned support AO. The MEB staff will ensure close, continuous coordination with the higher headquarters staff and AO tenant and transient units to ensure security, protection, movement, continuous support, and defense. The MEB will aggressively execute detection, early warning, and rapid response to threats and coordinate responsive ADC to minimize effects.

6-32. The MEB will synchronize security operations, integrate ISR, and develop the COP and share it will all units in the AO. The MEB will C2 the collective defense within the AO. The MEB may direct and employ transiting combat forces with the approval of higher headquarters. The MEB will defeat level III threats or conduct battle handoff to other combat forces.

ASSESS

6-33. The MEB must fuse the assessments from the commander, staff, subordinates, supporting units and tenant units to monitor and evaluate the current situation and progress. The MEB conducts base threat and vulnerability assessments. Key areas the staff assesses include security, base defense preparations, and ADC preparations. The staff can use MOEs and MOPs from FM 7-15 to help it develop METT-TC measures for the assigned support area and required detailed tasks.

TERRAIN MANAGEMENT

6-34. The higher headquarters may position a number of other support brigades, functional brigades, and smaller units, various higher headquarters, contractors, and joint, interagency, and multinational organizations within the MEB support AO. Regardless of commander's ranks or size of units, the MEB commander has some C2 responsibilities over those in his or her AO. The MEB commander retains final approval authority for the exact placement of units and facilities within its AO, unless placement is directed by the MEB's higher headquarters. The commander must deconflict operations, control movement, and prevent fratricide. The MEB conducts many of the functions previously conducted by the division rear command post. The MEB has the authority to C2 tactical operations within the AO through subordinate commanders and the base/base cluster commanders.

6-35. Terrain management involves allocating terrain by establishing AOs and other control measures, by specifying unit locations, and by de-conflicting activities that are not complementary or that may interfere with operations. For example, indirect fire assets should not be located where their fires could interdict an active air corridor. It includes grouping units into bases and designating base clusters as necessary for common defense. A technique is for the MEB to designate subordinate TF AOs to increase the ability of unit leaders to develop improved relationship with local officials. Terrain management should facilitate current and future operations. Poor terrain management can result in congestion, interruption of tactical traffic patterns, and degradation of support operations. The failure to follow basic rules of coordination can cause disruption and create combat identification hazards. Good terrain management will enhance operations. This section establishes procedures for terrain management in the MEB support AO. Refer to FM 3-90 for more doctrinal guidance.

6-36. Having an AO assigned both restricts and facilitates the movement of units and the use of fires. It restricts units not assigned responsibility for the AO from moving through the AO without coordination. It also restricts outside units from firing into or allowing the effects of its fires to affect the AO. Both of these restrictions can be relaxed through coordination with the owning unit. It facilitates the movement and fires of the unit assigned responsibility for, or owning, the AO. In selected situations, subordinate AOs may be created to facilitate the movement of sustainment convoys or maneuver forces through the support AO. The MEB can conduct movement corridor operations as discussed in chapter 5.

6-37. Within its support AO, the MEB conducts the tactical coordination and integration of land and air units while employing firepower and maneuvering forces for positional advantage in relation to the enemy. Beyond the inherent responsibilities for adjacent unit coordination, the area operations section within the MEB deconflicts terrain coordination issues by collaborating with adjacent, passing, and supported units to reduce the likelihood of combat identification errors, trafficability problems, and to enhance situational understanding, security, and defense. Airspace management is also planned, coordinated, and monitored from the airspace management cell in the area operations section. Firepower integration and coordination, to include fires from rotary wing aircraft, is conducted by the MEB fire support element (FSE) through the targeting process to detect, decide, deliver, and assess targets and affects supporting mission requirements.

S-3 PROCEDURES

6-38. The MEB S-3 functions as the overall terrain manager for the brigade and assigns and reassigns AOs based on mission requirements to subordinate units. The brigade manages and is responsible for any terrain in its AO not assigned to a subordinate unit. Within the MEB the area operations section serves as primary terrain manager for the brigade and reports directly to the S-3. The S-3 is responsible for overall AO surveillance and reconnaissance plans and integrates subordinate unit and base plans.

6-39. The MEB performs a detailed IPB for their AO and shares it with all tenants. The detailed terrain analysis is key to MEB terrain management. The MEB must consider the defensibility of the terrain and primary units missions when constructing new bases and assigning units to existing bases. The MEB considers the military aspect of terrain and other applicable aspects. (See the JCOB Protection Handbook and FM 5-103.) The MEB S-3 will engage the entire staff, particularly the S-2, the engineer, the provost marshal (PM), and the CBRN officer when analyzing factors essential to assigning territory and locating bases and facilities within its AO. These factors include—

- Locating bases on the best defensible terrain. The S-2, S-3, terrain analysis team, engineer, and maneuver commander (if a TCF is assigned) collaborate on this effort. This will significantly reduce the resources need to effectively defend them.
- Locating the sustainment brigade (if in the AO) with access to transportation infrastructure.
- Constructing a base defense can be viewed as constructing a strong point (360-degree defense).

6-40. These factors also include an assessment of—

- The availability of drop zones/LZs protected from the enemy's observation and fire is a main consideration in selecting and organizing the location.
- Geographical boundaries.
- Concept of the operation.
- Mission requirements.
- Mission priority.
- Tactical maneuver plans.
- Likely enemy avenues of approach.
- Direct and indirect fire weapons capabilities.
- Deconflict fires (fire control measures/fire control plan) and airspace coordinating measures.
- Equipment density.
- Consequence management.
- Accessibility for sustainment.
- Storage space for supply units.
- Indigenous civil considerations.
- Trafficability (ideally level, well drained, and firm ground).
- Access to MSR, roads, transportation infrastructure.
- Available facilities.
- Environmental considerations.
- Room for dispersion.
- Natural obstacles and canalized areas.
- Cover, concealment, and camouflage (natural or man-made structures).
- Security and mutual support.
- Ease of evacuation.
- Key facilities.
- WMD research, production, and storage sites.
- Toxic industrial material (TIM) hazard sites/areas.
- Decontamination sites.

6-41. The S-3 remains informed and involved in ongoing, potential, and planned unit movements and major activities by using various TTPs to synchronize the actions and efforts of the many units and subunits in the AO. Networked communication systems help provide real time visibility of unit movements in an AO and the MEB makes maximum use of these technologies to track every unit movement in its AO. Further, the MEB develops TTPs in the areas of unit reporting, adjacent unit coordination, higher to lower unit liaison, and movement information exchange to further enhance situation awareness in the MEB AO.

6-42. MEB elements may be tasked to conduct traffic regulation enforcement for major unit movements in the division/EAD AO in general or they may be tasked to enforce a specific circulation, control, or movement plan. For example, the division/EAD provost marshal's office, in conjunction with the division transportation officer (DTO), generally develops and disseminates a battlefield circulation plan of some type.

OTHER KEY STAFF INPUT TO TERRAIN MANAGEMENT

6-43. The MEB engineer cell supports the planning, integration, and assessment of engineer capabilities supporting the maneuver support and terrain management functions for the brigade. The brigade engineer cell plans and synchronizes engineer support for infrastructure development, and survivability and protection tasks in the MEB or sustainment areas of operation. Competing requirements at every echelon will drive commanders to carefully prioritize and synchronize engineer tasks and efforts to maximize their effectiveness consistent with the mission, threats and hazards, and time. Additional support includes:

- Identifying and coordinating with the area operations section for unit-specific terrain requirements that may require engineer preparation.
- Assisting the S-3 in analyzing terrain for placement of units.
- Assisting in coordination of assembly areas or other facilities in the MEB AO for incoming units.
- Assisting the intelligence section in the IPB process that supports the terrain management effort.
- Conducting engineer reconnaissance to facilitate terrain use and trafficability.
- Assessing facilities and bases and making recommendation on repair or upgrade.
- Designing and planning construction and security features of bases and facilities.

Note. Infrastructure development applies to all fixed and permanent installations, fabrications, or facilities that support and control military forces. Infrastructure development focuses on facility security modifications and includes ADC and repairs.

6-44. The MEB CBRN officer considers the vulnerability of facilities and supplies to CBRN attack and recommends locations and tasks to mitigate enemy effects. Potential decontamination sites and procedures are developed.

6-45. The MEB PM assists in AO vulnerability assessments and security requirement (the MEB may designate the senior MP as PM). The PM recommends allocation of assessment to protect critical facilities and high value targets.

INTELLIGENCE, SURVEILLANCE, AND RECONNAISSANCE

6-46. The MEB integrates organic ISR, tenants ISR, adjacent units ISR, and higher headquarters ISR efforts to develop information to conduct support area operations and conduct operations within other AOs. The MEB will provide assigned units, tenant units, and units passing through the support AO with intelligence updates and share the COP as needed.

6-47. The S-2 provides intelligence synchronization, support to security programs, and other intelligence assistance required to support units and organizations in the MEB AO. The S-2 will maintain and disseminate a continual IPB of the MEB AO and will be integrated into the terrain management process. The S-2 cell examines and reviews the positioning of friendly units and capabilities in relation to threat patterns and likely enemy responses. The S-2 cell remains nested with higher threat indicators and warning systems to advise commanders on protection postures, effects, and patterns, trends, and associations (PTA) that could threaten operations or LOCs.

6-48. The MEB requests ISR support from the higher headquarters and is supported by the BFSB when assigned to an Army division. This support could be provided through criminal intelligence (CI), human intelligence, signal intelligence, UAS systems, or ground surveillance systems. The BFSB has responsibility to conduct ISR in the division's unassigned areas. (See FM 2-0 and FM 34-10.) When the MEB is deployed in an AO without an assigned BSFB the MEB will typically be augmented and perhaps task-organized with ISR capabilities.

6-49. The MEB conducts detailed terrain analysis to site facilities, bases, and tenants based on their mission and capabilities. Terrain considerations include identifying the best defensible terrain, site drainage, existing infrastructure, communications, and mutual security/defense.

6-50. The MEB tasks units that it has a command or support relationship with within its AO to conduct parts of the ISR plan. The MEB must know enemy capabilities and intentions. It must anticipate and both receive and provide early warning of emerging threats in the AO. This requires access to all-source intelligence. Based on intelligence the MEB commander locates facilities and units and applies combat power to defeat threats early in the security area and if required relocate units at risk.

6-51. The MEB and base commanders use observation posts and patrols to gain intelligence and improve security. Base/base cluster commanders have an inherent responsibility to gather information and share intelligence with the MEB. Surveillance is inherent and continuous in all security operations.

6-52. Counterreconnaissance is also inherent in all security operations. It is the sum of all actions taken to counter the enemy reconnaissance and surveillance efforts. The focus is to deny the enemy information and destroy or repel enemy reconnaissance elements. Security forces operate either offensively or defensively when executing counterreconnaissance.

6-53. *Counterintelligence* is the information gathered and activities conducted to protect against espionage, other intelligence activities, sabotage, or assassinations conducted by or on behalf of foreign governments or elements thereof, foreign organizations, or foreign persons, or international terrorist activities. (JP 2-0) (See FM 3-13.) The Marine Corps defines counterintelligence as the active and passive measures intended to deny the enemy valuable information about the friendly situation, to detect and neutralize hostile intelligence collection, and to deceive the enemy as to friendly capabilities and intentions. The MEB S-2 will coordinate all CI measures and operations with the counterintelligence coordinating authority of the higher headquarters. (See FM 34-60.)

MOVEMENT CONTROL

6-54. *Movement control* includes the planning, routing, scheduling, and control of personnel and cargo movements over lines of communications personnel (the definition was shortened; the complete definition is printed in the glossary). Maintaining movement control, keeping LOCs open, managing reception and transshipment points, and obtaining host nation support are critical to movement control within a unit's AO. FM 4-01.30 discusses movement planning and control measures.

6-55. The MEB commander controls movement throughout the assigned AO unless the movement is conducted on MSRs or alternate supply routes (ASRs) designated by higher headquarters. The MEB provides movement coordination and regulation on these MRSs and ASRs. Units may not move through the AO without clearance from the MEB. The MEB designates, maintains, secures, and controls movement along the routes within the AO unless the higher headquarters directs otherwise. The sustainment brigade or higher headquarters assist the MEB in the conduct of movement control. Most routine movement control is handled by the unit conducting the movement or the supporting headquarters. The MEB must assert control when security conditions require it and stop, reroute, or delay movement even if coordinated or approved by others.

6-56. The echelon that designates the support AO must provide clear guidance on the roles and responsibilities for movement control, protection, and defense of forces moving through the AO or originating in the support area AO that move into other AOs. Active participation with higher headquarters planners will help to ensure proper guidance is provided. The MEB has responsibility for movement control, protection, and defense within its support AO, and may have a role within the higher headquarters AO as it conducts MANSPT operations for other units/forces. The higher headquarters, through its movement control battalion and movement control teams (MCTs), has primary responsibility for movement control within the larger AO. The convoy commander has primary responsibility for convoy protection, security, and defense. The MEB may be assigned TACON (JP 3-10 uses TACON in joint security area operations [JSAO]) while units are moving within the AO.

6-57. When a unit wants to move within the AO, it coordinates with the BDOC/BCOC. The BDOC/BCOC will coordinate with the MEB to obtain movement support: intelligence updates, additional security, fires, MANSPT operations, and final approval. When the unit plans to leave the support AO, the MEB will coordinate with the supporting MCT as required to obtain movement clearance for use of the MSRs/ASRs. The base/base cluster commander adjusts perimeter security after a unit loads out for movement or integrates a new unit into existing plans to ensure a comprehensive security posture.

6-58. When a unit moves through the support AO, it coordinates with the supporting MCT and the MEB. The MEB will provide needed support as it does for convoys originating within the support AO.

6-59. The division/EAD assistant chief of staff, operations (G-3) or assistant chief of staff, logistics (G-4) or their supporting sustainment brigade may establish control points and measures such as the first destination reporting points, a periodic movement control board (MCB) or the sustainment brigade mobility branch, to control the movement of forces into the division/EAD AO in a predictable or deliberate manner. The MEB may want to consider placing an LNO at the higher headquarters movement control board. The responsible MCT coordinates all sustainment movement into and out of the MEB AO. The MEB area operations section may have reporting, regulating, or response force responsibilities to major movements and convoys in coordination with the responsible provost marshal's office and DTO while supporting division/EAD movement priorities. For major movements the MEB may establish a movement control board to coordinate with higher headquarters G-4, movement control staffs, the sustainment brigade, convoy commanders, and AO owners that the movement will transit.

6-60. The MEB staff plans and conducts the required MANSPT operations to support movement. The CBRN officer determines likely areas for enemy use of CBRN, and designates decontamination sites for restoring contaminated units. The CBRN officer also coordinates with task-organized CBRN assets to position chemical detection sensors and to establish the corresponding process for receiving, validating, and disseminating chemical alerts, precautions, and downwind messages to subordinate, adjacent, and higher units. The engineer coordinates mobility support, monitoring route status and directing required route maintenance. The EOD staff, in coordination with the engineer and S-2, monitors and conducts trend analysis within the support AO. The MP coordinates traffic control. He directs required MP security. The S-6 ensures that the required codes, loads, administrative data, and procedures for accessing dedicated communication nets or networked systems are current, available, operational and packaged for dissemination by the operations section to organic, tenant or passing units. He coordinates with subordinate electronic warfare officers to ensure that electronic counter measure devices and equipment are properly installed, tested, and deconflicted with noncomplementary devices of similar purpose within the support AO.

OPERATIONAL AREA SECURITY

6-61. The MEB may perform any required security task within their AO. This discussion focuses on the Army Universal Task List task of conducting operational area security. The MEB commander is responsible for the security of all units operating with the support AO. Each unit commander retains responsibility for his unit's local security. (See FM 3-90.)

6-62. The MEB conducts operational area security to protect the force. They provide time and maneuver space in which to react to the enemy and develop the situation. Security operations include—

- Conducting reconnaissance to reduce terrain and enemy unknowns.
- Gaining and maintaining contact with the enemy to ensure continuous information.
- Providing early and accurate reporting of information to the protected force.

6-63. Security is an essential part of all operations. Security operations are those operations undertaken by a commander to provide early and accurate warning of enemy operations, to provide the force being protected with time and maneuver space in which to react to the enemy, and to develop the situation to allow the commander to effectively use the protected force. The ultimate goal of security operations is to protect the force from surprise and reduce the unknowns in any situation. The MEB commander does not have to conduct area security operations throughout his AO. This may occur with a large AO and noncontiguous bases. He must provide security forces to prevent surprise and provide time for units within the AO to effectively respond. The MEB commander must inform tenants and transients of his security plans and capabilities. (See FM 3-90.)

6-64. The main difference between security operations and reconnaissance operations is that security operations orient on the force or facility being protected, while reconnaissance is enemy and terrain oriented. Security operations are shaping operations.

6-65. Successful security operations are planned and performed using the five fundamentals of security:

- **Orient on the main body (base)**. The security force operates at a specified distance between the base and known or suspected enemy units. The security force commander must know the scheme of maneuver for defensive operations to remain between the base and the enemy and conduct battle handover as appropriate. The value of terrain occupied by the security force lies in the protection it provides to the base.

- **Perform continuous reconnaissance**. Security is active. The security force performs continuous, aggressive reconnaissance to gain all possible information about the enemy and terrain. Surveillance and patrolling required in security use the same techniques as in reconnaissance.
- **Provide early and accurate warning**. Early warning of enemy activity provides the main body commander the time and information needed to retain the tactical initiative and to choose the time and place to concentrate against the enemy. Ground scouts are positioned to provide long-range observation of expected enemy avenues of approach and are reinforced with electronic surveillance devices and aerial platforms when available. Flexibility and depth are built into the surveillance plan.
- **Provide reaction time and maneuver space**. The security force operates as far from the main body as possible, consistent with the factors of METT-TC. This distance provides the reaction time and maneuver space required by the MEB commander. It fights, as necessary, to ensure adequate time and space for the brigade commander to maneuver and concentrate forces to meet the enemy.
- **Maintain enemy contact**. Once contact is made with the enemy, the security force keeps contact to protect the brigade. The security force uses redundant surveillance methods, direct and indirect fires, freedom of maneuver, and depth to achieve continuous contact.

6-66. There are five primary types of security—screen, guard, cover, area security, and local security. The MEB would not be assigned a screen, guard or cover mission by a higher headquarters, but can use all except guard and cover as part of their conduct of support AO security operations.

6-67. A screen unit is tasked to maintain surveillance; provide early warning to the main body/base; or impede, destroy, and harass enemy reconnaissance without becoming decisively engaged. Depending on the screening unit's capabilities, they may be able to impede and harass the enemy force with indirect and or direct fires. A screen may be static or moving. Any subordinate element that can maneuver can be given a screening mission. The assigned maneuver unit should be trained on these doctrinal tasks. The engineer and MP units may need training to perform these security missions.

6-68. Area security is a form of security that includes reconnaissance and security of designated personnel, airfields, unit convoys, facilities, MSRs, LOCs, equipment, and critical points. An area security force neutralizes or defeats enemy operations in a specified area. It screens, reconnoiters attacks, defends, and delays as necessary to accomplish the mission. The MEB conducts area security to deny the enemy the ability to influence friendly actions in a designated area or to deny the enemy use of an area for his own purposes. Area security often entails route security, convoy security, and checkpoint operations.

6-69. Local security consists of low-level security operations conducted near a unit to prevent surprise by enemy forces. All units of the MEB are capable of, and required to, conduct local security operations as an inherent part of self-protection and mission assurance measures.

6-70. Other security operations include—
- Area and high value asset (HVA) security.
- Route security.
- Convoy security.

6-71. Area and HVA security is a form of security that includes reconnaissance and security of designated personnel, airfields, unit convoys, facilities, MSRs, LOCs, and other critical points. An area security force neutralizes or defeats enemy operations in a specified area. It screens, reconnoiters attacks, defends, and delays as necessary to accomplish the mission. The MEB performs area security missions to prevent the enemy from influencing friendly actions in a designated area, or to deny the enemy use of an area for its own purposes. Area security often entails route security, convoy security, and checkpoint operations. The MEB support AO security operations will involve both these forms of security.

6-72. The MEB conducts route security missions to prevent enemy ground maneuver forces or unconventional forces from coming within direct fire range of the protected route. MP or reconnaissance units execute this mission as part of battlefield circulation and may require augmentation during small scale contingency or major combat operations (MCOs) conflicts. A route security force operates on and to the flanks of a designated route. Route security operations are defensive in nature and, unlike guard operations, are terrain oriented. A route security force prevents an enemy force from impeding, harassing, containing, seizing, or destroying traffic along the route.

6-73. The MEB conducts convoy security operations when insufficient friendly forces are available to continuously secure LOCs in an AO. They also may be conducted in conjunction with route security operations. A convoy security force operates to the front, flanks, and rear of a convoy element moving along a designated route. Convoy security operations are offensive in nature and orient on the force being protected. A convoy security mission has certain critical tasks that guide planning and execution. (See FM 3-90.)

RESPONSE FORCE OPERATIONS

6-74. Each designated base commander is responsible for organizing and preparing a response force. The response force can be assigned, attached, or OPCON units or supporting/reinforcing combat forces directed to conduct combat operations in support of the unit. These forces operate under control of the BDOC to defeat level I and some level II threats and contain and maintain contact with level III threats until the MEB responds with their reserve or a TCF. A base cluster commander is also responsible for organizing and preparing a response force, for level II threats, from the assets available in assigned bases.

6-75. When needed, the base response force assembles and counterattacks by fire and maneuver to eliminate the threat. The base commander commits the response force, reconstitutes the response force and notifies the base cluster commander, if assigned, or the MEB commander. This notification becomes the WARNO for the base cluster or MEB reserve.

6-76. The commitment of a response force or reserve becomes a significant C2 and potential fratricide problem that rehearsals and SOPs can mitigate. Since the two friendly forces may converge, typically the higher commander assumes C2 of the engagement.

RESERVE

6-77. When assigned an AO the MEB dedicates a reserve. All base commanders may as well, but typically only have a response force. The reserve is a dedicated force withheld from action and committed at a decisive moment. The reserve provides the commander flexibility to exploit success or deal with a tactical setback. The force is not committed to perform any other task.

6-78. The reserve may be positioned to have a shaping effect. The reserve is positioned to respond quickly to unanticipated missions. A reserve maintains protection from enemy fires and detection by maximizing covered and concealed positions, wide dispersion, and frequent repositioning.

6-79. When resources (or METT-TC) permit, the MEB may begin defensive operations with a company reserve, and allocate additional forces to the reserve as operations progress. In other cases, the MEB's initial reserve force might be as small as a platoon. The commander and staff must look for opportunities to use other forces to assist with the reserve mission. Such forces may include fires, aviation, airmobile Javelin teams, and rapidly emplaced minefields. The MEB commander must strive for IS over his enemy to eliminate as much uncertainty as possible, and achieve decisive results. He must capitalize on the capabilities of digitization to apportion his available troops to the required defense tasks.

6-80. A reserve usually is assigned an assembly area or base. Maintaining and positioning a reserve is a key requirement for achieving depth within the defense. The commander and staff determine the size and position of the reserve based on the accuracy of knowledge about the enemy and the ability of the terrain to accommodate multiple enemy courses of action. When the MEB has good knowledge about the enemy and the enemy's maneuver options are limited, the MEB can maintain a smaller reserve. If knowledge of the enemy is limited and the terrain allows the enemy multiple COAs, then the MEB needs a larger reserve positioned more centrally in the AO. This gives the MEB the required combat power and reaction time to commit the reserve effectively throughout the AO.

6-81. To employ the reserve the MEB must be able to "see" the threat, assess information, and employ/control fires. The MEB may need air surveillance assets to look at NAIs and targeted areas of interest not under routine surveillance by base/base clusters or units in C2 of movement corridors. The MEB must plan and coordinate responsive fires when bases or convoys are attacked.

COMBINED ARMS TACTICAL COMBAT FORCE OPERATIONS

6-82. The MEB defeats level I, II, and III (if assigned a TCF) threats within their AO. Tennant units defeat level I and some II threats within their assigned base. The MEB employs a reserve combat force (may be engineer units and/or MP units) within their AO to assist tenants or convoy commanders to defeat level II threats when they are not capable of doing it themselves. The MEB employs a TCF as the designated MEB reserve, to defeat level III threats.

BASE SECURITY AND DEFENSE

6-83. A MEB will conduct base/base cluster security and defense when it is necessary to defend in all directions, when it must hold critical terrain in areas where the defense is not tied in with adjacent units, or when it has been bypassed and isolated by the enemy, and must defend in place. Within a support area, the MEB normally must defend in all directions and prepares perimeter base security and defense. Forward operating bases may be used by either the BCTs or MEBs. The MEB continually conducts base security and base defense within its AO.

6-84. The MEB is responsible for area security, base/base cluster security and defense within its AO. The designated base commanders within the MEB AO should be TACON to the MEB. The elements operating within the individual bases should be under OPCON or TACON of the base commander. The MEB tasks units within their AO to conduct collective ISR, security and defense operations.

6-85. Base security includes measures taken by military units, activities, and installations to protect themselves from acts designed to impair their effectiveness. It has four components: intelligence, base and base cluster self-defense, response force operations, and combined arms TCF operations.

6-86. The MEB integrates the base and base cluster security and self-defensive plans. The MEB commander designates tenant commanders as base commanders. The base commanders perform this additional responsibility under the oversight of the MEB commander. The MEB can mass forces, capabilities, or systems from several bases or base clusters to integrate, synchronize, and mass combat power at a decisive point where the threat exceeds a single base's security or defensive capabilities. Units conduct these tasks to improve security by—

- Establishing a perimeter with obstacles and access control.
- Preparing surveillance and reconnaissance plans.
- Establishing outposts.
- Conducting patrols.
- Preparing direct and indirect fire plans.
- Preparing overall base sector sketch.
- Emplacing TRPs to control fires, and for use of indirect fires.
- Conducting rehearsals.
- Identify an alarm or warning system to enable rapid execution of the defense plan (include in the SOP).
- Designating a reaction force/response force.

SECURITY AREA

6-87. Typically each base/base cluster has a boundary established beyond their perimeter to at least direct fire range (may be 3 to 5 kilometers) to execute their fire plans and within their ability to control; this is their security area. The MEB is responsible for the security of unassigned area within the MEB AO and may use it for the same purpose as a forward security area in a defense in depth. This security area should be wide enough to preclude enemy use of mortars and allow adequate time to detect enemy threats and engage with direct fire weapons. This security area provides early warning and reaction time, denies enemy reconnaissance efforts, and protects the bases. The MEB could divide the area around the bases into subordinate AOs and have each base commander provide a security force within their AOs. Commanders give their security force its boundaries to define its area, or control measures as part of the overall ISR plan. Within this security area responsible units conduct ISR and engage enemy forces. The commander clearly defines the objective of the security area. OPORDs state the tasks of the security force(s) in terms of time required or expected to maintain security, expected results, disengagement criteria, withdrawal criteria, and follow-on tasks. The OPORD identifies specific avenues of approach and NAIs the security force(s) must cover.

6-88. Early warnings of pending enemy actions ensure the commander time to react to any threat. The S-2 analyzes likely routes and methods the enemy could use to conduct reconnaissance. He templates likely locations and activities of enemy observation posts (OPs), patrols (mounted and dismounted), and other reconnaissance assets. NAIs are established at these locations to focus counterreconnaissance activities. Security forces use OPs, combat outposts, patrols, sensors, target acquisition radars, and aerial surveillance to locate high potential targets, and to confirm or deny the CCIR. This is a vital step in disrupting the enemy's plan and getting inside his decision.

DEFENSE IN DEPTH

6-89. The support AO can be viewed as a defense in depth. The depth extends from the range of the threat's indirect weapons, to the individual Soldier's response to threats inside the perimeter. The MEB commander can mass combat power at any of the bases or direct the response forces, reserve, or TCF to fight from one of the bases. The commander plans fires throughout the support area up to the maximum range of available weapons. He may place portable obstacles around critical locations within the AO or base perimeters during periods of reduced visibility to disrupt the enemy's plan based on visual reconnaissance and add depth to the defense.

6-90. The bases formed into base clusters provide mutual support to each other. The MEB can coordinate mutual support between bases and between base clusters. This provides a series of integrated defensive positions that adds to defense in depth.

STRONG POINT

6-91. In hostile fire areas, most bases are planned, prepared, and executed as modified strong points since their focus is not primarily anti-armor. Normally the modified strong point must defeat antipersonnel, car or truck bombs, and indirect fires. If the base is designated a strong point, then the MEB has sited and planned it based on a detailed analysis of the terrain to best use its defensive potential. A strong point is a heavily fortified battle position (BP) tied into a natural obstacle or restrictive terrain, to create an anchor for the defense. Any base can be viewed as a strong point with an engagement area around it, but would not be called a strong point. A strong point implies retention of terrain for the purpose of controlling key terrain and/or blocking, fixing, or canalizing enemy forces. Defending units require permission from the higher headquarters to withdraw from a strong point. Strong points are prepared for all-around defense. Strong points require extensive engineer effort and resources. All unit assets within the strongpoint require fortified positions. Also, extensive protective and tactical obstacles are required to provide an all-around defense. A strong point usually requires one full day of engineer effort by an engineer force equal in size to that of the force defending the strong point. Before assigning a strong point mission, the commander considers the following:

- Loss of survivability and countermobility effort to other areas within the defense.
- Potential for the defending force to be encircled or isolated by the attacking enemy.
- Availability of sufficient time and resources to construct the position.

COMBAT OUTPOSTS

6-92. A combat outpost is a reinforced OP capable of conducting limited combat operations. While the factors of METT-TC determine the size, location, and number of combat outposts established by a unit, a reinforced platoon typically occupies a combat outpost. Both mounted and dismounted forces can employ combat outposts. Combat outposts are usually located far enough in front of the protected force to preclude enemy ground reconnaissance elements from observing the actions of the protected force. Considerations for employing combat outposts—

- Allow security forces to be employed in restrictive terrain that precludes mounted security forces from covering the area.
- Can be used when smaller OPs are in danger of being overrun by enemy forces infiltrating into and through the security area.
- Enable a commander to extend the depth of his security area.
- Should not seriously deplete the strength of the main body.

6-93. Forces manning combat outposts can conduct aggressive patrolling, engage and destroy enemy reconnaissance elements, and engage the enemy main body before their extraction. The commander should plan to extract his forces from the combat outpost before the enemy has the opportunity to overrun them.

AREA OF OPERATIONS

6-94. If the MEB commander does not assign units an AO, then the MEB is responsible for terrain management, security, clearance of fires, and coordination of maneuver within the entire AO. The MEB can designate subordinate AO. This gives subordinates freedom of maneuver and fire planning within a specific area.

6-95. Major avenues of approach should be defended within a single AO. AOs require continuous coordination with bordering units for security and to maintain a coherent defense. During base defense preparations, the commander and staff use confirmation brief, back briefs, inspections, supervision, and rehearsals to ensure base defenses are coordinated, and that unacceptable gaps do not develop.

PENETRATIONS

6-96. The MEB must develop plans to find, fix, and destroy enemy forces in the support AO. This is accomplished in the security area and within the bases when there is a penetration. Each base commander or unit assigned an AO is responsible for identifying enemy forces. Enemy threats may originate within the support area or be a larger element that penetrates the security area or a base perimeter.

6-97. If a base is threatened with a penetration, the MEB commander may take several actions in order of priority:

- Allocate immediate priority of all available indirect fires, including attack aviation or CAS, to the threatened unit. This is the most rapid and responsive means of increasing the combat power of the threatened unit.
- Direct and/or reposition adjacent units to engage enemy forces that are attacking the threatened unit. This may not be possible if adjacent units are already decisively engaged.
- Commit the TCF (if available) to defeat the level III threat.
- Commit the reserve to reinforce the threatened unit.
- Commit the reserve to block, contain, or destroy the penetrating enemy force.

6-98. The MEB or base commander can use the following steps to counter a penetration:

- **Maintain contact with the penetrating enemy force.** Security area forces may be able to delay the penetrating force, with which to maintain contact. The commander seeks to determine the penetrating enemy force's size, composition, direction of attack, and rate of movement. Forces in contact must also adjust indirect fires and CAS against the enemy to disrupt, delay, or divert his attack.

- **Take immediate actions to hold the shoulders of the penetration.** This may require changing task organization, adjusting adjacent boundaries and tasks, executing situational or reserve obstacles, or shifting priority of fires.
- **Move threatened units.** Based on the enemy's direction of attack, units may need to move away from the penetration. These movements must be controlled to ensure they do not interfere with counterattack plans or movements of combat forces.
- **Determine where and how to engage the penetrating enemy force.** Based on the enemy's size, composition, and direction of attack, the commander selects the best location to engage the enemy. The reserve may counterattack into the enemy's flank, or it may establish a defensive position in depth to defeat or block the enemy. The staff establishes control measures for the reserve's attack. The reserve can use an engagement area or objective to orient itself to a specific location to engage the enemy. A BP can be used to position the reserve along defensible terrain. When the situation is vague or the enemy has multiple avenues of approach, the commander may establish an AO for the reserve. This requires the reserve to locate, and move to intercept and engage the enemy anywhere in the assigned AO. The commander and staff develop a concept of fires and consider required adjustments to fire support coordination measures (FSCMs). They also decide on the commitment of directed, reserve, or situational obstacles to support the action. Traffic control is especially critical. Sufficient routes must be designated for the reserve to use, and provisions such as the use of MPs and combat engineers must be taken to ensure those routes remain clear.
- **Issue an order.** If the operation is not well controlled, the situation could easily deteriorate into a total force failure. Orders must be developed quickly and issued clearly, concisely, and calmly.
- **Plan effectively.** A simple, well thought-out plan, developed during the initial planning process, greatly improves the ability of subordinates to react effectively.

6-99. The MEB commander must keep his higher headquarters informed of any enemy penetrations and the base commanders must keep the MEB commander informed. The higher headquarters or MEB commander might reinforce the base commander with additional fires, attack aviation, security forces, or maneuver forces. Normally, in the case of a base penetration, the commander positions with the response force or reserve due to the criticality of the counterattack.

COUNTERATTACK

6-100. The MEB and base commanders use counterattacks to destroy an enemy within the AO or base perimeter. The units seek to slow the rate of penetration, weaken the enemy, and reduce his maneuver options, momentum, and initiative, then counterattack with all available force. Timing is critical to a counterattack. Assuring the mobility of the counterattacking force is critical.

6-101. Ideally, the response force or reserve must be given warning time to prepare and maneuver. A quick verbal WARNO or monitoring the command net or security forces net can give the response force or reserve some warning and allow them to begin immediate movement toward their attack position to begin a counterattack. The response force or reserve would issue situation reports and oral fragmentary orders on the move. Planning and preparation to a battle drill standard are needed. Within the support area, a successful defense is the defeat of enemy forces within the security area or the main battle area (MBA), if designated.

FIRES

6-102. The MEB must plan for both Army and joint fires: indirect fires, attack aviation, and CAS. The best results are normally obtained when a ground or aerial observer has eyes on the target to call for and adjust fire. The commander of the AO where the munitions will impact must approve those fires. Commanders commit a ground force to ensure and confirm that all enemy forces are defeated.

AIRSPACE MANAGEMENT

6-103.   The MEB is staffed to conduct AC2 to synchronize use of airspace and enhance C2 of forces using airspace. (See FM 3-52 and JP 3-52.) The MEB manages the airspace over its assigned AO to include identification, coordination, integration, and regulation of airspace users. The MEB coordinates with the higher headquarters AC2 staff, the joint air operations center, or the theater airspace control authority as required to deconflict and integrate use of airspace within the MEB AO. The airspace management section has digital connectivity to theater level with the tactical airspace integration system. When assigned an AO, the MEB commander approves, disapproves, or denies airspace combat operations. Fires and airspace use is deconflicted in the FC. The MEB can use control measures such as a UAS holding area, base defense zone, restricted operations area, and restricted operations zone. Key tasks may include coordinating UAS brigade level operations and coordinating Army aviation support.

FIRE SUPPORT COORDINATION

6-104.   The MEB has the authority to determine surface targets and perform clearance of fires within their AO. The MEB integrates fires with security and defense plans and rehearses their employment. Within its AO, the MEB may employ any direct or indirect fire system without further clearance. FM 3-90 list three exceptions: munitions effects extend beyond the AO, restricted munitions, and restrictive FSCM.

6-105.   The MEB must do detailed fire support planning down to company and below target level detail for bases and movement corridors for those tenants without this capability. The MEB must integrate fire support planning (including nonlethal fires and the positioning of fire support personnel and assets) and targeting. The MEB staff will coordinate fires with the higher headquarters and base/base clusters staffs. The MEB could provide fires if the TCF is task organized with artillery or mortar systems. Much of the time, the MEB will receive fire support from the fires brigade. The MEBs must develop targeting and counterfire SOPs. See FM 6-20 and FM 3-13.

EMPLOYMENT EXAMPLE

6-106.   An example of MEB conduct of support area operations is shown in figure 6-1. In this example, the division support area was assigned to the MEB as AO BILL. Based on the templated company team (TM) mechanized armor threat, the division task organized an OPCON TCF to the MEB. The MEB located them in an area within the base closest to the templated threat. The division established TACON for the aviation and sustainment brigade to the MEB. The MEB designated the aviation brigade and chemical battalion commanders as base commanders. The sustainment brigade designated one of its battalion commanders as a base commander. The MEB designated the sustainment brigade as base cluster commander and established TACON for the MEB MP company TM assigned to a small base within the sustainment brigade's boundary. The division located its headquarters in a base commanded by the aviation brigade. The MEB also established TACON for the MEB MP company located within the aviation brigade's base. The MEB created a unit boundary, an MP battalion TF, an engineer battalion TF, and assigned them each about half of the AO. The division TAA has a proposed DHA and LZ to be developed later. (See chapter 5.) The MEB established a proposed movement corridor from the sustainment brigade to division unassigned area along MSR WHITE. Within the proposed movement corridor, the MEB established an air corridor and ACPs to their current AO boundary. The MEB prepared ISR and fires plans and designated NAIs and TRPs.

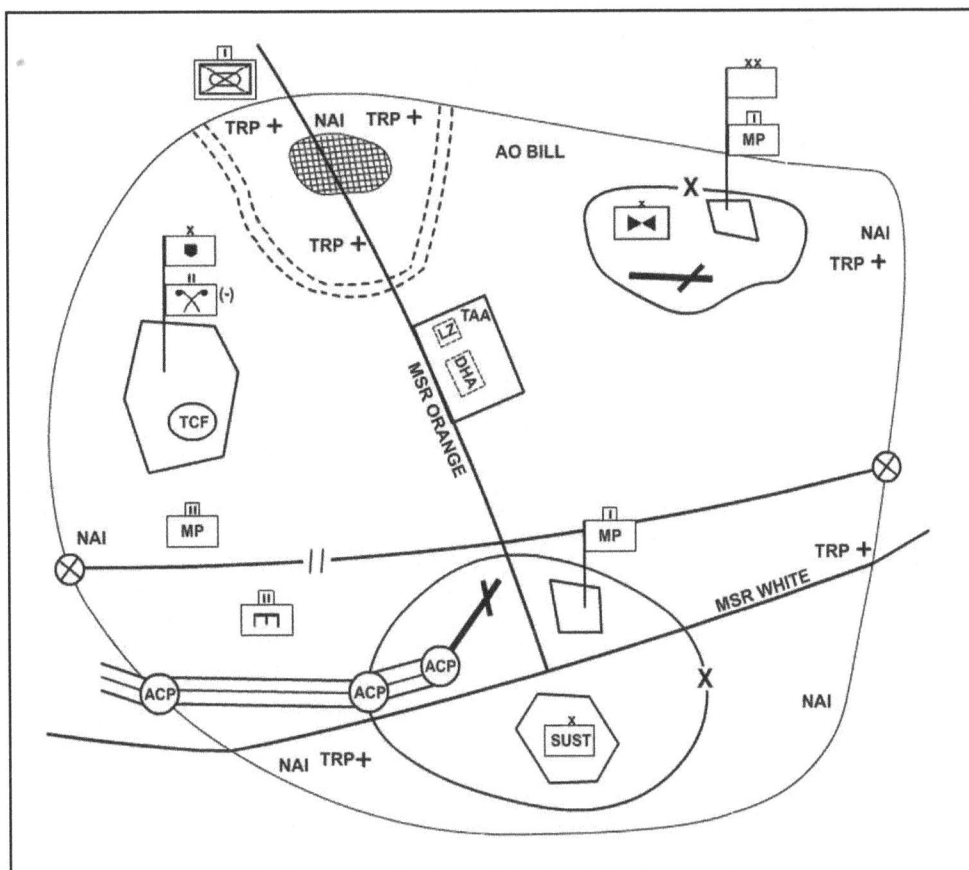

Figure 6-1. Example of MEB conducting support area operations

AREA DAMAGE CONTROL

6-107.   The MEB conducts ADC to respond to incidents within the support area. (See chapter 7.) FM 3-90 discusses the actions following an enemy attack. The MEB or base commander may need to reorganize. *Reorganization* is action taken to shift internal resources within a degraded unit to increase its level of combat effectiveness (FM 100-9). ADC and reorganization may include such measures as—

- Reestablishing security.
- Assessing the situation and damage.
- Treating and evacuating casualties.
- Cross-leveling equipment and personnel.
- Matching operational weapons systems with crews.
- Forming composite units (joining two or more reduced units to form a single mission-capable unit).
- Redistributing ammunition and supplies.
- Reestablishing the chain of command, C2 facilities, and key staff leaders lost during the attack.
- Eliminating pockets of enemy resistance.
- Destroying captured enemy equipment and processing enemy prisoners of war (EPWs) and detainees.

- Reorganizing or reconstituting a response force or reserve.
- Reconstructing facilities.
- Improving security or defenses.
- Capturing lessons learned.
- Replacing or shifting ISR assets and observers.
- Conducting emergency resupply and refueling operations.
- Recovering and repairing damaged equipment.
- Submitting reports to higher headquarters.
- Repairing/restoring critical routes within the AO.

EMPLOYMENT EXAMPLE

6-108.   One example of MEB performing ADC is shown in figure 6-2. In this example, the BCT area from the movement corridor employment example (figure 5-1, page 5-7) is shown in more detail. An enemy rocket attack destroyed the bridge on MSR BLACK and produced a CBRN incident with a corresponding downwind prediction. The BCT requested ADC support from the division to allow the BCT to focus their capabilities on an expected enemy attack on their base. The MEB task organized and prepared a chemical battalion TF which included the chemical battalion, an engineer construction company, a bridging company, and two MP companies. The division detached the TF from the MEB and placed it in DS to the BCT. The BCT created a new unit boundary and placed the TF within it to allow the BCT to mass their organic capabilities on the expected ground attack. The TF is required to conduct area security, highway regulation, decontamination, construction of ASR INDIGO, and emplacement of a bridge upstream from the contaminated and destroyed bridge.

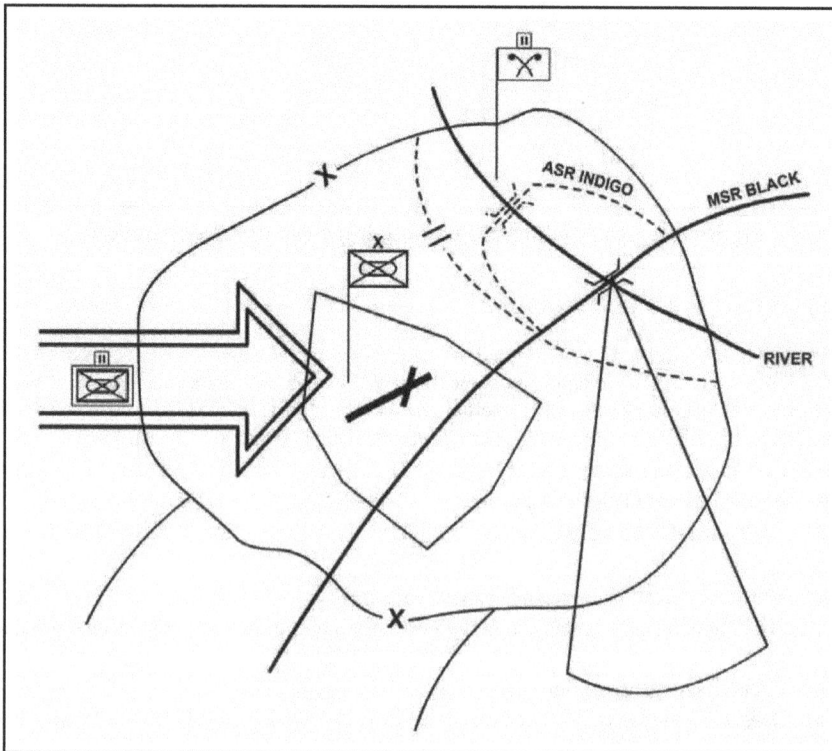

Figure 6-2 Example of an MEB performing ADC

Chapter 7

Consequence Management Operations

The MEB is capable of conducting many of the missions that may be associated with consequence management operations. It has the most complete multifunctional staff of any Army brigade with the staff skills needed to C2 consequence management operations. The MEB is designed to integrate many of the types of units that have the greatest applicability in support to consequence management (CBRN, engineer, EOD, and MP). Other brigade units are optimized for specific consequence management functions but the MEB has the broadest consequence management capabilities and the training to integrate them. The MEB may be the ideal type of brigade for certain consequence management incidents because of its capability to C2 an AO and perform other related requirements. The brigade is trained to C2 airspace and interface with others that control airspace. This is particularly important in large-scale disasters with DOD aviation support. The MEB can conduct consequence management depending on the nature of the incident and its task organization. The MEB may be called upon to function as the on-site DOD or Army headquarters or complement or support another headquarters such as a JTF or the CBRNE Operational Headquarters to respond to specific consequence management missions. The MEB can provide ADC as part of support area (see chapter 6) or MANSPT operations (see chapter 5) performed in support of its higher headquarters and assigned units. For further guidance on consequence management refer to Chairman, Joint Chiefs of Staff instruction (CJCSI) 3125.01, CJCSI 3214.01A, JP 3-07.6, JP 3-28, JP 3-40, JP 3-41, FM 3-11.21 (FM 3-21), FM 3-07, FM 3-90, and FMI 3-90.10.

FUNDAMENTALS

7-1. *Consequence management* involves actions taken to maintain or restore essential services and manage and mitigate problems resulting from disasters and catastrophes, including natural, manmade, or terrorist incidents (JP 3-28). JP 3-41 contains doctrine on chemical, biological, radiological, nuclear, and high-yield explosives consequence management.

7-2. This manual discusses consequence management operations in support of full spectrum operations. With applicability in both domestic and foreign operations, consequence management is focused on DHS and Department of State (DOS) related actions. Although ADC is distinct from consequence management, it is included in the discussion here given the numerous similarities between it and consequence management. ADC is focused on DOD related actions and typically has a tactical connotation unlike consequence management which focuses on actions taken during or after an event, ADC also includes actions taken before an event. For domestic crisis management or crisis response, see the National doctrine in the NIMS, and NRF.

7-3. Land power includes the ability to address the consequences of catastrophic events—both natural and manmade—to restore infrastructure and reestablish basic civil services. Consequence management could be a joint military operation generally conducted under the operational theme of limited intervention. (See FM 3-0.) Consequence management operations can also be conducted under foreign humanitarian assistance. (See JP 3-0.)

7-4. There is currently no consistent use of the term consequence management in Army doctrine. This manual provides a framework for the MEB to understand how to view consequence management in support of full spectrum operations.

7-5. Consequence management supports domestic civil authorities, foreign civil authorities, or military authorities. Consequence management operations support foreign civil authorities or military authorities when conducted in support of stability operations. Consequence management in support of stability operations may be referred to in some publications as Foreign Consequence Management (FCM). Consequence management operations support domestic civil authorities when conducted in support of civil support operations. Consequence management operations support military authorities when conducted in support of offensive or defensive operations. Army commanders that are assigned AOs use ADC to respond to incidents. ADC has similar tasks as consequence management. ADC may be conducted as part of support area operations or MANSPT operations. ADC could support joint and multinational forces.

DOMESTIC INCIDENT MANAGEMENT, EMERGENCY MANAGEMENT, CRISIS RESPONSE, AND INCIDENT RESPONSE

7-6. The National Doctrine in the NIMS and the NRF employ the term incident to include any occurrence or event, natural or manmade, that requires a response to protect life or property (NIMS). Therefore, at the national level, incident is the most inclusive official term.

7-7. Incidents include, major disasters, emergencies, terrorist attacks, terrorist threats, civil unrest, wildland and urban fires, floods, hazardous materials spills, nuclear accidents, aircraft accidents, earthquakes, hurricanes, tornadoes, tropical storms, tsunamis, war related disasters, and public health and medical emergencies. Within this manual, incidents also include hostile action or enemy attacks on DOD forces that require ADC.

AREA DAMAGE CONTROL

7-8. Area damage control is the measures taken before, during, or after hostile action or natural or manmade disasters, to reduce the probability of damage and minimize its effects (JP 3-10). ADC is separate but similar to consequence management. This is a DOD lead action and what an AO unit commander does initially within existing capabilities or a unit does to support others.

7-9. When the MEB provides ADC support to others, it is typically viewed as part of MANSPT operations. (See chapter 5.) ADC is also listed as a key element of operational area security. (See chapter 6.) The preventative part of ADC (before an event) is less evident in consequence management. ADC is focused on DOD related actions and typically has a tactical connotation.

CBRNE/CBRN CONSEQUENCE MANAGEMENT

7-10. JP 3-0 and JP 3-41 contain doctrine on chemical, biological, radiological, nuclear, and high-yield explosives consequence management. This chapter uses the task Respond to CBRNE Incident as part of consequence management operations and ADC.

7-11. FM 3-11.21 contains doctrine on CBRN consequence management operations at the tactical level.

TECHNICAL OPERATIONS

7-12. Technical operations are activated to address aspects of CBRNE materials when encountered in consequence management operations. Technical operations may occur before the operation to support the crisis management response and continue to support the consequence management response. Technical operations include actions to identify, assess, dismantle, transfer, dispose of, or decontaminate personnel and property exposed to explosive ordnance or weapons of mass destruction. The lead federal agency for technical operations depends on the material involved and the location of the incident. (See JP 3-41.)

7-13. This manual takes an inclusive view of consequence management to conduct the response to a broad range of incidents. Where consequence management is performed and who the designated lead is define the different categories of consequence management and whether it is considered to be ADC rather than consequence management. The MEB can conduct consequence management or ADC in support of each of these operations for the responsible authority, to include—

- Stability operations with DOS or DOD for lead for foreign civil authorities. (See FM 3-07.)
- Civil support operations and domestic support operations with a DHS, Department of Justice, or DOD lead for domestic civil authorities.
- CBRNE consequence management operations with a DOD lead for civil or military authorities. (See JP 3-41.)
- ADC with an AO commander lead for military units. (See FM 3-90.)

7-14. The nature of consequence management environment is often complicated by the following factors:

- Interagency coordination.
- Overwhelming scope of consequences.
- Large number and types organizations providing support.
- Complex C2 arrangements.
- Rapidly changing situations.
- Uncertainty and conflicting information.
- A loss of hope by many.

7-15. Consequence management activities manage the problems and consequences and mitigate, contain, and reduce the effects of the incident or attack. Most of these purposes apply equally to ADC. The purpose of consequence management includes—

- Preventing, limiting, or containing consequences.
- Assessing consequences.
- Coordinating responses.
- Protecting public health and safety.
- Maintaining or restoring essential services.
- Providing emergency relief to governments, businesses, and individuals.
- Eliminating or alleviating human suffering.
- Alleviating damage, loss and hardship.

7-16. The first priority in civil support operations is to save lives. In the aftermath of a manmade or natural disaster, the first military forces to arrive focus on rescue, evacuation, and consequence management. (See FM 3-0.) Essential services and priorities are defined by the supported agency. DOD consequence management support is typically provided to a lead agency.

7-17. Domestic or foreign governments have primary responsibility to plan, prepare, prevent, and to manage crises and coordinate consequence management responses. Geographic combatant commanders (GCCs) have consequence management responsibility for support to U.S. forces and on U.S. controlled installations.

7-18. For consequence management as part of civil support operations, State governments are responsible and have the authority to respond and the Federal Government provides assistance. DHS is the "Primary Agency" for consequence management during civil support operations.

7-19. Military support for consequence management during civil support operations will be provided through Commander, United States Northern Command; Commander, United States Southern Command; or Commander, United States Pacific Command depending upon the location of the incident.

7-20. The Joint Director of Military Support (JDOMS) in the J-3, Joint Staff serves as the action agent for the Assistant Secretary of Defense-Homeland Defense and America's Security Affairs who has the executive agent responsibility delegated by the Secretary of Defense. The JDOMS plans for and coordinates the DOD civil support mission and is the primary DOD contact for all federal departments and agencies during DOD involvement in most domestic civil support operations.

7-21. For consequence management during stability operations the DOS is normally the federal agency with lead responsibility although in some cases it may be the DOD. U.S. military support to consequence management operations during stability operations normally will be provided to the foreign government through the GCC within whose AOR the incident occurs. (See FM 3-07.) FCM includes—

- Support to DOS on U.S. installations such as embassies.
- FHA operations in support of foreign governments or people.
- CBRNE consequence management.

7-22. The MEB can conduct the consequence management operations supporting tasks outlined in chapter 2 and shown in the left column of table 7-1 as part of consequence management operations. This table shows what key tasks may be performed during stability, civil support, and ADC operations.

Table 7-1. MEB consequence management operations tasks relationships to other operations

	Stability Operations	Civil Support Operations	ADC Operations
Respond to CBRNE incident	X	X	X
Provide support to law enforcement	X	X	
Conduct post incident response operations	X	X	X

7-23. ADC may also include key additional tasks that are not necessarily performed as a part of consequence management operations. These include but are not limited to—

- Overcome barriers, obstacles, and mines.
- Provide illumination.
- Provide general engineering support.
- Provide high-value site security.
- Identify local resources, facility.
- Conduct personnel recovery operations.
- Conduct AT activities.
- Conduct survivability operations.
- Conduct CBRNE operations.
- Conduct consolidation and reorganization activities.
- Respond after an enemy attack.
- Conduct recovery (often an Air Force term for what an air base does after an attack).
- Assess and repair battlefield damage assessment and repair.

7-24. Consequence management operations can be categorized several ways; by location where they occur, what they provide, after what type incident, and for whom they provide support. Location may be foreign or domestic. In both locations, consequence management may occur on U.S. government controlled installations and directly support U.S. forces. The types of incidents are disasters and catastrophes. Causes of incidents are natural, manmade, or terrorist. In this manual "man-made or terrorist incidents" include hostile actions against military forces that require consequence management or ADC. The types of military response for consequence management include C2, resources, equipment, supplies/sustainment, services, and advice to decisionmakers. (See FM 3-07.)

CONSIDERATIONS

PLAN

7-25. All Army units develop incident response plans to prevent, mitigate, or limit consequences, contain consequences, coordinate responses, and reestablish operations. Consequence management is often provided in a complex environment characterized by uncertainty, multiple service providers, unclear roles and responsibilities, and the potentially overwhelming nature of catastrophic consequences. If requested, the MEB could participate in pre-incident planning to support military units or civil authorities. Local civil authorities may have a prepared plan for some incidents but may be quickly overwhelmed with a major incident and request support. The MEB would then conduct parallel and collaborative planning with the lead agency to modify a plan and create new incident response plans. See FM 3-90 for ADC planning guidance. See FM 3-11.21 for planning guidance for CBRN consequence management.

7-26. In emergency preparedness planning, the DHS plans for manmade and natural disasters and incident and executes the plans as civil support operations. See the NIMS and NRF for essential services Army forces provide in response to disaster.

7-27. While the MEB may be the lead DOD unit on-site, it will typically be in support of another military or civilian organization. The MEB coordinates all planning with whoever is in the lead to determine required support. The MEB considers support functions that may be required during consequence management to include communications, transportation, engineering, maintenance, medical, and public affairs.

7-28. The MEB will typically develop plans for all of the potential consequence management operations that the MEB is projected to participate in. Anticipate those operations that may require MEB support as a C2 headquarters. Plan sequential responses; initial, subsequent, follow-on, and transition to other authorities. Develop a plan that defines the conditions when additional functional headquarters should be requested to C2 functional requirements that overload the span of control or expertise of the MEB. Military OPLANs/OPORDs currently use Annex T-Consequence Management (CM). (See FM 5-0.) Much of the C2 information, except combat operations in chapter 6, titled conduct support area operations, applies to the MEB's conduct of consequence management. Task organization of subordinates, terrain management, and assignment of AOs are similar.

7-29. The MEB must assess the probable requirements for medical assets required to respond to given consequence management incidents. Ideally, the command or support relationship of the medical assets to the MEB would be determined before deployment, but changes in their requirement may only become evident as certain incidents occur.

7-30. The MEB task organizes subordinates, conducts terrain management, and assigns AOs in much the same manner as it does during the conduct of support area operations. (See chapter 5.)

7-31. The MEB conduct of risk management in consequence management is more important due to the uncertainty, complexity, and unfamiliarity of the OE during most incidents. Besides the standard risk management process, the MEB may consider the following:

- Detailed IPB continually updated with input from the on-scene command post, first responders, and MEB ISR plan.
- Risk assessment of all phases of the operation from any required deployment, through execution, to any redeployment.
- Both natural and manmade incidents often have follow-on incidents that can complicate the operation and affect the initial risk assessment.

PREPARE

7-32. Form, train, and rehearse crisis response teams to include medical, CA, CBRN, engineer, EOD, MP, damage assessment, fire, search and rescue and other capabilities. Prepare equipment and supplies for deployment or stage response equipment and supplies.

7-33. MEB elements may be deployed in anticipation of an incident if there is sufficient warning. When authorized, quickly deploy to the incident location and establish contact with the on-site lead. Continue to support crisis planning, and potentially support protection and security efforts, or pre-positioning of resources.

7-34. Based on guidance from the higher headquarters that will be supported and mission analysis, project necessary task organization or augmentation to include units, technical experts, specialized equipment, and supplies. Conduct rehearsals of known or probable support tasks.

7-35. Continue mission analysis and conduct or request ISR operations to develop SA and SU. Share your COP with the supported headquarters/agency.

7-36. Conduct survivability operations before an incident to reduce the probability of damage and minimize its effects. Vulnerability assessment can be conducted on fixed locations and a risk assessment supported by CRM can help to identify potential preemptive or preparatory actions.

EXECUTE

7-37. All Army units execute consequence management (or ADC) within their ability. Commanders assigned AOs provide ADC for those units located within their AO. AO commanders take actions to maintain and restore essential services, C2 capabilities, and mission support. Actions are taken to manage and mitigate the effects of incidents.

7-38. Commanders act quickly to control events. Acting faster than the situation deteriorates can change the dynamics of a crisis. (See the discussion of tempo in FM 3-0.) The capability to act quickly helps prevent, contain, or recover from incidents.

7-39. Domestically, first responders should establish a local command post at the incident location. Determining on-site who is in charge of various response efforts may be a challenge as response grows for a large incident. Coordinate and integrate all support with the on-site command post, commander, or manager.

7-40. Continually update and share your COP with the lead agency. The MEB may employ capabilities to support the lead agency's COP and SA. Quickly adjust efforts based on changing situations and new priorities. This also supports risk management.

7-41. Coordinate all information operations with the supported agency. The media can have a significant impact on public support, legitimacy of local authorities, views of our military, and changes in priority of effort.

7-42. Decide when to hand off to functional brigades/other units or civil authorities (foreign or domestic) and when to request additional support or release assets no longer required. Initial or follow-on support requirements could include C2 and support to movement and maneuver, protection, and sustainment support.

ASSESS

7-43. Before an incident, assess measures that could prevent, limit, or contain consequences. Assess readiness to respond. Assess MEB sustainment requirements before deployment.

7-44. After an incident, conduct an initial assessment of the consequences (immediate and long-term) and provide advice on response measures. Assess needs and the organizations capabilities and resources to respond. UAS can assist in aerial damage assessment (ADA) and MEB technical experts can assess beyond most units' capabilities. Assess the requests for assistance. Continually asses if additional forces or resources are required to meet approved levels of support. Be aware of unintended mission creep.

7-45. Assess response efforts using MOEs and MOPs as in any operation.

RESPOND TO CBRNE INCIDENTS

7-46. This task includes respond to CBRN or CBRNE incidents as discussed in other chapters and reference manuals. Depending on the nature of the incident and initial assessment, the task organization of the MEB may need to be frequently changed. The controlling headquarters may also change the command or support relationship of the MEB as additional units or organizations respond to the incident. Key response tasks may include: assessing CBRN hazard, conducting risk management, responding to chemical/biological EOD incidents, responding to WMD incident, planning/preparing for CBRN CM support, responding to a CBRN CM incident, and providing mass casualty decontamination support.

PROVIDE SUPPORT TO LAW ENFORCEMENT

7-47. The MEB conducts this task in both domestic and foreign locations and is governed by the applicable laws and policies. The efforts are similar to the stability tasks; establish civil security and establish civil control. Key law enforcement tasks may include conducting law and order operations, providing guidance on MP operations, planning L&O operations, and providing operational law support.

CONDUCT POST INCIDENT RESPONSE

7-48. The MEB organic staff has many of the skills required to conduct most post incident response tasks. MEB requirements could include many of the tasks from stability and civil support operations to include tasks from support area operations and MANSPT operations. Some disasters would require the MEB to C2 AC2, UAS employment, debris removal, medical care, and the employment of specialized search and rescue teams. The MEB can C2 most search and rescue tasks on land but may require augmentation and task organized capabilities depending on the mission. In a domestic incident, United States Northern Command has a capability area of protection that includes search and rescue. The USACE provides organic and contracted land based search and rescue capabilities.

EMPLOYMENT EXAMPLE

7-49. One example of an MEB conducting consequence management within CONUS is shown in figure 7-1, page 7-8. In this example, a plane has crashed into a major industrial site and mass casualties have resulted; a CBRNE incident has occurred with downwind prediction that affects a built up area and state Highway 5, and there is an environmental hazard of runoff into the river that provides water to a built up area downstream. This example could also be viewed as civil support operations as part of full spectrum operations. The local officials responded but were overwhelmed. The state governor declared a state of emergency, directed the state emergency management agency (SEMA) to take over incident command, management and response, and requested support from a neighboring state. That state has an ARNG MEB ready to respond to the mission based upon an existing support agreement.

7-50. The ARNG MEB immediately deploys the DCO with an ECCP to collocate with the SEMA on-site command post while the rest of the MEB mobilizes and moves to the incident site. The MEB is task organized with one engineer battalion, two MP battalions, a CA battalion, two chemical battalions, and one mechanized infantry battalion. The SEMA also put their state medical battalion, Chinook squadron, local and state search and rescue teams, and a volunteer local construction company OPCON to the MEB. The SEMA assigned the MEB an area to control and in which they will conduct the operations. The key tasks include conducting risk management, responding to CBRNE incident, providing support to law enforcement, conducting post incident response, conducting MANSPT operations; improving movement, and supporting area security in and around the industrial site. Finally, they are to conduct sustainment support operations (general engineering to construct a berm to control surface runoff) and other critical requirements that may be identified.

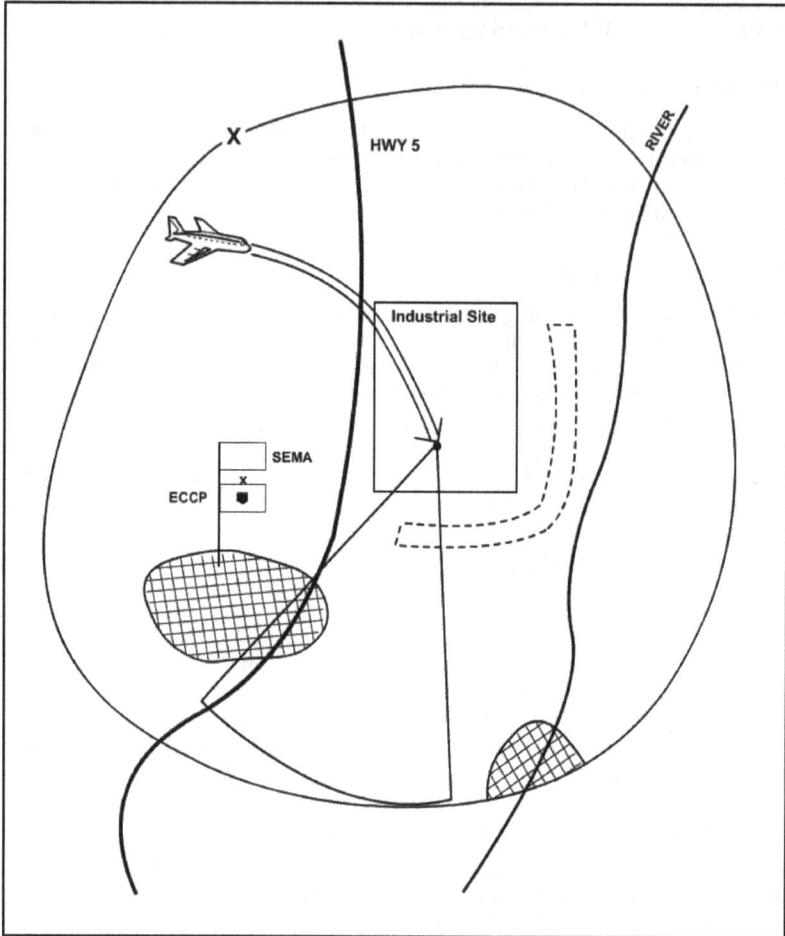

Figure 7-1 Example of an MEB conducting consequence management

Chapter 8

Stability Operations

The specialized organization and training focus of the MEB make it an important contributor to stability operations. The MEB may be required to conduct some stability operations for its supported echelon within an assigned AO while concurrent MCO are occurring in the larger AO of the headquarters they are supporting. In this case the MEB would effectively perform in an economy of force role in one area with the relative weight of the effort on stability operations as other units focus the relative weight of their effort on combat operations in another area. The MEB may be required to conduct stability operations simultaneously with support area operations, consequence management operations, and MANSPT operations. (See FM 3-0, and FM 3-07 for additional information on stability operations.)

OVERVIEW

8-1. *Stability operations* is an overarching term encompassing various military missions, tasks, and activities conducted outside the United States in coordination with other instruments of national power to maintain or reestablish a safe and secure environment and provide essential government services, emergency infrastructure reconstruction, and humanitarian relief (JP 3-0). Stability operations can be conducted in support of an HN or interim government or as part of an occupation when no government exists. Stability operations involve both coercive and constructive military actions. They help to establish a safe and secure environment and facilitate reconciliation among local or regional adversaries. Stability operations can also help establish political, legal, social, and economic institutions and support the transition to legitimate local governance. Army stability operations will take place in continuous, simultaneous combinations with offensive and defensive operations. The mission determines the relative weight among these elements. (See FM 3-0.)

STABILITY TASKS AND PURPOSES

PRIMARY TASKS OF STABILITY OPERATIONS

8-2. Military stability tasks include—
- Civil security.
- Civil control.
- Restoration essential services.
- Support to governance.
- Support to economic and infrastructure development.

8-3. The MEB can conduct or support the five primary military stability tasks; however, they have little unique capability to conduct the primary tasks: support to governance and support to economic development. The MEB does have capability to conduct support to infrastructure development. These tasks are conducted in a complementary, reinforcing, and concurrent manner with other agencies or multinational forces. While the five stability tasks are essential for success, without complementary information engagement that explains these actions to the population, success may be unattainable. The MEB could be the primary military unit conducting selected stability tasks in an environment with a low level of violence or following a natural disaster. However, it would more likely conduct stability operations concurrently in support of other Army or joint forces. The MEB may conduct stability operations within their assigned AO. The brigade may also provide forces in a command or support relationship when commanders of other AOs require MEB capabilities.

8-4.   The MEB and its subordinate elements may support HN or other civilian agencies. When the HN or other agencies cannot provide basic government functions, MEB forces may be required to do so directly. The MEB conducts both coercive and constructive actions. The brigade has the capability to C2 many of the types of units needed to establish and maintain stability. The MEB establishes fusion cells to integrate intelligence from all organizations. It assesses requirements and conducts operations integrated and synchronized with others to shape the civil conditions. The MEB interacts with the populace and civil authorities and conducts MANSPT operations to provide full freedom of movement for friendly forces while denying it to the enemy. The MEB's organic staff is best suited to conduct civil security, civil control, and restore essential services. They can use reachback or staff augmentation to better conduct these tasks. See FM 3-07 for a discussion of essential stability tasks, subordinate stability tasks, and supporting information engagement tasks. The MEB may be called upon to conduct any of their key tasks in the conduct of stability operations.

8-5.   Many stability operations require Soldiers to interact with the populace in the AO often for prolonged periods of time to a greater extent than in offensive and defensive operations. NGOs may be assisting some efforts or conducting parallel efforts. There can be a large range of small unit technical or constructive tasks along several lines of operation that the commander must integrate and synchronize. This makes the environment complex and suited to the MEB staff capabilities and probable task organization of CBRN, EOD, and engineer units, especially if major offensive or defensive operations are not required in the MEB AO, or are small enough to be conducted by the MEB with a task organized maneuver battalion.

Civil Security

8-6.   The MEB provides major capabilities through MANSPT operations to establish civil security, and could conduct support area operations. The objective is to provide a safe and secure environment to create conditions for political, economic, and humanitarian activities to succeed. Civil security involves protecting individuals, infrastructure, and institutions from external and internal threats. Ideally, Army forces defeat external threats posed by enemy forces that can attack population centers. Simultaneously, they assist HN police and security elements as the HN maintains internal security against criminals and small, hostile groups. In some situations, there is no adequate HN capability for civil security and Army forces may provide most of it while developing HN capabilities. Civil security is required for the other stability tasks to be effective. The MEB may be required to secure and account for conventional or CBRNE weapons and materials before appropriate EOD or technical escort units render safe if required/disposal/or preparation/transport for subsequent disposition. Responsibility is transferred to competent and legitimate local authorities when they can perform the task. Stability subordinate tasks may include—

- Enforce cessation of hostilities, peace agreements, and other agreements.
- Determine disposition of constitution and national armed and intelligence services.
- Conduct disarmament, demobilization, and reintegration.
- Conduct border control, boundary security, and freedom of movement.
- Support identification programs.
- Protect reconstruction and stabilization personnel and facilities.
- Clear unexploded ordnance.

8-7.   MEB key supporting tasks may include coordinating interface/liaison between U.S. military forces and local authorities/NGOs, conducting area security operations, planning HN police building operations, and planning security operations.

Civil Control

8-8.   The MEB provides major capabilities through MANSPT operations to establish civil control. The objectives of civil control are to establish civil administration and provide for social reconciliation. Civil control regulates selected behavior and activities of individuals and groups. This control reduces risk to individuals or groups and promotes security. Civil control channels the population's activities to allow the establishment of security and essential services. Civil control may be required while coexisting with a military force conducting operations. The MEB may use MP, engineer, CBRN, CA units, or a combat force to impose martial law, impose curfews, conduct information engagement, or close borders. Stability subordinate tasks may include—

- Establish public order and safety.
- Establish interim criminal justice system.
- Support law enforcement and police reform.
- Support judicial reform.
- Support property dispute resolution processes.
- Support legal system reform.
- Support human rights initiatives.
- Support corrections reform.
- Support war crimes courts and tribunals.
- Support public outreach and community rebuilding programs.

8-9.   MEB key supporting tasks may include planning populace and resource control operations, advising commanders of obligation to civilian population, providing EOD support to weapons storage site inspection, planning civil disturbance operations, and a variety of MP tasks.

Restore Essential Services

8-10. The MEB provides major capabilities through MANSPT operations and conduct consequence management operations to restore essential services. The objective is to provide immediate and essential humanitarian relief in coordination with NGOs and international government organizations. Normally, Army forces support other government, intergovernmental, and HN to establish or restore the most basic services and protect them until a civil authority or the HN can provide them. This military stability task includes programs conducted to relieve or reduce the results of natural or manmade disasters or other endemic conditions such as human suffering, disease, or privation that might represent a serious threat to life or that can result in great damage to or loss of property. When the HN or other agency cannot perform its role, MEB Army forces may provide the basics directly. The MEB has the staff to assess most needs and plan for the provision of most essential services. They can use reachback or staff augmentation to better plan and control some tasks. Stability subordinate tasks may include—

- Restore essential civil services.
- Perform tasks related to civilian dislocation.
- Support famine prevention and emergency food relief programs.
- Support shelter and nonfood relief programs.
- Support humanitarian de-mining
- Support public health programs.
- Support education programs.

8-11. MEB key supporting tasks may include coordinating support with HN/multinational representative(s), performing an initial infrastructure assessment, installing prime power generation equipment, and other general engineering tasks.

Support to Governance

8-12. The MEB has no special capabilities to support governance. The short-term objective may be to establish a military government, support an interim or HN government and to create an environment conducive to stable governance. The objective is to support legitimate authorities, assess formal and informal power arrangements, encourage dialogue among leaders, and work with local leaders in coordination with interagency objectives. The MEB can help establish conditions that enable interagency and HN actions to succeed. This could include providing military governance on a temporary basis to include societal control functions that include regulation of public activity, rule of law, taxation, maintenance of security, and essential services, and normalizing means of succession of power. The MEB could establish security and control, conduct MANSPT operations, and conduct information engagement to provide a foundation for transitioning authority to other government or intergovernmental agencies and eventually to the HN. Stability subordinate tasks may include—

- Support transitional administrations.
- Support development of local governance.
- Support anticorruption initiatives.
- Support elections.

Support to Economic and Infrastructure Development

8-13. The MEB provides capabilities through MANSPT operations and some pure functional engineer tasks to support infrastructure development. Without staff augmentation, the MEB has no major capabilities to support economic development, except to support economic generation by conducting local infrastructure projects and providing security and protection. The objective is to prevent infrastructure from further deterioration and decay, to rebuild infrastructure to provide basic services to the populace and restore functioning of economic production and distribution. Civilian agencies have the lead for this task. Support to economic and infrastructure development helps a HN develop capability and capacity in these areas. It may involve direct and indirect military assistance to local, regional, and national entities. Infrastructure has four major subsystems: utilities, transportation, industry, and public facilities. The CA, CBRN, engineer, EOD, and capabilities typically task organized to an MEB are often needed in the support of economic and infrastructure development. Infrastructure reconnaissance will be an important piece of this support. For more information on infrastructure reconnaissance, see FM 3-34.170. Stability subordinate tasks may include—

- Support economic generation.
- Support monetary institutions and programs.
- Support national treasury operations.
- Support public sector investment programs.
- Support private sector development.
- Protect national resources and environment.
- Support agricultural development.
- Restore transportation infrastructure.
- Restore telecommunications infrastructure.
- Support general infrastructure reconstruction programs.

PURPOSES OF STABILITY OPERATIONS

8-14. Stability purposes include—

- Providing a secure environment.
- Securing land areas.
- Meeting the critical needs of the populace.
- Gaining support for HN government.
- Shaping the environment for interagency and HN success.

8-15. Stability operations focus on achieving the military end state and creating conditions where the other instruments of national power predominate. The design and training focus of the MEB make it a valuable contributor to stability operations. The following paragraphs discuss the purposes of stability operations.

Provide a Secure Environment

8-16. Isolate enemy fighters from the local populace and protect the population. By providing security and helping HN authorities control civilians, Army forces begin the process of separating the enemy from the general population. Information engagement complements physical isolation by persuading the populace to support an acceptable, legitimate HN government. This isolates the enemy politically and economically.

Secure Land Areas

8-17. Help to secure land areas by developing HN capabilities. Areas of population unrest often divert forces that may be urgently needed elsewhere. In contrast, stable areas may support bases and infrastructure for friendly forces, allowing commitment of forces elsewhere. In stability operations, friendly bases may be key terrain.

Meet the Critical Needs of the Populace

8-18. MEB forces can provide many essential services until the HN government or other agencies can do so. Examples of essential services include sanitation, emergency health care, shelter, and food.

Gain Support for HN Government

8-19. Successful stability operations depend on the legitimacy of the HN government—its acceptance by the population as the governing body. All stability operations are conducted with that aim.

Shape the Environment for Interagency and HN Success

8-20. The MEB may provide part of the security and control necessary for HN and interagency elements to function and may support them in other key related functions. The MEB will likely conduct simultaneous combat and stability operations. The MEB applies its mix of combat power to enhance the shaping of the environment. At the conclusion of MCO, the purpose of the stability operations must link with the DOS efforts.

STABILITY OPERATIONS CONSIDERATIONS

PLAN

8-21. The MEB considerations for stability operations planning are very similar for civil support operations planning because the supporting tasks outlined in chapter 2 are similar. The MEB will normally plan stability operations. The MEB will typically conduct MANSPT and support area operations during stability operations. The MEB may need to plan to conduct or support each of the military stability tasks. MEB leaders must understand the Army doctrine in FM 3-07 to conduct or support stability operations.

8-22. The MEB must understand any linkage to the DOS stability sectors. (See FM 3-07.) The MEB must be involved in the early stages of stability support planning to ensure higher level planners understand the capabilities and limitations of the MEB and effect force tailoring. The MEB staff must understand the conditions and objectives to achieve the strategic and military end states to develop the MEB operations. The end state can evolve and the MEB adjust operations.

8-23. Stability operations are designed using lines of effort to create the conditions that define the end state. See figure 8-1, page 8-6. Some lines of effort may be decisive or shaping. (See FM 3-07.)

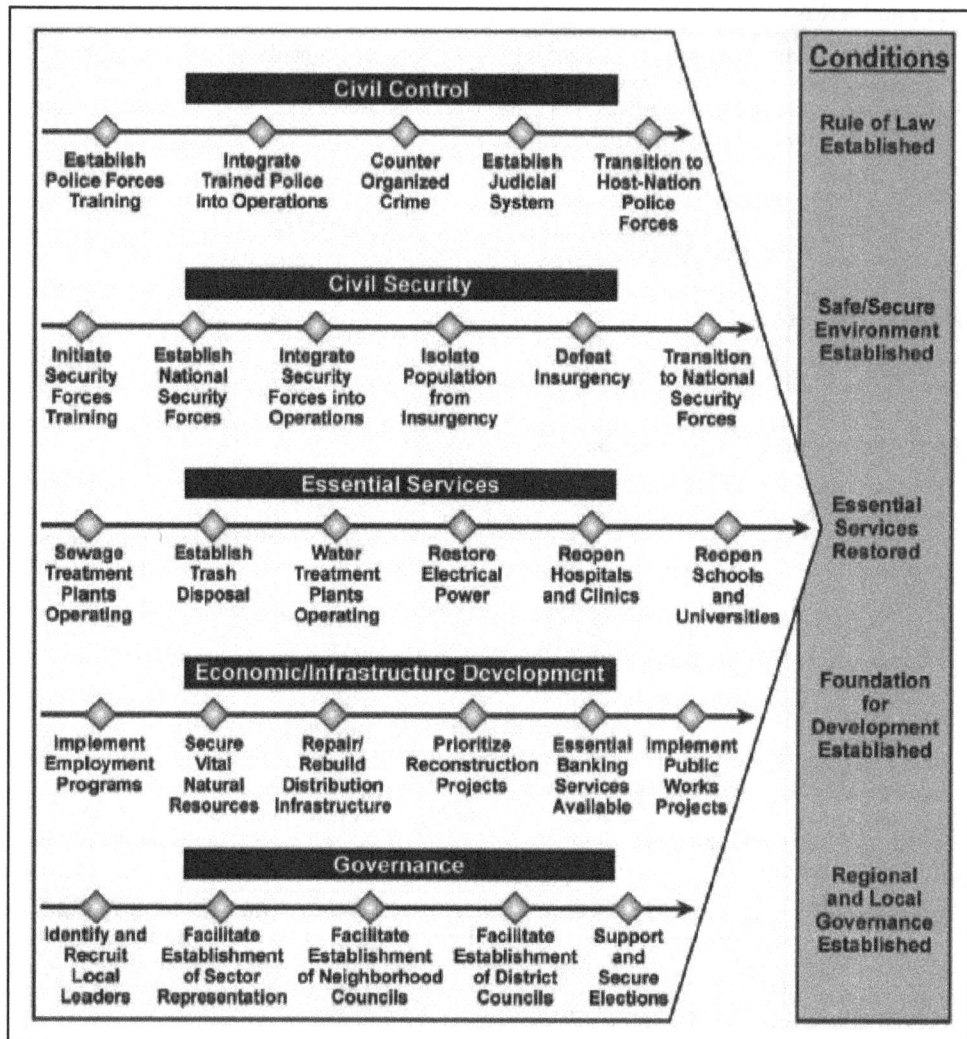

Figure 8-1. Examples of lines of effort

8-24. A stability mechanism is the primary method through which friendly forces focus affect civilians in order to attain conditions that support establishing a lasting stable peace. As commanders and their staffs frame an operation, they determine an appropriate combination of stability mechanisms to contend with the civil population and civil considerations required for successful operations. The situation may require a combination of defeat (dislocation, isolation, destruction, and disintegration) and stability mechanisms. This sets in motion the process that will ultimately create the conditions that define the desired end state. (See FM 3-0.) The four stability mechanisms are—

- Compel.
- Control.
- Influence.
- Support.

8-25. CA operations are fundamental to executing stability tasks. CA operations are those activities that establish and maintain relations among U.S. military forces, HN, NGOs, DOS agencies, other U.S.

governmental agencies, and the civilian populace. CA units provide commanders with the means to shape their OE with regard to these significant factors and to synchronize their actions with those of the military force. Additionally, CA units perform important liaison functions between the military force and the local civil authorities, international organizations, and NGOs. The MEB plans CA operations nested within the use of stability mechanisms to attain conditions. (See FM 3-05.40.)

8-26. Planning considerations and necessary interagency coordination for stability operations are discussed in FM 3-0. The stages of stability operations and the necessary interaction with other agencies are further discussed in detail in FM 3-07. Within its AO the MEB must—

- Understand the drivers of conflict.
- Coordinate actions with other agencies.
- Enhance the capabilities and legitimacy of the HN.
- Empower at the lowest feasible levels.
- Project a credible force.
- Act decisively to prevent escalation.
- Apply force selectively and discriminately.
- Provide essential support to the largest number of people with focus on the most vulnerable.
- Collaborate on measures of effectiveness.
- Hand over to civilian agencies as soon as possible.
- Conduct all operations in as transparent a manner as possible.
- Be flexible and adaptable.

8-27. Army tactical tasks for stability are those tasks that must be performed to establish or maintain order when civilians cannot do so. Successfully performing these tasks can help secure a lasting peace and facilitate the timely withdrawal of U.S. and foreign forces. (See FM 3-0 and FM 3-07.)

8-28. Stability operations require the absence of major threats to friendly forces and the populace. The MEB must plan to secure critical infrastructure and populated areas, and provide essential services to minimize and relieve civilian suffering. Plan to minimize the effects of combat on the populace. As civil security is established, the force returns territory to civil authorities' control, as they are prepared to accept control. Transitions to civil authority require the coordination and integration of civilian organizations and military efforts. Unified action is crucial.

8-29. To ensure a unified effort, MEB commanders and their staff coordinate plans and actions with their higher headquarters and adjacent units, and with government and NGOs present in the AO. Use of liaison officers is vital for this requirement. The MEB may work with a variety of organizations and CA will be critical to the success of its operations. (JP 3-57, JP 3-57.1, FM 3-05.40, and FM 3-05.401 contain doctrine CA.)

8-30. The MEB augments its communications abilities to effect long-range communications, access to civilian telephones and data links, and proper liaison with necessary organizations. Commanders and their staff consider equipment compatibility, data encryption, information sharing, and security measures when working with SOF, joint forces, and multinational forces.

8-31. Stability operations involve numerous legal, religious, and cultural issues. The MEB Chaplain, CA, brigade judge advocate (BJA), and psychological operations (PSYOP) staff will play key roles in the planning and execution of stability operations in these areas. All staff members must incorporate these considerations in their planning and running estimates as they apply to each staff section. Legal implications will be largely the staff focus of the BJA and the religious and culture implications will typically be the focus of the Chaplain, CA officer, and PSYOP officer.

8-32. Stability operations are normally long-term endeavors requiring the commitment of forces and resources to achieve a lasting success. To account for this, the commander must develop a vision for the operation from initiation to the desired end state. The commander must guard against a tendency to expand the stated mission in an effort to accomplish more than is appropriate. The commander and staff should not expand their mission unless the accomplishment of additional tasks is critical to accomplishing the stated mission and achieving the desired end state.

8-33. Commanders and their staff analyze the current political and socioeconomic situation in the AO, the friendly situation, and the higher headquarters' order to determine the MEB's mission and requirements. Developing and articulating a desired end state in terms of the military and political socioeconomic conditions that have the greatest potential for lasting stability in the area is a commander's responsibility. For commanders of the MEB, much of this guidance will typically be provided by a higher headquarters. Commanders and their staff determine the required sequence of tasks and objectives that must be accomplished to meet the end state. The most critical tasks that normally provide at least a temporary suspension of violence, suffering, and chaos are undertaken immediately. These often include actions that separate the warring factions, restore basic security, and provide immediate relief to suffering people. Other critical actions include moving into the AO and the establishment of a base of operation and sustainment base for the MEB. As the immediate situation stabilizes, follow-on actions are taken to restore order, assist local governments, assist in repairing infrastructure, remove weapons, disarm factions, and enforce specified military aspects of political agreements. The commander and staff assign objectives and AOs to subordinate forces. They allocate forces and establish control measures for subordinate forces to accomplish their missions.

8-34. To maintain focus during this type of long-term operation, it is vital that commanders and their staff develop a concept of the operation that establishes objectives and time lines that meet the desired end state. The concept should cover the entire duration of the operation from deployment to the end state, defining how the MEB will accomplish its assigned mission. Fragmentary orders (FRAGOs) and subsequent OPORDs are used to control execution of each phase of operation and various missions as required.

Command and Support Relationships

8-35. With the exception of military forces under the command of a GCC, the ambassador to the country is responsible for U.S. operations, both civilian and military. The ambassador heads a country team that interfaces with civilian and military agencies. The term "country team" describes interdepartmental coordination among the members of the U.S. diplomatic mission within a specific country. Examples of team members include the—

- Economics officer.
- Director of the United States Agency for International Development.
- Commercial attaché.
- Agriculture attaché.
- Military attaché.
- Department of State.
- Chief, Security Assistance Office.

8-36. The U.S. area military commander is not a member of the diplomatic mission. The JTF interfaces with the senior military defense representative on the country team. If there is no JTF, a division or MEB headquarters may be responsible for interface with the country team and HN.

Fires

8-37. Although fire support planning for stability operations is the same as for traditional MCO, there will likely be additional limitations or restrictions on the use of certain indirect fire assets. The ROE and munitions restrictions may be established to decrease fratricide and prevent collateral damage.

8-38. MEB commanders integrate fire support into their tactical plans in accordance with the ROE, and any restrictions imposed within the AO (such as no-fire or restrictive fire areas, presence of noncombatants). Special considerations include—

- Procedures for the rapid clearance of fires (more complex due to avoidance of collateral damage and fratricide of noncombatants).
- Close communication and coordination with host country officials.

- Increased security for indirect firing positions.
- Restricted use of certain munitions such as dual-purpose improved conventional munitions or scatterable mines.
- Integration nonlethal effects.

Information Engagement

8-39. Information engagement in stability operations is critical to inform U.S. and friendly audiences and to influence foreign audiences. (See FM 3-0 and FM 3-07.) Successful information engagement helps to give MEB commanders the ability to affect the perception of the local population, belligerent factions, and local leaders, and to accomplish their missions. The MEB may have PSYOP, CA, and PA elements attached, OPCON, or otherwise operating in support of the MEB. As the staff coordinates and synchronizes their employment, they must consider the ROE, the order from higher headquarters, and the commander's intent. If these elements are operating in the MEB AO, the MEB could be responsible for providing security for them. Sources of information used by the MEB include—

- Neutral parties.
- Former warring factions.
- Civilian populace.
- Other agencies working in the AO.
- Media and information passed from organic and nonorganic assets.

8-40. The MEB commander must be aware of theater of operations positions and interests and the effects of events on the perceptions of Soldiers, opponents, and the population in general. The commander must understand the positions of and information environments created by—

- Neutral parties.
- Warring or formerly warring factions.
- The population and its major segments.
- Other agencies working in the AO.
- Media.
- Information gathered by elements of the MEB.

Sustainment

8-41. The MEB's ability to sustain itself in the AO depends on theater maturity, the sustainment structure, and the time flow of forces. Refugees, an inadequate infrastructure, and demands by the HN and multinational partners can make logistical support complex. Engineering support plays a critical role in delivering sustainment by enhancing its capabilities. General principles to consider when planning sustainment for stability operations include—

- Ability to implement logistical support in any stability operations area.
- Ability of the MEB to provide its own support.
- Ability of higher headquarters to provide support.
- Availability of local supplies, facilities, utilities, services, and transportation support systems by contract or local purchase.
- Availability of local facilities such as LOCs, ports, airfields, and communications systems.
- Local capabilities for self-support to facilitate the eventual transfer of responsibilities to the supported nation for development or improvement.
- Availability of resources.

8-42. The primary sustainment challenges of stability operations are to anticipate needs and to integrate assigned units and sources of supply into the operation. Informational needs include—

- Resources available in the AO.
- Status of critical supply items and repair jobs.
- Nature and condition of the infrastructure.

- Capabilities of general reconstruction units.
- Mission tasks.
- Overall material readiness of the MEB.
- Contracting. (In some cases, contracting can augment organic sustainment.)
- Contractor protection (MEBs may encounter contractor-provided services and supply operations in reconstruction operations environments. The MEB S-4 and commander must understand the terms and limitations of contractor reconstruction.)
- Liaison with civil authorities.
- Additional liaison teams. (Close coordination with civil authorities and nonstandard supporting relationships demand the use of digitized liaison teams to assure their greatest usefulness. They can also require the creation of additional liaison teams that may have to operate without the C2 INFOSYS.)

Army Health System Support

8-43. The Army Health System (AHS) is a component of the military health system that is responsible for operational management of the Army's HSS and FHP missions, including training and predeployment, deployment, and post-deployment operations. It is responsible for all mission support services performed, provided, or arranged by the Army Medical Department (AMEDD) for the Army and, as directed, for joint, intergovernmental, multinational, and multinational forces and agencies. Health service support includes all support and services to promote, improve, conserve, or restore the mental and physical well-being of personnel in the Army and other organizations as directed. This includes medical evacuation (MEDEVAC), medical logistics, and casualty care, encompassing a number of AMEDD functions, to include—

- Organic and area medical support.
- Hospitalization.
- Treatment aspects of dental care.
- Behavioral health/neuropsychiatric treatment.
- Clinical laboratory services.
- Treatment of CBRN patients.

8-44. Force health protection includes all measures to enable a healthy and fit force, prevent injury and illness, and protect the force from health hazards. It covers prevention aspects of a number of AMEDD functions, to include—

- Preventive medicine (PVNTMED), including medical surveillance and occupational and environmental health surveillance.
- Veterinary services, including food inspection and animal care missions.
- Prevention of zoonotic diseases (those transmissible from animals to humans).
- Combat and operational stress control (COSC).
- Dental services (preventive dentistry).
- Laboratory services (area medical laboratory support).

8-45. In stability operations, the MEB's BSB could be augmented with an area support medical company or supported by a brigade support medical company. Additional HSS augmentation could include a forward surgical team, a forward MEDEVAC team (forward support medical evacuation team [FSMT]) (from the general aviation support battalion), and hospital augmentation may be required. (See AR 40-3 for information on emergency medical treatment for local national civilians during stability operations.) Army Health System support for the MEB in stability operations depends upon the specific type of operations, anticipated duration of the operations, number of personnel deployed, evacuation policy, medical troop ceiling, and anticipated level of violence. Additional FHP requirements could include veterinary services, preventive medicine, laboratory, combat and operational stress control, and preventive dentistry support.

Contracting

8-46. Contracting can be an effective force multiplier and should be used to augment existing sustainment capabilities. Weak logistical infrastructures in the AO may make it necessary to contract some supplies and services. If he knows that contracting may be required, the MEB commander obtains guidance from higher headquarters concerning contracting during the initial planning stages. Hostilities can cause interruptions in the delivery of any contracted services, such as food and water. For this reason, the MEB must be prepared to sustain itself, attached forces, supporting forces, and the local populace for limited periods of time. A good plan anticipates large consumption rates of supplies in classes I, III, IV, and VIII and provides for reserve stockage of nonperishables. The MEB S-4 and the engineer coordinator are typically the members of the MEB staff to coordinate contracting efforts.

PREPARE

8-47. The MEB may conduct stability operations in its own AO or in support of other AOs within the larger AO of the unit it is supporting. When deploying from home station the typical sequence for an MEB committed to conducting stability operations will generally follow this sequence—

- Deploy and move into the AO.
- Conduct stability operations.
- Terminate operations and redeploy.

Deployment and Movement into the Area of Operations

8-48. The commander and staff must plan, synchronize, and control the movement of forces into the AO to maintain the proper balance of security and flexibility. In coordination with the MCT/MCB, commanders must decide the sequence in which their forces will enter the AO. The MEB must consider the number of suitable routes or lift assets available to meet the movement requirements of its subordinate elements. Other considerations include—

- Road and/or route improvement and maintenance.
- Route construction.
- Obstacles clearance.
- Bridge and culvert repair.
- Bridging rivers or dry gaps.
- Establishment of security along routes.
- Traffic control to permit freedom of or restrict civilian movements along routes.
- Communications architecture.

8-49. If the AO does not have the infrastructure to support the operation, it might be necessary to deploy an advance party heavy with logistical and engineering support into the AO. If the threat level is high, security elements will be a critical consideration. In other circumstances, it may be necessary for the commander or deputy commander and a small group of specialized key personnel such as CA, PA, or the BJA to lead the advance party. These personnel will set the groundwork for the rest of the force by conducting face-to-face coordination with local civilian or military leaders. In all cases, a well-developed movement order is essential. Infrastructure reconnaissance (to include the use of geospatial products) may be critical to early success. (See FM 3-34.170.)

NGOs and UN Relief Agencies and International Organizations

8-50. Commanders and their staff coordinate the MEB's actions with the higher headquarters, adjacent units, and governmental and NGOs in the AO to ensure a unified effort. The effective use of LNOs is vital for this requirement.

The Role of NGOs

8-51. NGOs may range in size and experience from those with multimillion dollar budgets and decades of global experience in developmental and humanitarian relief to newly created small organizations dedicated to a particular emergency or disaster. The professionalism, capability, equipment, and other resources and expertise vary greatly from one organization to another.

8-52. NGOs are involved in such diverse activities as education, technical projects, relief activities, refugee assistance, public policy, and development programs. It should be remembered that NGO objectives may be counter to the U.S. government objectives.

Civil-Military Operations Center

8-53. Conceptually, the civil-military operations center (CMOC) is the meeting place of NGOs and the population. Although not a new concept, the CMOC has been effectively employed as a means to coordinate CA operations and plays an execution role. The organization of the CMOC is theater and mission dependent, and flexible in size and composition. A commander at any echelon may establish a CMOC to facilitate coordination with other agencies, departments, organizations, and the HN.

8-54. The commander may form a CMOC as the action team to provide the following:

- Carry out guidance and institute decisions regarding CA operations.
- Perform liaison and coordination between military capabilities and other agencies, departments, and organizations to meet the needs of the populace.
- Provide a partnership forum for military and other engaged organizations.
- Receive, validate, and coordinate requests for support from the NGO and regional and international organizations.

Use of Force in Stability Operations

8-55. When using force, restraint is as important in stability missions as applying overwhelming force is in offensive and defensive operations. In stability operations, commanders at every level emphasize that violence not precisely applied is counterproductive. Speed, surprise, and shock are vital considerations in lethal actions; perseverance, legitimacy, and restraint are vital considerations in stability and civil support operations. The ROE may include procedures for warnings and the employment of lethal and nonlethal force. During preparation, all subordinate units must understand completely how to comply with the ROE.

8-56. Commanders address the apprehension caused by the presence of heavily armed Soldiers operating among the local populace. Discipline and strict adherence to the rules of engagement are essential but not sufficient to reassure the population. Commanders balance protecting the force, deterring attacks, and taking constructive action throughout the AO. They also stress cultural awareness in training and preparing for operations. Cultural awareness makes Soldiers more effective when operating in a foreign population.

8-57. Generally, stability operations require a greater emphasis on nonlethal actions. Often the mere presence of military force is enough to maintain stability and compel behavior. However, some belligerents may provoke forces conducting stability operations into an overreaction that can be further exploited through propaganda. Commanders may demonstrate restraint by employing coercive, nonlethal methods and capabilities that escalates force, including lethal force in a scalable manner enhancing the legitimacy of an operation.

EXECUTE

Nature of Stability Actions

8-58. The MEB may execute stability operations at any point along the full spectrum operations from stable peace to general war. Stability operations by nature are often decentralized in execution. Subordinate units (often at the company and platoon level) carry out the vast majority of critical tasks and must possess a complete understanding of the commander's intent. The MEB must maintain the ability to conduct coordinated small-scale operations over great distances quickly and securely. Subordinate units may conduct a wide range of tasks to support the stability subordinate tasks including, but not limited to,—

- Battalion level and below offensive tasks such as attacks, search and attack, and ambushes.
- Defensive tasks such as area defense.
- Cordon and search operations.
- Humanitarian assistance.
- Environmental assistance which may include environmental clean-up or environmental services.
- Security operations such as area security or convoy escort missions.
- Reconnaissance operations.
- Controlling civil disturbances.

8-59. Due to the multiple and unique demands of these operations, MEB forces must remain responsive and flexible. Task organization of units may change many times during the course of the operation. The MEB must ensure adequate support for its subordinate units and take active measures to create the conditions for its subordinates to succeed. The MEB focuses the majority of its efforts towards coordinating and supporting subordinate's actions, assigning subordinate objectives and responsibilities that support the concept of operations, and controlling all efforts to ensure they are working towards the brigade's overall objectives.

Complex and Uncertain Situations

8-60. Stability operations often take place in political, military, and cultural situations that are highly fluid and dynamic. Unresolved political issues, an unclear understanding or description of a desired end state, or difficulty in gaining international consensus may cause ambiguity. Complexity in these actions may also arise from—

- Troops dispersed throughout the AO.
- Difficulty in discriminating between combatants and noncombatants or between the many parties of a dispute.
- Undisciplined factions, uncontrolled by a central authority and unwilling to consent to the agreement.
- Absence of basic law and order.
- Violations of human rights.
- Widespread destruction or decay of physical and social infrastructure and institutions; collapse of civil infrastructure.
- Environmental considerations (damage, hazardous materials).
- Threats of disease or epidemics.
- Presence of many displaced persons.
- Presence and involvement of nongovernmental organizations, media, and other civilians.

8-61. Stability operations require detailed interagency planning and coordination. The Army's response to crises will have to address several components, such as political, diplomatic, humanitarian, economic, and security.

8-62. After the MEB has moved into its AO and established a base for future operations, a continuation of the stability effort commences. To successfully execute the mission, commanders at all levels must clearly understand the mission and the higher commander's concept of operation and intent. This knowledge enables the commander to prioritize tasks, begin stability operations, and allow subordinates to take initiative. Tactical tasks executed during the stability operation depend upon the factors of METT-TC. These tactical tasks include—

- Establishment of zones of separation.
- Combat operations including raids, checkpoints, patrols, and reconnaissance.
- Support to the HN.
- Security operations.

- Treaty compliance inspections.
- Negotiation or mediation.

Termination of Stability Operations

8-63. The MEB can terminate stability operation in four ways. First, the MEB may be relieved of its mission and conduct a mission handover of the operation to a follow-on force. This force could be another MEB, functional brigade, BCT, a UN force, or a nonmilitary organization. Second, the situation could become stabilized and not necessitate the continuance of operations. In this case, the HN or domestic community assumes responsibility for stability. Third, the MEB could be redeployed with no follow-on forces and without the area being stabilized. A condition such as this would place the MEB in a vulnerable situation. Security must be intense and the protection of the force during its exit must be well planned and executed. Finally, the MEB could transition to MCO. The commander must always ensure the MEB maintains the ability to transition quickly and forcefully. See FM 3-07 for more discussion on transitions during humanitarian response and between various stability missions.

ASSESS

8-64. The MEB must continually assess the OE to maintain SU. Running estimates are continuously updated to ensure the commander is provided with accurate data and staff assessments to make necessary decisions. Assessing stability operations requires a long-range horizon, coordinated short-term goals, and great flexibility to include "out of the box" thinking. The MEB must consider their assessments and variances from planning goals and variances from the assessments provided by supported civil authorities. The MEB has the ability to assess infrastructure, security requirements, mobility requirements, HN police capabilities, I/R requirements, general engineering requirements, and CBRNE materials. (See FM 3-07 and FM 7-15 for possible MOEs and MOPs related to stability operations.)

8-65. The MEB CA staff can provide detailed on the ground assessments to validate IPB and assess progress. Every Soldier must be trained and able to collect and report information of value. (See FM 3-07 for information on the role of CA in stability operations.)

SPECIALIZED CAPABILITIES OF THE MANEUVER ENHANCEMENT BRIGADE

8-66. The MEB has a broad range of capabilities to conduct stability operations. With adequate resources, the MEB can conduct stability tasks in its AO while simultaneously supporting offensive or defensive operations being conducted by its higher headquarters. The unique breadth and capabilities of the MEB staff and likely mix of units with constructive capabilities could make it the preferred headquarters to conduct some stability operations rather than use a BCT or other functional headquarters.

8-67. In some stability operations, the employment of an MEB rather than a BCT may prove less provocative and a much more effective alternative. MEB elements are suited to helping to set the conditions for post-conflict recovery in areas where active combat operations are not underway. Commanders may choose to use an MEB and its task organized elements in lower risk areas to economize combat power for decisive operations being conducted elsewhere in the supported echelon's AO.

8-68. An MEB is typically task organized with assets (such as CBRN, CA, engineer, EOD, and MP) capable of performing many of the essential stability tasks. These resources may come from higher-echelon Army or even joint, interagency, or multinational sources and must be integrated into MEB operations for successful use. Assets with high facility to conduct stability operations include components capable of security operations, engineering support, CA operations support, information engagement, police intelligence operations, hazard neutralization, and other capabilities required to meet the unique situations encountered in stability operations.

COMMAND AND CONTROL

8-69. The MEB headquarters allows it to deploy with a staff that is trained to conduct a wide range of technical and combat missions. It knows how to use these units frequently required in stability operations: CA, CBRN, EOD, engineer, and MP. With specific staff augmentation it can better use other more specialized assets in its AO. It can readily accept augmentation and quickly task organize to create the needed TFs and teams to conduct complex stability missions.

8-70. The MEB may be required to conduct stability operations in its own AO while other units are conducting major combat operations in their AOs. Depending on task organization, the MEB could simultaneously conduct MANSPT operations for its higher headquarters.

SUSTAINMENT

8-71. With its organic BSB the MEB has the baseline ability to integrate its sustainment in austere and undeveloped areas. This baseline ability allows it to rapidly accept other augmentation to include additional sustainment organizations.

COMMUNICATIONS

8-72. With its organic signal network support company the MEB can communicate with most organizations. With augmentation, it can interface with and support civil communications. The MEB uses its organic liaison teams to affect interagency coordination.

MANEUVER SUPPORT OPERATIONS

8-73. The MEB may conduct MANSPT operations in support of stability operations. Improving mobility in the supported units AO or within the MEB AO will almost certainly be a part of the unit's mission in stability operations. The freedom to move and maneuver is essential to the conduct of stability operations. The MEB may be tailored and task organized with a variety of engineer or other mobility assets. Providing protection support will also typically be required and will depend heavily on MP and other assets (Army, joint, multinational, HN, and potentially other contracted security).

8-74. The MEB has a staff that routinely integrates unit capabilities to conduct MANSPT operations that enhance the freedom of movement needed to conduct stability operations. MANSPT operations can support military forces or civil authorities. (See chapter 5.) The MEB has a staff that routinely fuses intelligence and plans and conducts operations to provide many aspects of protection to create a safe and secure environment.

SUPPORT AREA OPERATIONS

8-75. The MEB may conduct support area operations in support of stability operations. The ability to control terrain is key in most stability operations. The MEB is staffed to control terrain, own an AO, and influence the population to enhance freedom of action for the friendly force while denying it to the enemy. It will likely require ISR and fire support if there is a significant threat since these are not organic to the brigade. It may also require augmentation that includes a TCF when level III threats are likely within the AO it has been assigned.

EMPLOYMENT EXAMPLE

8-76. One example of an MEB conducting stability operations is shown in figure 8-2. In this example, the MEB is assigned AO Smith primarily to conduct stability operations within. The stability operations require the MEB to establish civil security, civil control, and restore essential services. The MEB is task-organized with a chemical, engineer, and MP battalion, and a CA and EOD company. Based on METT-TC, the MEB creates three battalion TFs task-organized based on the primary tasks within their assigned boundaries. The MP TF has responsibility for the MSR RED and construction of ASR BLUE to improve movement within the AO and bypass the built up area. Attachments to the MP TF include an engineer company and a CA team and it has detached a company and a platoon. The chemical battalion TF has TIC/TIM concerns and responsibility for the smaller built up area. Attachments to the chemical battalion TF include an MP platoon, and a CA team. The engineer TF has responsibility for the largest built up area, general engineering support to the BSB, and the largest area of demand to restore essential services. Attachments to the engineer TF include an MP company and a CA team and it has detached a company. The MEB and CA headquarters are collocated within the largest built up area to coordinate with and assist the regional civil authority. The MEB locates the BSA within a partially destroyed existing base near the built up area due to sources of local supplies and access to the road connecting to MSR RED.

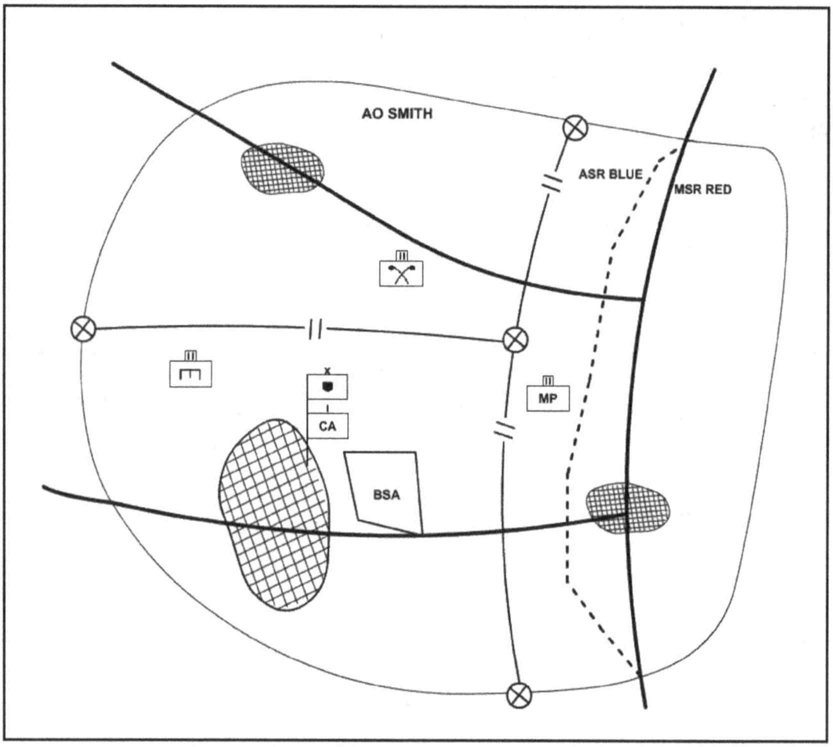

Figure 8-2. Example of an MEB conducting stability operations

Chapter 9

Sustainment Operations

Sustainment is the provision of logistics and personnel services required to maintain and prolong operations until successful mission accomplishment (JP 3-0). The endurance of Army forces is primarily a function of their sustainment. Sustainment determines the depth to which Army forces can conduct decisive operations, allowing the commander to seize, retain and exploit the initiative. The guiding principles of sustainment include responsiveness, anticipation, continuity, improvisation, and integration. MEB commanders use their assets to maintain the momentum of operations and enhance the capabilities of their forces. Digital C2 enablers enhance their sustainment operations. This chapter discusses sustainment of the MEB, not the conduct of sustainment tasks, as a part of MANSPT operations. Further information on sustainment operations can be found in FM 4-0, FM 63-2, and FM 3-90, appendix E. Information on contracting can be found in FM 100-10-2 and FM 3-100.21. See FM 3-34 or FM 3-34.400 for information on general engineering support (part of logistics).

PLANNING

9-1. The *sustainment warfighting function* is defined as the related tasks and systems that provide support and services to ensure freedom of action, extend operational reach, and prolong endurance (FM 3-0). Sustainment encompasses the sub-functions of logistics, personnel services, AHS support, and I/R operations required to maintain operations for mission accomplishment. Logistics is the science of planning, preparing, executing, and assessing movement and maintenance of forces. Personnel services are those sustaining functions related to Soldier's welfare, readiness, and quality of life. AHS support consists of all measures taken by commanders, leaders, individual Service members, and the military health system to promote, improve, conserve, or restore the mental and physical well-being of Service members.

9-2. The MEB staff synchronizes operations across all six warfighting functions to generate and maintain combat power. It plans tactical logistics. The sustainment warfighting function is synchronized with the higher echelon staff and supporting sustainment brigade. An MCT supporting the AO and other sustainment brigade assets may be located in the MEB brigade area. If required, the MEB will coordinate directly with the contracting support brigade (CSB) for contingency contacting. (See FM 100-10-2)

9-3. The MEB S-4, S-1, MEB brigade surgeon, and chaplain are the principal sustainment planners in the MEB. The BSB is the principal sustainment executer. Logistics synchronization for the brigade is done between the primary staff sections and the BSB support operations section. The MEB commander designates who will oversee logistics synchronization for the brigade. Traditionally this has been the XO. However, the MEB commander may elect to use the DCO for that mission while the executive officer focuses on other staff planning, integration, and synchronization functions in the main CP. The MEB obtains the logistics preparation of the theater information/products from the supporting sustainment brigade and the higher echelon headquarters concept of operations and integrates this with their IPB. The S-4, S-1, and BSB support operations officer maintain a continuous sustainment estimate during all operations. They use the logistics estimate to determine sustainment capabilities, anticipate support requirements, identify and resolve shortfalls, and develop support plans. They integrate into all planning what is needed to develop and synchronize sustainment with maneuver and fire plans. Sustainment commanders and planners must thoroughly understand the mission, tactical plans, and the MEB commander's intent.

They must know—
- Mission, task organization, and concept of operations for all subordinate battalions and attachments under MEB control.
- Higher headquarters sustainment plans.
- Known and anticipated branch plans and sequels.
- Density of personnel and equipment of each subordinate unit.
- Known and anticipated enemy situation and capabilities.
- Capabilities and limitations of subordinate units.
- HN support and contract capabilities.

9-4. The organic BSB supports the MEB employment, sustainment, and maintenance of organic and attached units. The BSB receives sustainment augmentation to expand capabilities as required. It task organizes as needed to support multiple simultaneous or sequential operations. It conducts sustainment for current operations and sets conditions for future operations. The BSB may command nonlogistics units when the MEB uses them as a TF or the BSB may form company teams to provide security as necessary. The BSB maintains visibility of the distribution system, theater infrastructure, and MSRs to provide the flexible support when and where it is needed.

9-5. The MEB establishes a BSA. The BSA could be a perimeter established by the BSB within a supported unit's AO, a base commanded by the BSB, or an area or base within the MEB's support AO. The MEB operations may require split based sustainment operations. The BSB may conduct replenishment operation within the MEB support AO or within the AO of a unit that the MEB is supporting. The MEB may establish an area within the support AO to support MSO for the MEB or support a BCT to establish an area for them in their AO or in the support AO.

PLANNING OVERVIEW

9-6. Logistics planners must understand the MEB's current and projected sustainment capabilities. They use information collected from personnel and logistics reports and operational reports to determine the personnel, equipment, and supply status of each unit within the MEB. They consider the disposition and condition of all supporting sustainment units and individual unit-level capabilities. They analyze this data and the current situation to determine the MEB's logistical capabilities and limitations.

9-7. Logistics planners must anticipate and understand support requirements of a tactical plan or COA. The S-1, S-4, and the BSB commander/BSB support operations officer analyze all COAs and modifications to current plans. They assess their sustainment feasibility, identify support requirements, and determine requirements for synchronization. The S-1 and S-4, like the commander, must visualize how the battle will unfold to determine critical requirements for each sustainment function. They logically consider the requirements for each sustainment function during the operational phases of before (prior to commitment), during (commitment to battle), and after (future missions). They analyze each COA/plan and consider the following:
- Type and duration of the operation.
- Task organization, tasks, and sustainment requirements of subordinate forces.
- Medical and maintenance profile of units to be assigned or attached.
- Ramifications of tactical operations such as gap (river) crossings, tactical pauses, long movements, preparatory fires, or defenses.
- Need for special equipment, supplies, or service.
- Requirements to separate, disassemble, configure, uncrate, or transload supplies above normal requirements.
- Requirements for reconstitution.
- Required varieties and quantities of all classes of supplies (especially class III, V, and IX).
- Requirements for support of reconnaissance forces, security operations, or deception efforts.
- Need for class IV/V obstacle material.

- Positioning of combat trains and other supporting logistics elements.
- Casualty numbers and likely locations.
- Large-scale decontamination operations in support of BCTs or consequence management mass casualty decontamination operations.
- ADC preparations and response.

9-8. The S-4's analysis also includes estimated attrition based on likely outcomes of subordinate missions. Analysis of estimated attrition primarily focuses on critical systems. The S-1 assists by projecting potential personnel losses. To perform this analysis, current unit personnel and equipment densities, standard planning factors, operations logistics software, and historical data are used in conjunction with operations logistics plan. When analyzing COAs, this projection helps the commander understand the potential losses and associated risks of each COA.

9-9. To understand the MEB's capabilities and determine support requirements, logistics planners apply a METT-TC analysis to the situation. Table 9-1 gives an example of general sustainment consideration for tactical operations.

Table 9-1. Logistics considerations for tactical operations

Mission	Enemy	Troops	Terrain and Weather	Time Available	Civil Considerations
• MEB mission and commander's intent. • Concept of operations. • Higher head-quarter's mission and concept of operations. • Higher head-quarter's concept of support. • Type and duration of operation. • Required supply rate. • Controlled supply rate.	• Enemy capabilities and tactics that could threaten sustainment operations. • Enemy unconventional tactics that could threaten sustainment operations. • Anticipated amount of EPWs.	• MEB's task organization to include supporting logistics units. • Location and condition of all units, including sustainment units. • Current and projected status of personnel, equipment, and classes of supply. • Availability and status of services. • Unit-level sustainment capabilities.	• Effects of weather and terrain on sustainment operations. • Additional sustainment require-ments of the MEB due to weather and terrain. • Condition of infra-structure such as roads and bridges.	• Impact on the ability to build-up supplies and replenish units. • Planning and preparation time for sustainment units. • Impacts of time on support require-ments and distribution methods.	• Host-nation support and contract services. • Impact of civilian and refugee movements. • Potential for hostile reactions by civilians against sustainment operations. • Potential detainee or resettlement requirements.

9-10. The S-4 and BSB support operations officer must balance support requirements and priorities with available sustainment capabilities. They consider existing stockages, anticipated receipts, capacities, and capabilities. They must assess the status of all logistics functions required to support the MEB and compare them to available capabilities. They identify potential shortfalls then take or recommend actions to eliminate or reduce their effect on the operation.

9-11. When a logistics shortfall is identified, the S-1, S-4, MEB surgeon, chaplain, and BSB support operations officer take every action available to eliminate or reduce its effect. They must understand its potential impact on the force, the risk it presents to mission accomplishment, its duration, and which requirement exceeded the unit's capabilities. They analyze the shortfall to determine its cause such as battle losses, supply availability, resource availability (equipment, man-hours), or distribution shortfall. They consider the following actions to resolve a shortfall:

- Shifting supplies or assets by phase of the operation.
- Requesting support or additional assets from higher headquarters.
- Using alternative distribution methods.
- Considering the use of host nation support.
- Considering pre-positioning supplies or attaching additional sustainment capabilities to subordinate forces.
- Modifying the COA or plan.

9-12. Based on the logistics estimate, the S-4, MEB surgeon, chaplain, and BSB support operations officer develop support plans. The overall sustainment plan is briefly described in the concept of support. The concept of support provides all commanders and staffs a general understanding of the commander's priorities and how the operation will be logistically supported. Detailed sustainment plans are outlined in a logistics annex to the MEB's OPORD or as part of a FRAGO. BSB commanders also issue an OPORD to all units under their control. BSB commanders in conjunction with the S-4 and executive officer closely monitor the implementation of the sustainment plan. They adjust sustainment operations, or shift resources to account for changing situations, changes in priorities (such as shifting the main effort) or to replace lost sustainment capabilities.

9-13. The MEB staff plans for sustainment of a frequently changing task organization with augmentation from other Army, joint, interagency, and multinational forces. Attachments to the MEB should arrive with their appropriate sustainment capability. When a company, team, or detachment is attached to the MEB, the S-4 integrates their sustainment augmentation pieces into the MEB support system. The S-4 must clearly state who will provide medical, maintenance, and recovery services, and provide support for class III, V, and IX supplies. When receiving attachments, sustainment planners require some basic information from the sending unit's S-4 to anticipate how to develop a synchronized concept of support. When the unit is detached, the MEB assists forwarding any on-hand supplies or equipment to the gaining unit. Some considerations are—

- Number and type of vehicles, personnel by specialty, and weapons systems.
- Current status and/or strength.
- Organic medical and maintenance capabilities.
- When attachment is effective and for how long.
- What support assets are coming with each attachment to the MEB.
- When and where linkup will occur, and who is responsible for linkup.

OPERATIONS

LOGISTICS

9-14. Logistics is primarily the responsibility of the MEB S-4 and provided primarily by the MEB's organic BSB. Logistics includes maintenance, transportation, supply, field services, distribution, contracting and general engineering. General engineering and I/R are primarily planned by the S-3 staff and not discussed in this chapter. Field services will be discussed further and include mortuary affairs, shower, laundry and light textile repair, and water purification. Contracting is discussed in greater detail since much of this information is new or emerging doctrine.

FIELD SERVICES

9-15. The MEB is dependent on augmentation for collection, processing and evacuation. A mortuary affairs team from the theater sustainment brigade provides mortuary services support to the MEB. The team operates from the BSA and is responsible for processing remains. The team has no transportation capabilities and coordinates with the support operations officer for evacuation back to the theater mortuary evacuation point. Internal to the MEB, handling teams are pre-designated at the unit level. It is the unit's responsibility to evacuate remains to the BSA.

9-16. There is no organic laundry or bath capability in the MEB. Support must be coordinated with the sustainment brigade.

9-17. The BSB has the organic capability to produce, store and transport purified water to meet the MEB's support requirements.

OPERATIONAL CONTRACT AND OTHER ACQUISITION LOGISTICS AND TECHNOLOGY SUPPORT

Overview

9-18. Acquisition, logistic, and technology (ALT) support consists of a myriad of unique support functions on the modern battlefield to include rapid equipment fielding support, technical equipment support, prepositioned stock support, and contracting support. Most of this ALT support is conducted through two colonel (O-6) level (United States Army Materiel Command [USAMC]) units—the Army field support brigade (AFSB) and the CSB. AFSB and CSB ALT support to the MEB will normally be executed in a GS manner under the C2 of the theater sustainment command (TSC) or expeditionary support command (ESC).

Army Field Support Brigade

9-19. The AFSB is the primary ALT unit for the Army and is responsible to control all ALT functions, less theater support contracting and logistic civil augmentation program (LOGCAP) support in the AO. The AFSB is a small TOE and augmented table of distribution and allowance (TDA) headquarters. It leverages reach (for technical support) and call-forward procedures to bring the requisite USAMC and Assistant Secretary of the Army for Acquisition, Logistics and Technology (ASA[ALT]) program executive offices (PEOs) (such as PEO Ground Combat Systems) and their subordinate product/ project manager (such as project manager Stryker brigade combat team) capabilities forward to the AO. These capabilities are organized in a USAMC-wide contingency TDA consisting of nearly 2,000 personnel. (Additional AFSB information can be found in FMI 4-93.41.) Specific AFSB functions include, but are not limited to—

- Army Logistics Assistance Program (LAP) U.S. Army Materiel Command support.
- System support contract management.
- Army preposition stocks offload support.
- USAMC research and development call forward support.
- USAMC Life Cycle Management Command (LCMC) call forward support.
- Project manager/PEO rapid-fielding and equipment modification support.
- Contractor personnel accountability and deployment support.

9-20. Two key AFSB subordinate units are the Army field support battalion and the brigade logistics support team (BLST). Army field support battalions are small, tailorable, deployable, lieutenant colonel (O-5) level TDA organizations of about 22 personnel, mostly LCMC logistics assistant representatives, aligned to specific division headquarters. BLSTs are similar to Army field support battalions, but are smaller major (O-4) level organizations (can also be lead by a warrant officer) that provide DS LAP support to a specific BCT or aviation brigade. Since MEBs do not have a DS BLST, they receive GS ALT support (less theater support contracting and LOGCAP from a designated Army field support battalion commander on GS basis.

Contracting Support Brigade

9-21. The Army has recently consolidated its theater support contracting capabilities into separate TOE units. These units include the CSB, contingency contracting battalions, senior contingency contracting teams, and contingency contracting teams (CCTs). These consolidated units are made up of primarily 51C military occupational specialty officers and NCOs. Like the AFSB, these units are currently assigned to the ASC, but are scheduled to come under the command of the new U.S. Army Contracting Command, and its subordinate expeditionary contracting command in the near future. The CSB and its subordinate unit's primary missions include—

- Providing theater support contracting capabilities to deployed Army forces, and as other military forces, governmental agencies and/or nongovernmental agencies, as directed.
- Developing contracting support plans; normally at the Army force (ARFOR) level. These plans will include mission specific LOGCAP support information.
- Coordinating execution of LOGCAP support to ensure that it is not in competition with existing or planned theater support contracts.
- Staying in close coordination with the supporting AFSB, providing contracting advice and planning assistance to senior maneuver and sustainment commanders.

9-22. In major operations, the CSB will normally be OPCON to the TSC or a separate joint theater support contracting command. In these situations, theater support contracting actions in support to the MEB will be executed in a GS manner.

9-23. For more information on operational contract support, see FM 3-100.21 and FM 100-10-2. For more specific postings of questions and discussions of operational contract support issues, see the Combined Arms Support Command battle command knowledge system on logistics data network (array) (LOGNET) <https://lognet.bcks.army.mil/>. Click on "Battlefield Contracting." For online training covering basic contracting familiarization, go to <https://scoe.learn.army.mil/webapps/portal/frameset.jsp>, browse the course catalogues, select "Software Center of Excellence (SCOE) courses," and enroll in "151-CAF-DL, Contractors Accompanying the Force (CAF)."

Maneuver Enhancement Brigade's Role in Planning and Managing Operational Contract Support

9-24. Contracting is a key source of support for deployed armed forces across the full spectrum operations. Because of the importance and unique challenges of operational contract support, the MEB commander and staff need to fully understand their role in planning and managing contracted support in the AO. Current doctrine describes three broad types of contracted support—theater support, external support and systems support.

- **Theater support contracts** support deployed operational forces under prearranged contracts, or contracts awarded from the mission area, by contracting officers under the C2 of the CSB. Theater-support contractors are utilized to acquire goods, services, and minor construction support, usually from the local commercial sources, to meet the immediate needs of operational commanders. Theater support contracts are the type of contract typically associated with contingency contracting. MEBs will often be the requiring activity for theater support contract support actions related to both internal and external missions. Theater support contracts in support of the MEB's missions are normally executed through a GS CCT or regional contracting office.
- **External support contracts** provide a variety of mission support to deployed forces. External support contracts may be prearranged contracts or contracts awarded during the contingency itself to support the mission and may include a mix of U.S. citizens, third country nationals, and local national subcontractor employees. The largest and most commonly used external support contract is LOGCAP. This Army program is commonly used to provide life support, transportation support, and other supporting functions to deployed Army forces and other elements of the joint force as well. In most operations, the MEB is a supported unit, but not the requiring activity when it comes to LOGCAP support.

- **System support contracts** are prearranged contracts by the USAMC LCMCs and separate ASA (ALT) PEO and project manager offices. Supported systems include, but are not limited to, newly fielded weapon systems, C2 infrastructure, such as the ABCS and STAMIS, and communications equipment. System contractors, made up of U.S. citizens, provide support in garrison and may deploy with the force to both training and real-world operations. They may provide either temporary support during the initial fielding of a system, called interim contracted support, or long-term support for selected materiel systems, often referred to as contractor logistic support. The MEB does not normally have a significant role to play in planning or coordinating system support contracts other than coordinating and executing support of system support contract related personnel.

9-25. For the MEB, the major challenge is ensuring theater support and external contract support (primarily LOGCAP related support) actions are properly incorporated and synchronized with the overall MEB support effort. It is imperative the MEB S-4 and its BSB support operations officer (SPO) work closely work with the TSC/ESC SPO, the ARFOR G-4, the CSB and the supporting Team LOGCAP-Forward. It is also important to understand that MEBs do not have any dedicated contingency contracting officers on their staff and that this support will be provided on a GS basis through the supporting CSB. Because of these new modular force contracting support arrangements, it is imperative the MEB S-4 and BSB SPO staff be trained on their roles in the operational contract support planning and execution process as described below:

- **Contract planning.** The sustainment brigade must to be prepared to develop "acquisition ready" requirement packets for submission to the supporting contracting activity. The packets must include a detailed performance work statement (PWS) (sometimes referred to as a statement of work [SOW]) for service requirements or detail item description(s)/capability for a commodity requirement. In addition to the PWS, packets must include an independent cost estimate for the item or service required along with an O-6 level and resource manager staff approved DA Form 3953, (*Purchase Request and Equipment*). Depending upon local ARFOR or joint force command policies, certain items or specific dollar amount requests may require formal acquisition review board packet review.
- **Contract management.** One of the most important MEB staff tasks is to nominate and track contract officer representatives (CORs) (sometimes referred to as contract officer technical representatives [COTRs]) for every service contract and a receiving official for all supply contracts. Quality COR and receiving official support is key to ensuring contractors provide the service or item according to the contract. The MEB must also manage funding for each contract and request funds in advance of depletion of current funds or all contract work will stop until adequate funds are available.
- **Contract close out.** The MEB is responsible for completing receiving reports, certifying that contracted goods or services were received by the Army, and submitting the receiving report to the contracting officer so the contract can be closed out and the contractor paid.

PERSONNEL SERVICES

9-26. Personnel services complement logistics by planning for and coordinating efforts that provide and sustain personnel. Personnel services are an integral part of unit readiness. The MEB S-1 is the staff officer responsible for personnel services. MEB capabilities include human resources support, legal support, and religious support.

9-27. Human resources (HR) support is an important component of sustainment. The MEB S-1 is responsible for providing or coordinating the operational and tactical level HR support that sustains the combat potential of the force, and the morale and welfare of Soldiers.

9-28. HR activities are divided into three categories—manning the force, personnel services, and personnel support. During the early phases of operations, HR support for the MEB focuses on the critical tasks of strength management, casualty operations, and replacement operations. Other HR key tasks will be completed via reachback operations or as the situation allows.

MANNING THE FORCE

9-29. The MEB S-1 section serves as a conduit between subordinate units and the division HR organization (G-1). Because of distances and communications capabilities, all reports are submitted through the MEB S-1 for forwarding to the appropriate agency. Initial personnel data is submitted by subordinate and attached units of the MEB by using digital technology. The MEB S-1 also provides information to subordinate units on status of evacuated/hospitalized personnel and adjusts personnel requirements accordingly.

9-30. There are four critical HR systems/functions that combine to form the task of manning the force—personnel readiness management, replacement management, personnel accounting, and personnel information management. The S-1 is responsible for integrating the elements of this task at the MEB level.

9-31. The purpose of the personnel readiness management system is to distribute Soldiers to units based on documented requirements or authorizations to maximize mission preparedness and provide the manpower needed. Personnel accounting is the system for recording by-name data on Soldiers when they arrive in and depart from units, when their duty status changes (such as from duty to hospital), and when their grade changes. Strength reporting is a numerical end product of the accounting process. It starts with strength-related transactions submitted at unit level and ends with a database update through all echelons to the Total Army Personnel Database. Personnel information management encompasses the collection, processing, and storing of critical information about Soldiers, units, and civilians. Personnel readiness managers, casualty managers, and replacement managers all utilize a personnel information database when performing their missions.

9-32. Replacement companies under C2 of replacement battalions at theater or corps level, receive, support, and process replacements. They coordinate movement with the appropriate movement control element. The division replacement section coordinates with the G-4 and division transportation officer for movement to the BSA. The MEB S-1 processes and assigns replacements to battalions. The battalion S-1 further assigns replacements to company level.

PERSONNEL SERVICES

9-33. Personnel services are an integral part of unit readiness. The MEB S-1 is the staff officer responsible for personnel services. This includes casualty reporting, military pay, and other essential services such as awards and decorations, evaluation reports, and enlisted promotions. While many of these functions are completed via reach operations, casualty operations are a critical function that must be completed throughout all operations, and with 100 percent accuracy.

Casualty Operations

9-34. The casualty reporting system is a by-name personnel accounting system that begins at unit level with the person who knows that a casualty has occurred. DA Form 1156 (*Casualty Feeder Card*) is forwarded as soon as possible. Reports are prepared using the Army Casualty Information Processing System–Light and are sent directly to HQDA, with copies furnished to other higher headquarters, as appropriate. Patient evacuation and mortality reports and treatment and disposition logs are provided daily to the MEB S-1 from the area support medical company.

Personnel Support

9-35. The third element of HR is personnel support. It includes postal operations management; morale, welfare, and recreation; and community support. The MEB has no unique capabilities in these areas.

FINANCIAL MANAGEMENT

9-36. The MEB has no special financial management capability. The MEB S-1 coordinates for support from mobile finance teams. Finance organizations provide support to the MEB units and individual Soldiers on an area basis. During deployments, mobile teams from corps-level finance organizations provide support to forward units. A finance battalion typically supports a division, with detachments providing financial management services as required.

LEGAL SUPPORT

9-37. The brigade legal section (BLS) provides and supervises legal support to MEB C2, sustainment, and support operations. The BLS provides and coordinates all legal support for the MEB. Paralegal Soldiers in the MEB and subordinate battalions provide paraprofessional and ministerial support for legal actions. The U.S. Army Trial Judiciary and U.S. Army Trial Defense Service are independent organizations that provide military judge and trial defense services to the MEB.

RELIGIOUS SUPPORT

9-38. The MEB chaplain is the staff officer responsible for implementing the commander's religious support program. Included in this program are worship opportunities; administration of sacraments; rites and ordinances; pastoral care and counseling; religious education; ministry to casualties to include support of combat operational stress reaction casualty treatment; and development and management of the unit ministry team (UMT). The chaplain advises the commander and staff on matters of morals, morale as affected by religion, the impact of local religion on the military mission, and the ethical impact of command decisions. The UMT is composed of a chaplain and one enlisted chaplain assistant. The chaplain assistant is an active member of the NCO support channel. The assistant assesses the Soldiers and other authorized personnel's well being that can affect the unit's fighting spirit. (See AR 165-1 and FM 1-05.)

HEALTH SERVICE SUPPORT

9-39. Health service support includes limited organic medical support and relies on area medical support. The MEB has limited medical logistics planning capability. The MEB surgeon ensures that all AHS support functions are considered and included in operation plans and operation orders. The MEB surgeon is a full-time special staff officer answering directly to the MEB commander on matters that pertain to the health of the command. The MEB surgeon coordinates AHS support for both HSS and FHP. The MEB surgeon coordinates AHS support operation with both the supported division surgeon and the medical brigade (MEDBDE) commander and establish medical guidelines for the MEB. The duties and responsibilities of the MEB surgeon include both HSS and FHP functions.

9-40. The MEB surgeon's duties and responsibilities for AHS may include—
- Advising the commander on the health of the MEB units.
- Planning and coordinating for HSS for MEB units (including but not limited to medical treatment, medical logistics, medical evacuation, hospitalization, dental support, preventive medicine, behavioral health, and clinical medical laboratory support.
- Developing and coordinating the HSS portion of AHS operation plans to support the MEB commander's decisions, planning guidance, and intent in support of full spectrum operations. (See FM 4-02.12 and FM 8-55.)
- Determining the medical workload requirements (patient estimates).
- Advising the MEB commander on policy regarding the eligibility of care for non-U.S. military personnel.
- Maintaining situational understanding by coordinating for current HSS information with surgeons of the next higher, adjacent, and subordinate headquarters.
- Recommending task organization of medical units/elements in support to MEB units to satisfy all HSS mission requirements.
- Recommending policies concerning medical support of stability operations (that include civil-military operations).
- Monitoring troop strength of medical personnel and their utilization.
- Coordinating, and synchronizing health consultation services.
- Evaluating and interpreting medical statistical data.
- Monitoring medical logistics and blood management operations in the theater. (See FM 4-02.1.)

- Monitoring medical regulating and patient tracking operations for MEB personnel. (See FM 4-02.2.)
- Determining MEB training requirements for first aid and for maintaining wellness of the command.
- Ensuring field medical records are maintained on each Soldier assigned to the TSC at their primary care medical treatment facility per AR 40-66 and FM 4-02.4.
- Establishing, in coordination with the chain of command, and promulgating a plan to ensure individual informed consent is established before administering investigational new drugs as described in Executive Order 13139.
- Recommending disposition instructions for captured enemy medical supplies and equipment. (Refer to FM 4-02 for additional information on the Geneva Conventions).
- Submitting to higher headquarters those recommendations on medical problems/conditions that require research and development.
- Coordinating, and synchronizing—
    - Health education and combat lifesaver training for the MEB.
    - Mass casualty plan developed by the S-3.
    - Medical care of EPWs, detainees, and civilians in the MEB's operations area.
    - Treatment of sick, injured, or wounded Soldiers.
- Performing medical evacuation, including use of both the Army's dedicated MEDEVAC platforms (air and ground).
- Coordinating medical logistics including class VIII resupply, blood management, and medical maintenance.
- Creating health-related reports and battlefield statistics.
- Collecting and analyzing operational data for on-the-spot adjustments in the medical support structure and for use in postoperations combat and materiel development studies.
- Providing Army Health System support for stability and civil support operations.

Force Health Protection

9-41. The MEB surgeon's duties and responsibilities for FHP may include:
- Identifying potential medical-related commander's critical information requirements (priority intelligence requirements and friendly force information requirements) as they pertain to the health threat; ensuring they are incorporated into the command's intelligence requirements.
- Coordinating for veterinary support for food safety, animal care, and veterinary preventive medicine to include zoonotic diseases transmissible to man.
- Planning for and implementing FHP operations to counter health threats. (See FM 4-02.17.) Force health protection operations may include:
- Planning for and accomplishing redeployment and postdeployment health assessments. Establishing and executing a medical surveillance program (refer to AR 40-5, AR 40-66, and FM 4-02.17 for an in-depth discussion).
- Establishing and executing an occupational and environmental health surveillance program. (See FM 3-100.4.)
- Recommending combat and operational stress control, behavioral health, and substance abuse control programs. (See FM 4-02.51.)
- Ensuring the general threat, health threat, and medical intelligence considerations are integrated into AHS support operation plans and orders.
- Advising MEB commanders on FHP CBRN defensive actions, such as immunizations, use of chemoprophylaxis, pretreatments, and barrier creams.
- Identifying health threats and medical-related commander's critical information requirements.
- Maintaining situational understanding by coordinating for current FHP information with surgeon staffs of the next higher, adjacent, and subordinate headquarters.

- Coordinating, and synchronizing—
  - Combat and operational stress control program with the division surgeon section (DSS) and supporting medical brigade.
  - Veterinary food inspection, military working dogs and other animal care, and veterinary preventive medicine activities of the command, as required.
  - Preventive medicine services to include identification of health threats.
  - Preventive dentistry support program for the prevention of cavities and gum disease.
  - Support of area medical laboratories support to include the identification of biological and chemical warfare agents, as required.

Brigade Surgeon Section

9-42. The brigade surgeon section (BSS) assists the surgeon with responsibilities listed above. The BSS monitors and tracks operations with medical communications for applicable automated systems (see FM 4-02.21) and provides updated information to the surgeon and the SPO chief for building capabilities to meet the MEB's medical requirements identified by the surgeon. Other functions include—

- Planning for the AHS support for the MEB units.
- Identifying and coordinating through the DSS and as authorized directly with medical brigade elements to support requirements of the MEB.
- Coordinating/managing medical evacuation and treatment capabilities.
- Coordinating/managing class VIII resupply capabilities and ensuring medical support is integrated and synchronized with the MEB's operational support plan.

Medical Plans and Operations

9-43. The BSS is normally staffed with medical operations officers Major 04, AOC 70H00, and a medical operations NCO (E-7, military occupational specialty 68W40). The primary function of this BSS is medical planning to ensure that adequate AHS support is available and provided in a timely and efficient manner for the MEB and its attached units. This BSS coordinates with the DSS and, as authorized, with medical brigade for the placement and support requirements of medical units and elements located in the MEB's operations area. For additional information on medical staff planning, see FM 8-55.

Medical Treatment Team

9-44. The medical treatment team assigned to the BSS and supports the MEB headquarters. The team provides Role 1 HSS for MEB headquarters personnel. The medical treatment leader is a physician assistant and works under the supervision of the MEB surgeon.

Health Threat

9-45. The health threat to Soldiers comes from enemy action and environmental situations. Effective and timely FHP initiatives are essential factors in sustaining combat power during continuous operations. The MEB's first line of protection is the use of preventive medicine measures and the units' field sanitation teams. For additional support, the MEB's subordinate units coordinate through their medical treatment team or the BSS for PVNTMED and COSC support. The PVNTMED and mental health elements from the MEDBDE provide DS as required that includes—

- Preventive medicine advice and consultation in the areas of disease and nonbattle injury, environmental sanitation, epidemiology, entomology, medical surveillance, limited sanitary engineering services, and pest management. See FM 4-02.17 for definitive information on PVNTMED.
- Training and advice in the promotion of positive combat and operational stress behaviors; the mental health element can provide early identification, handling, and management of misconduct stress behavior and Soldiers with combat and operational stress reactions. It assists and counsels personnel with personal, behavioral, or psychological problems and may refer suspected neuropsychiatric cases for evaluation. (See FM 4-02.51, FM 6-22.5 and FM 22-51 for definitive information on COSC.)

This page intentionally left blank.

Appendix A

Unit Manning Charts

Since there is no predecessor and little awareness of the MEB structure, this appendix provides the organizational and manning charts for the organic elements of the MEB as described in chapter 2. The manning charts for the MEB headquarters company, BSB, and NSC are based upon unit reference sheet decisions concerning duty title or position, rank, and military occupational skill (MOS).

Note. There are differences between these generic unit manning charts and the specific manning provided to each MEB in their TOE or MTOE. This information is provided to give a general understanding of the breadth and depth of manning for this new unit. Use this web site to see TOEs, MTOEs, and TDAs: <https://webtaads.belvoir.army.mil/usafmsa/>.

INTRODUCTION

A-1. The manning charts found in this appendix relate directly to the organizational charts in chapter 2. Chapter 2 provides additional details on the structures of all organic MEB organizations. Note the 01C00 MOS coding that specifies certain positions as being reserved for only CBRN, engineer, or MP personnel.

MEB HHC

A-2. Tables A-1 through A-21, pages A-1 through A-7, are MEB HHC manning charts.

Table A-1. Command section

Duty Title	Rank	MOS
Commander	Colonel (COL)	01C00
Deputy Commander	Lieutenant Colonel (LTC)	01C00
Executive Officer	LTC	01C00
Command Sergeant Major	CSM	00Z50
Driver	Sergeant (SGT)	88M20
Executive Administrative Assistant	Specialist (SPC)	42A10
Vehicle Driver	Private First Class (PFC)	31B10

Table A-2. Personnel section

Duty Title	Rank	MOS
S-1	Major (MAJ)	42H00
Strength Manager	Lieutenant (LT)	42B00
Military Personnel Tech	Chief Warrant Officer 2(CW2)	420A0
Senior Human Resources Sergeant	Master Sergeant (MSG)	42A50
Human Resources Sergeant	Staff Sergeant (SSG)	42A30
Human Resources Sergeant	SGT	42A20
Human Resources Sergeant	SGT	42A20
Human Resources Systems Management Specialist	SGT	42F20
Human Resources Specialist	SPC	42A10
Human Resources Specialist	SPC	42A10
Human Resources Specialist	SPC	42A10
Human Resources Systems Management Specialist	SPC	42F10

Table A-3. Intelligence section

Duty Title	Rank	MOS
S-2	MAJ	35D00
Vulnerability Assessment Officer	Captain (CPT)	31A00
Intelligence Officer	CPT	35E00
Criminal Intelligence/ Operations Officer	Chief Warrant Officer 3 (CW3)	311A0
Chief Intelligence Sergeant	MSG	35F50
Vulnerability Assessment NCO	Sergeant First Class (SFC)	31B40
Intelligence Sergeant	SSG	35F3I0
UAS Operator	SGT	15W20
Intelligence Analyst	SGT	35F20
UAS Operator	SPC	15W10
Intelligence Analyst	SPC	35F10
Intelligence Analyst	PFC	35F10

Table A-4. Operations section

Duty Title	Rank	MOS
S-3	LTC	01C00
Operations Officer	MAJ	01C00
Operations Officer	MAJ	57A00
Chief Operations Sergeant	Sergeant Major (SGM)	11Z50
Operations Sergeant	MSG	11Z50
Vehicle Driver	PFC	21B10
Vehicle Driver	PFC	31B10

Table A-5. Logistics section

Duty Title	Rank	MOS
S-4	MAJ	90A00
Maintenance Officer	CPT	91A00
Mobility Officer	CW2	882A0
Property Assessment Technician/Property Book Officer	CW2	920A0
Command Food Service Technician	CW2	922A0
Senior Food Operations Sergeant	MSG	92G50
Senior Supply Sergeant	MSG	92Y50
Senior Movements NCO	SFC	88N40
Movements Supervisor	SSG	88N30
Property Book NCO	SGT	92Y20
Assistant Supply Sergeant	SGT	92Y20
Supply Specialist	SPC	92Y10

Table A-6. Plans section

Duty Title	Rank	MOS
Plans Officer	MAJ	21B00
Plans Officer	MAJ	31A00
Plans Officer	MAJ	74A00
Power Systems Technician	CW3	210A5
Operations Sergeant	SFC	11B40

Table A-7. Communications section

Duty Title	Rank	MOS
S-6	MAJ	25A00
Information System Management Officer	CPT	53A00
Information System Technician	CW2	251A0
Signal Support System Chief	MSG	25U50
Senior Local Area Network (LAN) Manager	SGT	25B20
LAN Manager	SPC	25B10
Signal Support System Maintenance	SPC	25U10
Signal Information Service Support	SPC	25U10
LAN Manager	PFC	25B10
Signal Support System Support	PFC	25U10

Table A-8. Civil-military plans and operations

Duty Title	Rank	MOS
Civil Affairs Officer	MAJ	39C00
Civil Affairs Sergeant	SFC	38B40

Table A-9. MP operations cell

Duty Title	Rank	MOS
Operations Officer	MAJ	31A00
Assistant S-3	MAJ	31A00
Assistant Operations Officer	CPT	31A00
Maneuver and Mobility Support Operations Officer	CPT	31A00
Maneuver and Mobility Support Operations Officer	CPT	31A00
Protective Services Officer	CW3	311A0
Operations NCO	MSG	31B50
Operations NCO	MSG	31B50
Operations NCO	SFC	31B40
Operations NCO	SFC	31B40
Operations NCO	SFC	31B40
Internment/Resettlement NCO	SFC	31E40
Operations Sergeant	SSG	31B30
Operations Sergeant	SSG	31B30
Military Police	SPC	31B10

Table A-10. Fires cell

Duty Title	Rank	MOS
FSCOORD	LTC	13A00
FSO	MAJ	13A00
Assistant FSO	CPT	13A00
Targeting Officer	CW3	131A0
Operations Sergeant	MSG	13Z50
Effects NCO	SFC	13F40
Targeting NCO	SSG	13F30
Fire Support Specialist	SPC	13F10

Table A-11. CBRNE operations cell

Duty Title	Rank	MOS
Operations Officer	MAJ	74B00
Assistant Operations Officer	CPT	74B00
Intelligence Officer	CPT	74B00
EOD Officer	CPT	89E00
Chemical Operations NCO	MSG	74D50
Operations Sergeant	MSG	89D50
CBRN Staff NCO	SFC	74D40
CBRN NCO	SSG	74D30
CBRN NCO	SSG	74D30
CBRN Operations Specialist	SPC	74D10
CBRN Operations Specialist	PFC	74D10

Table A-12. Engineer operations cell

Duty Title	Rank	MOS
Operations Officer	MAJ	21B00
Engineer Tactical Assistant Officer in Charge (OIC)	CPT	21B00
Assistant Operations Officer	CPT	21B00
Operations Sergeant	MSG	21Z50
Assistant Operations Sergeant	SFC	21B40
Assistant Operations Sergeant	SFC	21C40
Reconnaissance Sergeant	SSG	21B30
Reconnaissance Sergeant	SSG	21B30
Terrain Data Sergeant	SGT	21U20
Terrain Data Specialist	SPC	21U10
Terrain Data Specialist	PFC	21U10
Terrain Data Specialist	PFC	21U10

Table A-13. Brigade unit ministry team

Duty Title	Rank	MOS
Chaplain	MAJ	56A00
Chaplain Assistant NCO	SSG	56M30

Table A-14. Brigade legal section

Duty Title	Rank	MOS
Brigade Judge Advocate	MAJ	27A00
Operational Law Judge Advocate	CPT	27A00
Paralegal NCO	SSG	27D30

Table A-15. Public affairs section

Duty Title	Rank	MOS
Public Affairs Operations NCO	SFC	46Z40
Public Affairs Sergeant	SGT	46Q20

Table A-16. Brigade surgeon section

Duty Title	Rank	MOS
Brigade Surgeon	MAJ	62B00
Medical Operations Officer	CPT	70H67
Health Care NCO	SFC	68W40

Table A-17. Medical treatment team

Duty Title	Rank	MOS
Physician Assistant	CPT	65D00
Health Care Sergeant	SSG	68W30
Health Care Specialist	SPC	68W10
Health Care Specialist/Driver	PFC	68W10

Table A-18. Company headquarters

Duty Title	Rank	MOS
Commander	CPT	01C00
First Sergeant	1SG	31B5M
Food Operations Management NCO	SFC	92G40
Senior First Cook	SSG	92G30
Supply Sergeant	SSG	92Y30
Human Resources Sergeant	SGT	42A20
Equipment Receipt/Parts Specialist	SGT	92A20
First Cook	SGT	92G20
Equipment Receipt/Parts Specialist	SPC	92A10
Supply Specialist	SPC	92Y10
Cook	SPC	92G10
Cook	SPC	92G10
Cook	PFC	92G10

Table A-19. Liaison team

Duty Title	Rank	MOS
Team Chief	MAJ	01C00
Liaison Officer	MAJ	31A00
Liaison Officer	CPT	21B00
Liaison Officer	CPT	74A00
Construction Inspector	SFC	21N40
Liaison NCO	SFC	31B40
Liaison NCO	SSG	74D30

Table A-20. Airspace management section

Duty Title	Rank	MOS
Airspace Management Officer	MAJ	15B00
Assistant Operations Officer	CPT	14A00
C2 System Integrator	CW3	140A0
AC2 Sergeant	SFC	15Q40
Operations Sergeant	SSG	14J30
Electronic Warfare System Operator	SPC	14J10
Tactical Airspace Integration System Operator	SPC	15Q10
Electronic Warfare System Operator	PFC	14J10

Table A-21. Area operations section

Duty Title	Rank	MOS
Operations Officer	MAJ	03A00
Operations Officer	MAJ	03A00
Engineer Operations Officer	MAJ	21B00
Area Security/Protection Officer	MAJ	31A00
Chemical Officer	MAJ	74A00
Area Damage Officer	CPT	21B00
Civil Engineer	CPT	21B00
Area Security/Protection Officer	CPT	31A00
Assistant Operations Officer	LT	74B00
Chief Operations Sergeant	SGM	11Z50
Operations Sergeant	MSG	11Z50
Operations Sergeant	MSG	21X50
Operations NCO	MSG	31B50
Construction Inspector	SFC	21H40
Construction Inspector	SFC	21N40
Senior Technical Engineer NCO	SFC	21T40
Operations NCO	SFC	31B40
CBRN Staff NCO	SFC	74D40
Technical Engineer Specialist	SPC	21T10
Vehicle Driver	PFC	21B10
Vehicle Driver	PFC	31B10

NETWORK SUPPORT COMPANY

A-3. Tables A-22 through A-32 and pages A-7 through A-9 are NSC manning charts.

Table A-22. Company headquarters

Duty Title	Rank	MOS
Commander	CPT	25A00
Executive Officer	LT	25A00
First Sergeant	1SG	25W5M
CBRN NCO	SGT	74D20
Supply Sergeant	SGT	92Y20
Armorer	SPC	92Y10

Table A-23. Signal maintenance section

Duty Title	Rank	MOS
Senior Signal Support System Maintainer	SGT	25U20
Cable System Installer/ Maintainer	SPC	25L10
Support Electronic Devices Repairer	SPC	94F10

Table A-24. Network/chemical network defense team

Duty Title	Rank	MOS
Network Management Tech	CW2	250N0
COMSEC Custodian	SFC	25B40
Battlefield Spectrum Manager	SFC	25W40
Automated Data Processing (ADP) Security Team Chief	SSG	25B30
Assistant COMSEC Custodian	SSG	25B30
Network System Maintainer	SSG	25F30
Network System Maintainer	SSG	25F30
SATCOM Operations NCO	SSG	25S30
ADP Security Specialist	SPC	25B10
ADP Security Specialist	PFC	25B10

Table A-25. Range extension platoon headquarters

Duty Title	Rank	MOS
Platoon Leader	LT	25A00
Platoon Sergeant	SFC	25U40

Table A-26. Small command post support team (X2)

Duty Title	Rank	MOS
Senior Transmission (XMSN) Operator/Maintainer	SGT	25Q20
Information System Support	SPC	25B10
XMSN Operator/Maintainer	SPC	25Q10
Information System Support	PFC	25B10

Table A-27. Retransmission team (X3)

Duty Title	Rank	MOS
Team Chief	SGT	25U20
Radio Retransmission Operator	SPC	25U10
Radio Retransmission Operator	PFC	25U10

Table A-28. Network extension platoon

Duty Title	Rank	MOS
Platoon Leader	LT	25A00
Platoon Sergeant	SFC	25W40

Table A-29. Joint nodal network team

Duty Title	Rank	MOS
External Switch Supervisor	SSG	25F30
Senior Switch System Operator/Maintainer	SGT	25F20
TACSAT System Team Chief	SGT	25S20
Range Extension Operator	SPC	25F10
External Switch Operator/Maintainer	SPC	25F10

Table A-30. Line of sight V3 team

Duty Title	Rank	MOS
Senior XMSN System Operator/Maintainer	SGT	25Q20
XMSN System Operator/Maintainer	SPC	25Q10
XMSN System Operator/Maintainer	PFC	25Q10

Table A-31. Data support team

Duty Title	Rank	MOS
Senior Info Systems Specialist	SGT	25B20
Cable System Installer/Maintainer	SPC	25L10

Table A-32. Retransmission team

Duty Title	Rank	MOS
Team Chief	SGT	25U20
Radio Retransmission Operator	SPC	25U10
Radio Retransmission Operator	PFC	25U10

BRIGADE SUPPORT BATTALION

HHD BSB

A-4. Tables A-33 through A-43 and pages A-9 through A-12 are HHD, BSB manning charts.

Table A-33. Command section

Duty Title	Rank	MOS
Commander	LTC	90A00
Executive Officer	MAJ	90A00
Command Sergeant Major	CSM	00Z50
Chauffeur	SPC	88M10

Table A-34. Personnel section

Duty Title	Rank	MOS
S-1	CPT	90A00
Senior Human Resources Sergeant	SFC	42A40
Human Resources Sergeant	SSG	42A30
Human Resources Sergeant	SGT	42A20
Human Resources Sergeant	SGT	42A20
Paralegal Specialist	SPC	27D10
Human Resources Specialist	SPC	42A10
Human Resources Specialist	PFC	42A10

Table A-35. Unit ministry team

Duty Title	Rank	MOS
Chaplain	CPT	56A00
Chaplain Assistant	SPC	56M10

Table A-36. Logistics section

Duty Title	Rank	MOS
S-4	CPT	90A00
Supply Sergeant	SFC	92Y40
Supply Sergeant	SGT	92Y20
Supply Specialist	SPC	92Y10

Table A-37. Intelligence/operations section

Duty Title	Rank	MOS
S-2	CPT	35D00
S-3	CPT	90A00
Operations Sergeant	MSG	92A50
Intelligence Sergeant	SSG	35F30
Operations Sergeant	SSG	63H30
CBRN NCO	SSG	74D30
Movements NCO	SGT	88N20
Intelligence Analyst	SPC	35F10

Table A-38. Communications section

Duty Title	Rank	MOS
S-6	CPT	25A00
Section Chief	SFC	25U40
LAN Manager	SPC	25B10
Signal Information Service Specialist	SPC	25U10
LAN Manager	PFC	25B10
Signal Support System Specialist	PFC	25U10

Table A-39. Support operations office

Duty Title	Rank	MOS
Support Operations Officer	MAJ	90A00
Transportation Officer	CPT	88A00
Ammunition Officer	CPT	91A00
Operations Officer	CPT	92A00
Operations Sergeant	MSG	92A50
Ammunition Logistics Sergeant	SFC	88B40
Ammunition Inspector	SSG	89B40
Material Management NCO	SSG	92A30
Mortuary Affairs NCO	SSG	92M30
Transportation Management NCO	SGT	88N20
Material Contract/Accounting Specialist	SPC	92A10

Table A-40. Combat service support automation management office

Duty Title	Rank	MOS
Material Management NCO	SSG	92A30
Senior Information Systems Specialist	SGT	25B20
Patient Services NCO	SGT	68G20
Supply Sergeant	SGT	92Y20
Information Systems Specialist	SPC	25B10
Supply Specialist	SPC	92U10

Table A-41. Plans section

Duty Title	Rank	MOS
Plans Officer	CPT	90A00
Movements Supervisor	SSG	88N30

Table A-42. Readiness operations division

Duty Title	Rank	MOS
Maintenance Officer	CPT	91A00
Maintenance Management NCO	SFC	63X40

Table A-43. Detachment headquarters

Duty Title	Rank	MOS
Commander	CPT	90A00
First Sergeant	1SG	92Y5M
Senior Food Operations Sergeant	SFC	92G40
Senior First Cook	SSG	92G30
CBRN Decontamination Specialist	SPC	74D10
Cook	SGT	92G20
Cook	SGT	92G20
Supply Sergeant	SGT	92Y20
Cook	SPC	92G10
Cook	SPC	92G10
Cook	SPC	92G10
Cook	SPC	92G10
Cook	SPC	92G10
Armorer	SPC	92Y10
Cook	PFC	92G10
Cook	PFC	92G10
Cook	PFC	92G10
Cook	PFC	92G10

DISTRIBUTION COMPANY

A-5. Tables A-44 through A-53 and pages A-12 through A-15 are distribution company manning charts.

Table A-44. Company headquarters

Duty Title	Rank	MOS
Commander	CPT	90A00
Operations Officer	LT	92A00
First Sergeant	1SG	92A5M
Supply Sergeant	SSG	92Y30
CBRN Specialist	SPC	74D10
Armorer	SPC	92Y10

Table A-45. Distribution platoon headquarters

Duty Title	Rank	MOS
Platoon Leader	LT	88A00
Platoon Sergeant	SFC	88M40
Dispatcher	SGT	88M20

Table A-46. Truck squad (X2)

Duty Title	Rank	MOS
Squad Leader	SSG	88M30
Heavy Vehicle Driver	SSG	88M30
Heavy Vehicle Driver	SGT	88M20
Heavy Vehicle Driver	SGT	88M20
Heavy Vehicle Driver	SGT	88M20
Heavy Vehicle Driver	SPC	88M10
Heavy Vehicle Driver	SPC	88M10
Heavy Vehicle Driver	SPC	88M10
Heavy Vehicle Driver	PFC	88M10
Heavy Vehicle Driver	PFC	88M10

Table A-47. Supply platoon headquarters

Duty Title	Rank	MOS
Platoon Leaders	LT	92A00
Platoon Sergeant	SFC	92A40

Table A-48. Stock control section

Duty Title	Rank	MOS
Supply Systems Technician	CW2	920B0
Material Contract/Accounting Supervisor	SSG	92A30
Material Contract/Accounting NCO	SGT	92A20
Material Contract/Accounting Specialist	SPC	92A10
Material Contract/Accounting Specialist	SPC	92A10
Material Contract/Accounting Specialist	SPC	92A10
Material Contract/Accounting Specialist	PFC	92A10
Material Contract/Accounting Specialist	PFC	92A10

Table A-49. General supply section

Duty Title	Rank	MOS
Material Management Supervisor	SSG	92A30
Material Storage/Handling Sergeant	SGT	92A20
Material Storage/Handling Sergeant	SGT	92A20
Material Storage/Handling Specialist	SPC	92A10
Material Storage/Handling Specialist	SPC	92A10
Subsistence Supply Specialist	SPC	92A10
Subsistence Supply Specialist	SPC	92A10
Material Storage/Handling Specialist	PFC	92A10
Material Storage/Handling Specialist	PFC	92A10
Material Storage/Handling Specialist	PFC	92A10
Subsistence Supply Specialist	PFC	92A10
Subsistence Supply Specialist	PFC	92A10

Table A-50. Class IX section

Duty Title	Rank	MOS
Stock Control Supervisor	SFC	92A40
Material Management Supervisor	SSG	92A30
Material Storage/Handling Sergeant	SGT	92A20
Material Storage/Handling Sergeant	SGT	92A20
Material Storage/Handling Sergeant	SGT	92A20
Material Contract/Accounting NCO	SGT	92A20
Material Contract/Accounting Specialist	SPC	92A10
Material Storage/Handling Specialist	SPC	92A10
Material Storage/Handling Specialist	SPC	92A10
Material Storage/Handling Specialist	SPC	92A10
Material Storage/Handling Specialist	PFC	92A10
Material Storage/Handling Specialist	PFC	92A10
Material Storage/Handling Specialist	PFC	92A10
Material Storage/Handling Specialist	PFC	92A10

Table A-51. Fuel and water platoon headquarters

Duty Title	Rank	MOS
Platoon Leader	LT	92F00
Platoon Sergeant	SFC	92W40
Petroleum Lab Sergeant	SGT	92L20

Table A-52. Class III storage/issue section

Duty Title	Rank	MOS
Section Chief	SSG	92F30
Petroleum Heavy Vehicle Operator	SGT	92F20
Petroleum Heavy Vehicle Operator	SGT	92F20
Petroleum Heavy Vehicle Operator	SGT	92F20
Petroleum Heavy Vehicle Operator	SGT	92F20
Petroleum Heavy Vehicle Operator	SGT	92F20
Petroleum Heavy Vehicle Operator	SGT	92F20
Petroleum Light Vehicle Operator	SPC	92F10
Petroleum Heavy Vehicle Operator	SPC	92F10
Petroleum Heavy Vehicle Operator	SPC	92F10
Petroleum Heavy Vehicle Operator	SPC	92F10
Petroleum Heavy Vehicle Operator	SPC	92F10
Petroleum Heavy Vehicle Operator	SPC	92F10
Petroleum Heavy Vehicle Operator	SPC	92F10
Petroleum Heavy Vehicle Operator	SPC	92F10
Petroleum Heavy Vehicle Operator	SPC	92F10
Petroleum Heavy Vehicle Operator	SPC	92F10
Petroleum Heavy Vehicle Operator	SPC	92F10
Petroleum Light Vehicle Operator	PFC	92F10
Petroleum Light Vehicle Operator	PFC	92F10
Petroleum Light Vehicle Operator	PFC	92F10

Table A-53. Water section

Duty Title	Rank	MOS
Water Treatment Supervisor	SSG	92W30
Water Treatment NCO	SGT	92W20
Water Treatment Specialist	SPC	92W10
Water Treatment Specialist	SPC	92W10
Water Treatment Specialist	SPC	92W10
Water Treatment Specialist	PFC	92W10
Water Treatment Specialist	PFC	92W10

SUPPORT MAINTENANCE COMPANY

A-6. Tables A-54 through A-66 and pages A-16 through A-21 are support maintenance company manning charts.

Table A-54. Company headquarters

Duty Title	Rank	MOS
Commander	CPT	91A00
Executive Officer	LT	91A00
First Sergeant	1SG	63Z5M
Motor Sergeant	SFC	63X40
Senior Food Operations Sergeant	SFC	92G40
Senior Mechanic	SSG	63B30
CBRN NCO	SSG	74D30
Senior First Cook	SSG	92G30
Supply Sergeant	SSG	92Y30
Human Resources Sergeant	SGT	42A20
Power Generator Equipment Repairer	SGT	52D20
Wheeled Vehicle Mechanic	SGT	63B20
Wheeled Vehicle Mechanic	SGT	63B20
Cook	SGT	92G20
Forward Signal Support Specialist	SPC	25U10
Human Resources Specialist	SPC	42A10
Utilities Equipment Repairer	SPC	52C10
Construction Equipment Repairer	SPC	62B10
Wheeled Vehicle Mechanic	SPC	63B10
Wheeled Vehicle Mechanic	SPC	63B10
Tracked Vehicle Mechanic	SPC	63H10
Equipment Receipt/Parts Specialist	SPC	92A10
Cook	SPC	92A10
Cook	SPC	92A10
Armorer	SPC	92Y10
Power Generator Equipment Repairer	PFC	52D10
Wheeled Vehicle Mechanic	PFC	63B10
Wheeled Vehicle Mechanic	PFC	63B10
Wheeled Vehicle Mechanic	PFC	63B10
Equipment Receipt/Parts Specialist	PFC	92A10
Cook	PFC	92G10
Supply Specialist	PFC	92Y10

Table A-55. Maintenance control section

Duty Title	Rank	MOS
Maintenance Control Officer	LT	91A00
Maintenance Control Sergeant	MSG	63Z50
Equipment Receipt/Parts Sergeant	SGT	92A20
Equipment Receipt/Parts Specialist	SPC	92A10
Equipment Receipt/Parts Specialist	PFC	92A10
Equipment Receipt/Parts Specialist	PFC	92A10

Table A-56. Service/recovery section

Duty Title	Rank	MOS
Allied Trades Warrant Officer	CW3	914A0
Section Chief	SSG	44E30
Metal Worker/Repairer	SGT	44B20
Metal Worker/Repairer	SGT	44B20
Machinist	SGT	44E20
Recovery Vehicle Operator	SGT	63B20
Metal Worker/Repairer	SPC	44B10
Machinist	SPC	44E10
Recovery Vehicle Operator	SPC	63B10
Welder	PFC	44B10
Welder	PFC	44B10
Machinist	PFC	44E10

Table A-57. Automotive/armament maintenance platoon

Duty Title	Rank	MOS
Platoon Leader	LT	91A00
Senior Automotive Maintenance Warrant Officer	CW3	915E0
Platoon Sergeant	SFC	63X40
Armament Maintenance Technical Inspector	SSG	45K30
Technical Inspector	SSG	63B30
Technical Inspector	SSG	63B30
Technical Inspector	SSG	63H30

Table A-58. Tank/automotive maintenance section

Duty Title	Rank	MOS
Section Sergeant	SFC	63X40
Shop Foreman	SSG	63B30
Senior Mechanic	SSG	63B30
Wheeled Vehicle Mechanic	SGT	63B20
Wheeled Vehicle Mechanic	SGT	63B20
Wheeled Vehicle Mechanic	SGT	63B20
Wheeled Vehicle Mechanic	SGT	63B20
Tracked Vehicle Mechanic	SGT	63H20
Wheeled Vehicle Mechanic	SPC	63B10
Wheeled Vehicle Mechanic	SPC	63B10
Wheeled Vehicle Mechanic	SPC	63B10
Wheeled Vehicle Mechanic	SPC	63B10
Wheeled Vehicle Mechanic	SPC	63B10
Tracked Vehicle Mechanic	SPC	63H10
Wheeled Vehicle Mechanic	PFC	63B10
Wheeled Vehicle Mechanic	PFC	63B10
Wheeled Vehicle Mechanic	PFC	63B10
Wheeled Vehicle Mechanic	PFC	63B10
Wheeled Vehicle Mechanic	PFC	63B10
Wheeled Vehicle Mechanic	PFC	63B10
Wheeled Vehicle Mechanic	PFC	63B10
Tracked Vehicle Mechanic	SPC	63H10

Table A-59. Armament maintenance section

Duty Title	Rank	MOS
Armament Systems Maintenance Warrant Officer	CW3	913A0
Section Chief	SFC	45K40
Small Arms/Artillery Repairer	SGT	45B20
Fire Control Repairer	SGT	45G20
Armament Repairer	SGT	45K20
Small Arms/Artillery Repairer	SPC	45B10
Fire Control Repairer	SPC	45G10
Armament Repairer	SPC	45K10
Armament Repairer	SPC	45K10
Small Arms/Artillery Repairer	PFC	45B10
Small Arms/Artillery Repairer	PFC	45B10
Fire Control Repairer	PFC	45G10
Fire Control Repairer	PFC	45G10
Armament Repairer	PFC	45K10

Table A-60. Electronic equipment maintenance platoon

Duty Title	Rank	MOS
Platoon Leader	LT	91A00
Electrical Systems Maintenance Warrant Officer	CW3	948B0
Platoon Sergeant	SFC	94W40
Electrical Maintenance Quality Assurance (QA)/Quality Control (QC) Technical Inspector	SFC	94W40
Technical Inspector/Quality Control	SSG	25P30
Special Electronic Devices QA/QC Technical Inspector	SSG	94F30
Radio Repair QA/QC Technical Inspector	SGT	94E20

Table A-61. Radio and communications security repair section

Duty Title	Rank	MOS
COMSEC/Radio Supervisor	SSG	94E30
Senior COMSEC/Radio Repairer	SGT	94E20
COMSEC/Radio Equipment Repairer	SPC	94E10
COMSEC/Radio Equipment Repairer	SPC	94E10
COMSEC/Radio Equipment Repairer	SPC	94E10
COMSEC/Radio Equipment Repairer	PFC	94E10
COMSEC/Radio Equipment Repairer	PFC	94E10
COMSEC/Radio Equipment Repairer	PFC	94E10

Table A-62. Computer/automated systems repair section

Duty Title	Rank	MOS
Special Electronic Devices Repair Supervisor	SSG	94F30
Senior Special Electronic Devices Repairer	SGT	94F20
Special Electronic Devices Repairer	SPC	94F10
Special Electronic Devices Repairer	PFC	94F10
Special Electronic Devices Repairer	PFC	94F10

Table A-63. Microwave/radar repair section

Duty Title	Rank	MOS
Microwave Team Chief	SGT	25P20
Microwave Operator-Maintainer	SPC	25P10
Radar Repairer	SPC	94M10
Microwave Operator-Maintainer	PFC	25P10
Radar Repairer	PFC	94M10

Table A-64. Special electronic devices/wire systems repair section

Duty Title	Rank	MOS
Special Electronic Devices Repair Supervisor	SSG	94F30
Senior Special Electronic Devices Repairer	SGT	94F20
Senior Special Electronic Devices Repairer	SGT	94F20
Special Electronic Devices Repairer	SPC	94F10
Special Electronic Devices Repairer	SPC	94F10
Special Electronic Devices Repairer	SPC	94F10
Special Electronic Devices Repairer	PFC	94F10
Special Electronic Devices Repairer	PFC	94F10
Special Electronic Devices Repairer	PFC	94F10

Table A-65. Ground support equipment platoon

Duty Title	Rank	MOS
Platoon Leader	LT	91A00
Engineer Equipment Maintenance Warrant Officer	CW3	919A0
Platoon Sergeant	SFC	52X40
Technical Inspector	SSG	52D30

Table A-66. Ground support equipment maintenance section

Duty Title	Rank	MOS
Special Purpose Equipment Repair Supervisor	SFC	52X40
Senior Quartermaster and Chemical Equipment Repairer	SSG	52C30
Senior Utilities Equipment Repairer	SSG	52C30
Senior Power Generator Equipment Repairer	SSG	52D30
Senior Construction Equipment Repairer	SSG	62D30
Utilities Equipment Repairer	SGT	52C20
Power Generator Equipment Repairer	SGT	52D20
Power Generator Equipment Repairer	SGT	52D20
Construction Equipment Repairer	SGT	62B20
Quartermaster and Chemical Equipment Repairer	SGT	63J20
Utilities Equipment Repairer	SPC	52C10
Power Generator Equipment Repairer	SPC	52D10
Power Generator Equipment Repairer	SPC	52D10
Construction Equipment Repairer	SPC	62B10
Quartermaster and Chemical Equipment Repairer	SPC	63J20
Utilities Equipment Repairer	PFC	52C10
Utilities Equipment Repairer	PFC	52C10
Power Generator Equipment Repairer	PFC	52D10
Power Generator Equipment Repairer	PFC	52D10
Construction Equipment Repairer	PFC	62B10
Construction Equipment Repairer	PFC	62B10
Quartermaster and Chemical Equipment Repairer	PFC	63J20
Quartermaster and Chemical Equipment Repairer	PFC	63J20

This page intentionally left blank.

Appendix B
MEB Command Post

MEB commanders organize their C2 systems discussed in chapter 3 into CPs for optimum use (to include their staffing, layouts, and INFOSYS) based on the factors of METT-TC. This appendix provides solutions for the MEB CPs and provides examples of potential CP layouts using cells and staff sections. See FM 3-90, FMI 5-0.1, and FM 6-0 for additional possibilities and a discussion of how to optimize CP performance.

COMMAND POST

B-1. The MEB commander considers effectiveness and survivability factors when organizing CPs. (See FMI 5-0.1.) Normally, the MEB will establish a main CP and may also choose to establish a TAC CP. Additionally, the brigade may use command groups (away from the main or TAC CPs) or an early-entry command post (ECCP) as ad hoc or temporary CPs. (See chapter 2.) The MEB commander may choose to use the staff sections, S1 through S6, align with the modular division or supported headquarters cell or directorate organization, or use a mix of staff sections and cell as shown in the example below. FMI 5-0.1 should be the primary reference for considerations in establishing MEB CPs. It provides doctrine for the overall function of each functional and integrating cell. It also describes the roles, functions, and relationships between each type of CP. FMI 5-01 discusses the cells within a CP as functional cells (intelligence; movement and maneuver; fire support; protection; sustainment; and command, control, communications, and computer operations) and integrating cells (current operations, future operations, and plans). Any staff member and C2 capability augmentation to the MEB must be integrated into the various CPs.

B-2. CPs help commanders control operations by coordinating and synchronizing the warfighting functions. Activities common to all CPs include—

- Maintaining running estimates and the common operating picture. (See FMI 5-0.1.)
- Integrating the information superiority contributors—the Army information tasks, ISR, knowledge management, and information management. (See FM 3-0.)
- Developing and disseminating orders. (See FM 5-0.)
- Controlling operations. (See FMI 5-0.1.)
- Assessing operations. (See FMI 5-0.1.)
- Coordinating with higher, lower, and adjacent units.
- Administering the CP to include—
  - Displacing.
  - Providing security.
  - Organizing for operations
  - Maintaining continuity of operations.

B-3. In most instances, both the TAC CP and main CP must be operational to support C2 over extended distances. If the MEB is only conducting operations in the support AO then they might be able to operate with only the main CP and have the TAC CP or BSB CP prepared as an alternate CP to make the C2 system more survivable. All CP initial locations and subsequent locations must be integrated into the MEB's communication plan to ensure continuous connectivity is maintained. Only the main CP is discussed in more detail here.

B-4. The main CP is the commander's principal C2 facility. It is positioned to maintain communications with subordinate units and control MEB operations. Considerations for positioning the main CP include—

- Where the enemy can least affect the main CP operations.
- Where the main CP can achieve the best communications (digital and voice).
- Where the main CP can control operations best.

B-5. When assigned an AO, the MEB main CP can locate in and control one of the bases. If the MEB is located in another unit's AO then that unit will locate the MEB CP. Staffs develop a plan that addresses each CPs initial and subsequent position.

CP EQUIPMENT

B-6. See the MTOE for each MEB. The major equipment used to establish the CPs is the standard integrated command post system (SICPS). SICPS is the CP facility systems to support digitized units. SICPS provides the flexibility, commonality, and operational capabilities needed to enhance unit mobility and integrate ABCS and associated communication and networking equipment. SICPS can serve as a stand-alone CP facility or as an integrated element in a larger CP facility.

B-7. The SICPS has seven CP variants (not all will be organic to the MEB headquarters, some may come from augmentation units), including tracked and wheeled vehicle mounted vans, tents, and hard shelters. The MEB collocates staff sections and supporting communications systems to facilitate both face-to-face interaction and digital data exchange. The BSB CP is not shown in the MEB CP examples because they normally would not be collocated with the MEB main CP. The NSC CP is also not shown in the examples.

B-8. The CP's physical setup must facilitate communication and analysis of information, as well as accommodate computer hardwire requirements. Within the CP, information is processed at two locations— individual workstations and the combat information center (CIC). The focus of the individual workstation is the individual automated system and the specific warfighting function it supports. At the individual workstations, staff members input and monitor data within their sphere of responsibility. They also accesses data posted to web pages and shared files by other staff sections in the LAN and wide area network to carry out their warfighting function and duties. The focus of the CIC is integrated battle monitoring and decisionmaking. It is a special location within the CP for the display of information. The CIC is the central area for viewing information in order for commanders and their staff to maintain SU. The large screen display (LSD) accomplishes this, and is the only area in the CP where all key automated system data can be viewed simultaneously. It is therefore the place where battlefield vision is supported best. Commanders use the CIC to illustrate their guidance and with their staff's assistance, to develop and maintain the COP.

B-9. CICs vary by unit MTOE. However, the typical CIC has two LSDs, each capable of displaying nine sub-screens. Each sub-screen can display the COP and can be configured in various ways to best support the commander's information display preferences. The more sub-screens used, the lower the resolution of the image. For this reason, each LSD screen should use no more than four sub-screens.

B-10. The CP examples show the MEB C2 system organized in seven SICPS tents. It also displays vehicles/shelters with some of the C2 INFOSYS positioned both inside and outside of the tents. The MEB also uses a large number of items not discussed here to establish the CPs. Some of these include barrier materials, access control facilities, generators, lights, heaters, and cables. The MEB could establish some CPs in fixed facilities if available and desirable.

EXAMPLE MEB CP LAYOUT

B-11. This example provides one potential layout for the CPs (main CP and the tactical CP) of the MEB. Other layouts are possible based on a specific METT-TC analysis. Included in this example is a way to lay out the SICPS tents and position cells and staff sections (as named in appendix A) to take advantage of the potential INFOSYS that are provided to the MEB.

B-12. Figure B-1 provides an overall view of the MEB main CP SICPS layout and titles and the MEB HHC tent, which will normally be collocated with the main CP.

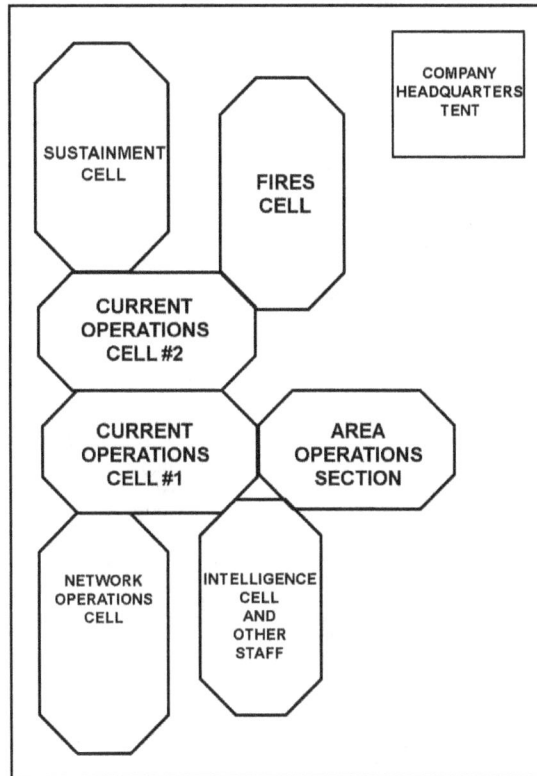

Figure B-1. MEB main CP

B-13. Figure B-2, page B-4, highlights the TAC CP and a recommended option for its layout using its single SICPS. In this option, the DCO has a position in the TAC CP. A combat service support automated information system interface (CAISI) bridge is necessary for the TAC CP.

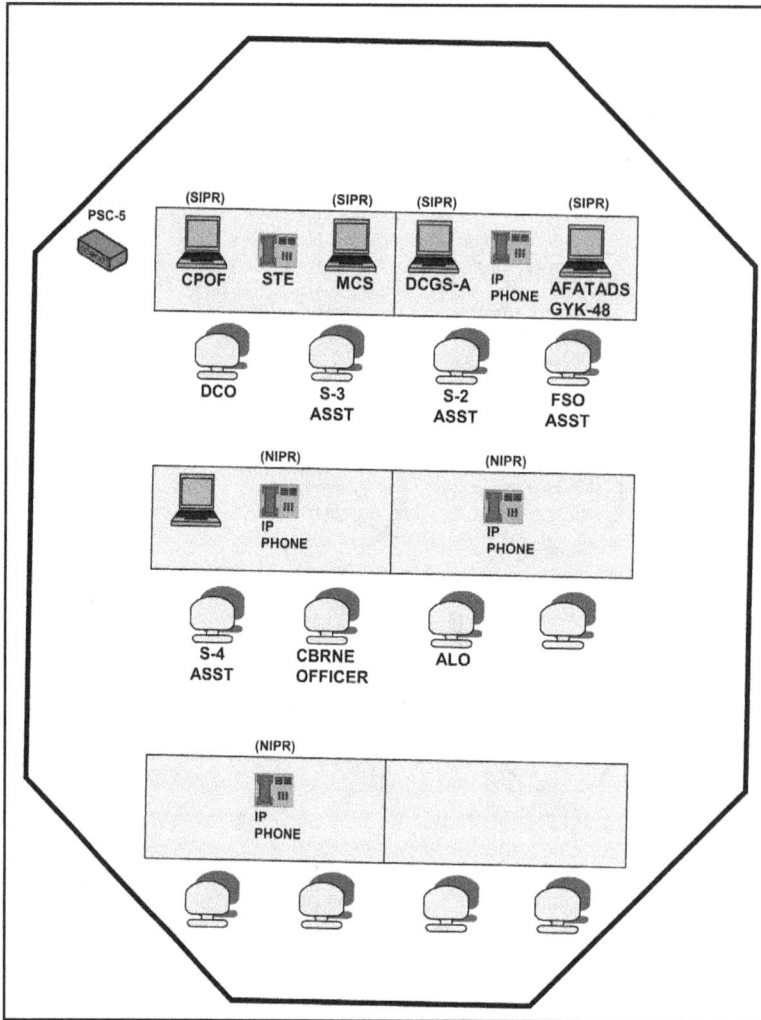

Figure B-2. Tactical operations center

B-14. Figure B-3 highlights the current operations cell #1, the SICPS location identified for the MEB commander and DCO when they are at the main CP and includes a portion of the complete operations cell (primarily the plans section). A position is also allocated for the DCO in the TAC CP (figure B-2). In this option, the XO has a position in the current operations cell #1. The LSD in this cell is one of two in the headquarters.

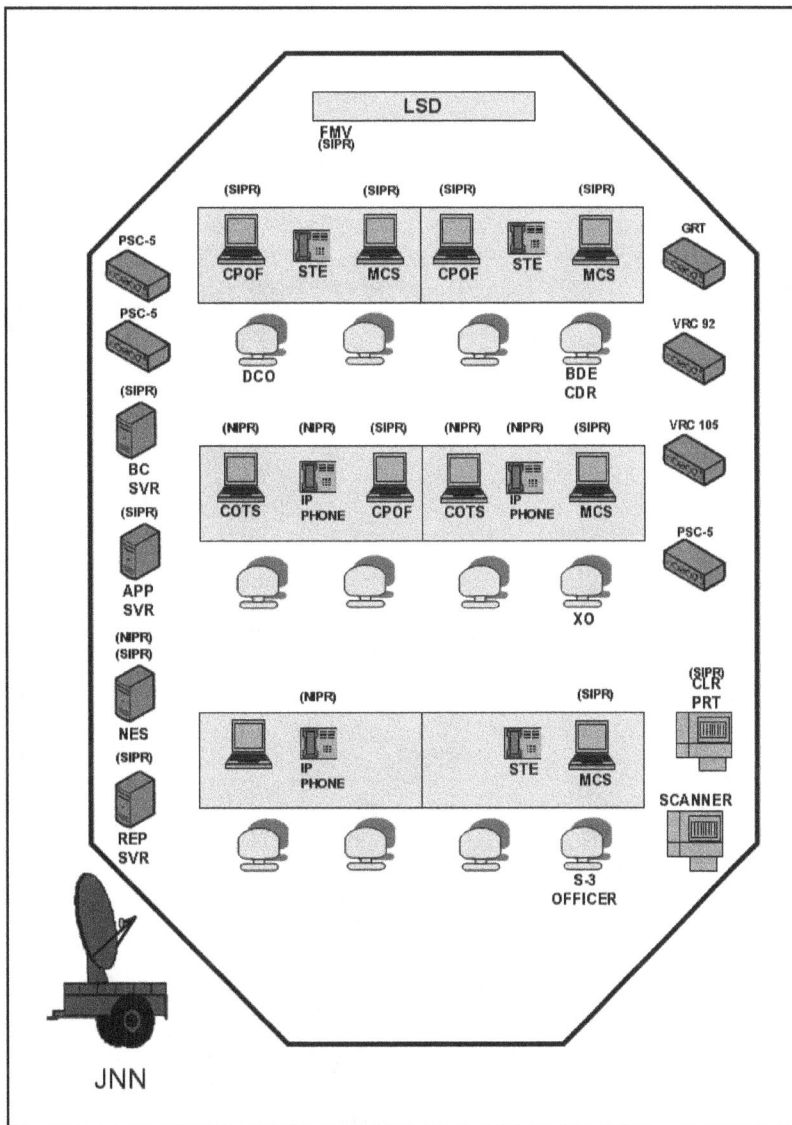

Figure B-3. Current operations cell number 1

B-15. Figure B-4, page B-6, highlights the remainder of the current operations cell not shown in figure B-3. Included in this SICPS are the engineer operations cell, CBRNE operations cell, MP operations cell, civil-military plans and operations, plans section, and the liaison teams.

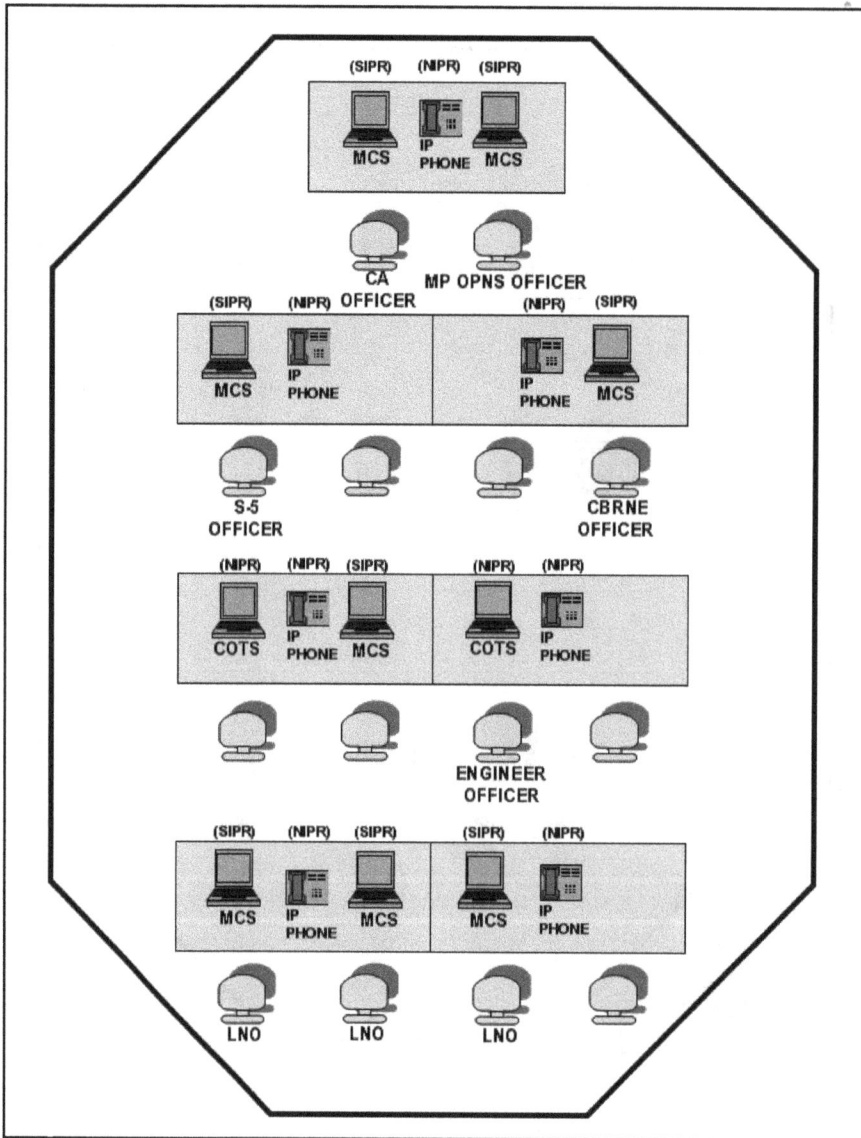

Figure B-4. Current operations cell number 2

B-16. Figure B-5 highlights the area operations section. This is where the second LSD is positioned in this example to facilitate the responsibilities associated with conducting support area operations.

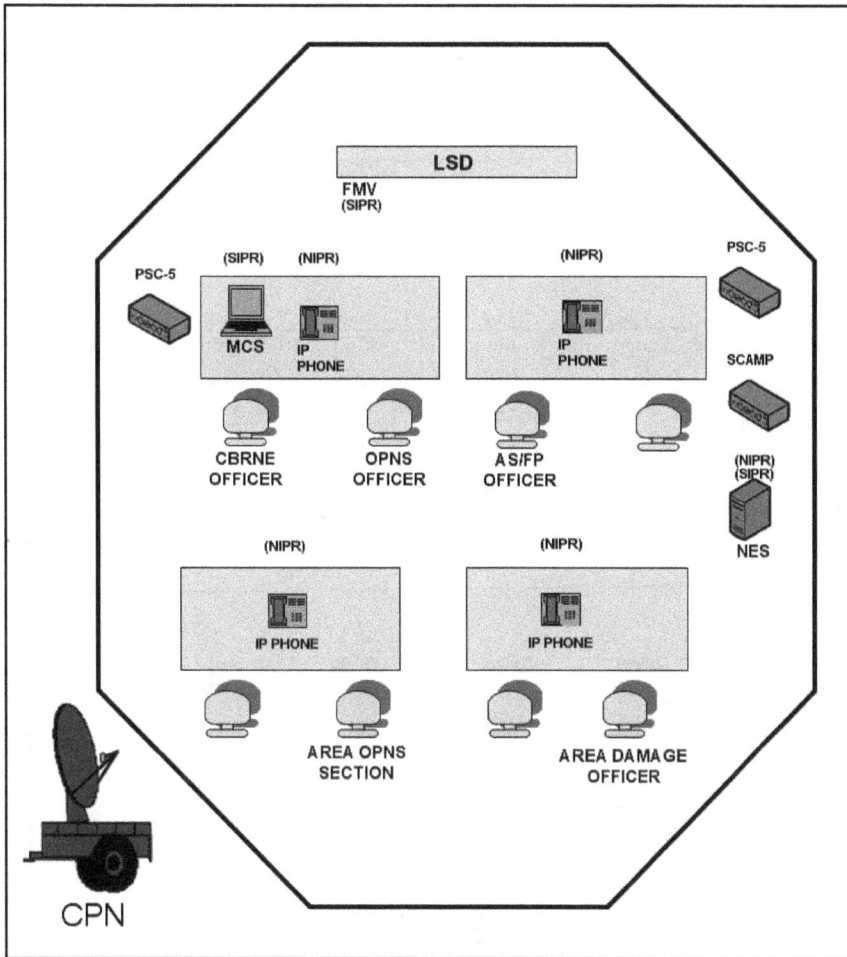

Figure B-5. Area operations section

B-17. Figure B-6, page B-8, highlights the intelligence cell. It includes not only the intelligence cell but also other staff (the public affairs section, brigade legal section, and brigade unit ministry team) that has been included in the lower half of this SICPS but may need to be positioned in a different SICPS if there is room.

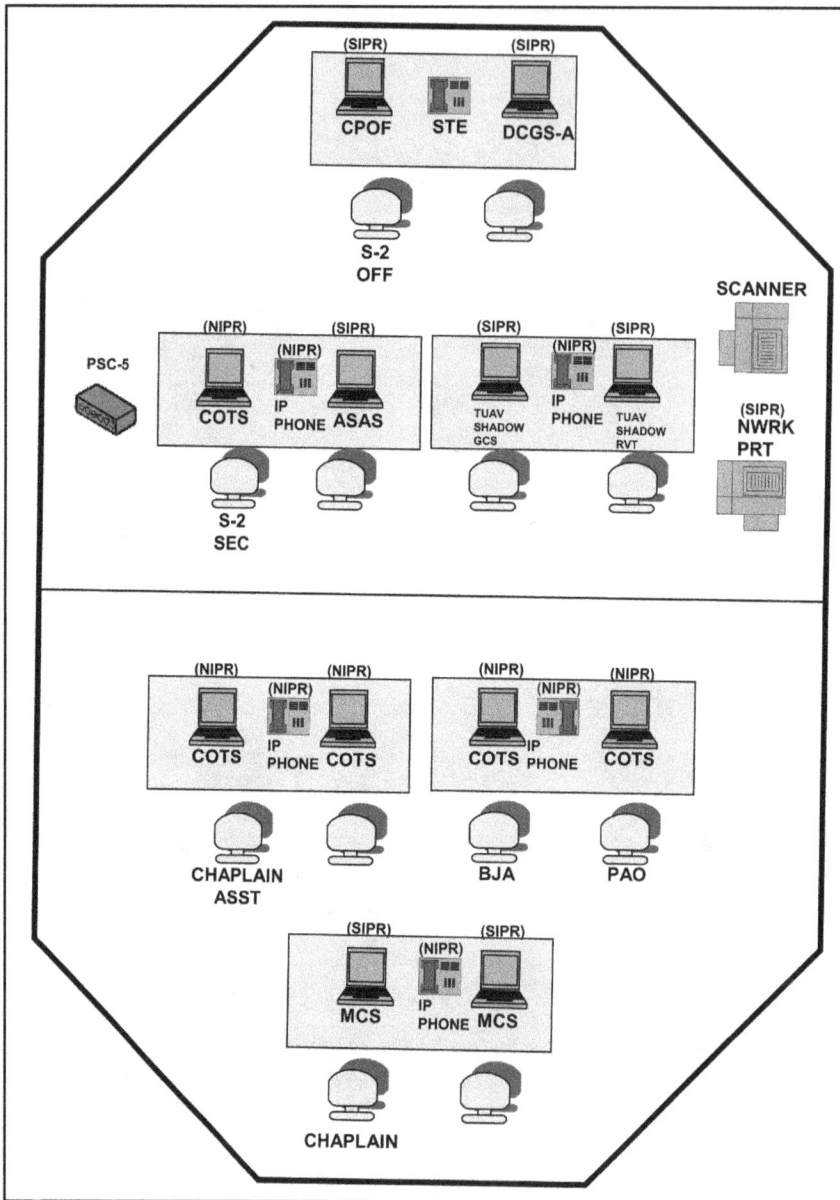

Figure B-6. Intelligence cell and other staff

B-18. Figure B-7 highlights the fires cell. This SICPS includes the fires cell, airspace management section, geospatial portion of the engineer operations cell, brigade surgeon section and medical treatment team (the surgeon section and medical treatment team should usually be in the sustainment cell if there is room for them). Note the three shelters that are linked to this SICPS.

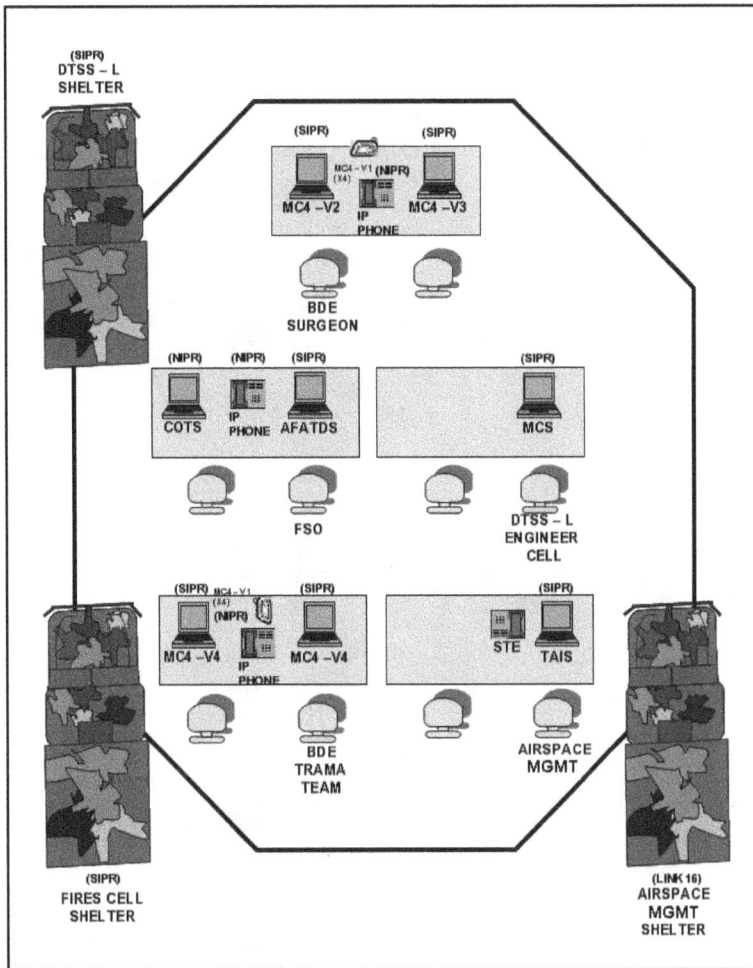

Figure B-7. Fires cell

B-19. Figure B-8, page B-10, highlights the sustainment cell. This SCIPS includes the personnel section and the logistics section. The CAISI bridge for the main CP is located in this SICPS.

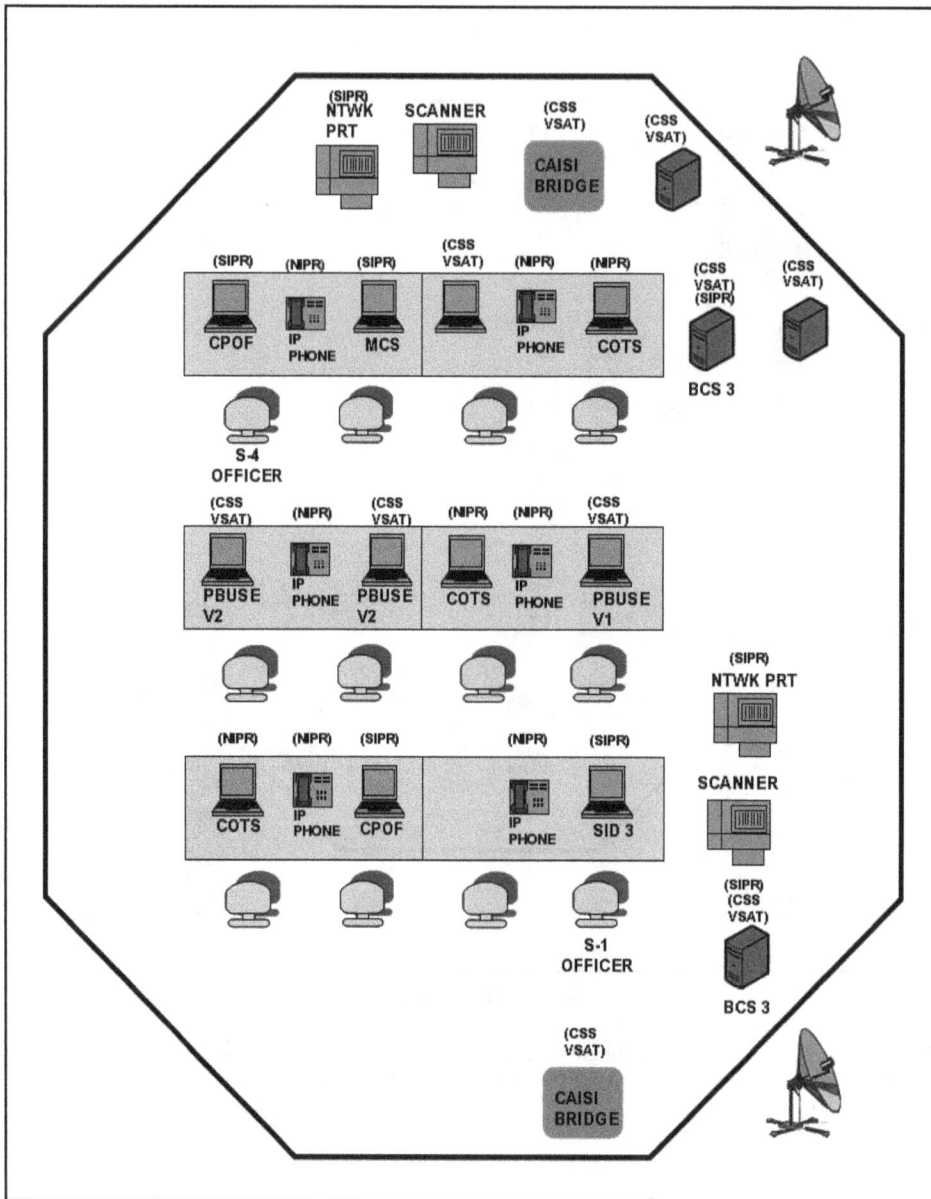

Figure B-8. Sustainment cell

B-20. Figure B-9 highlights the command, control, communication, and computer operations cell and the communications section. Note the two shelters that are linked to this SICPS.

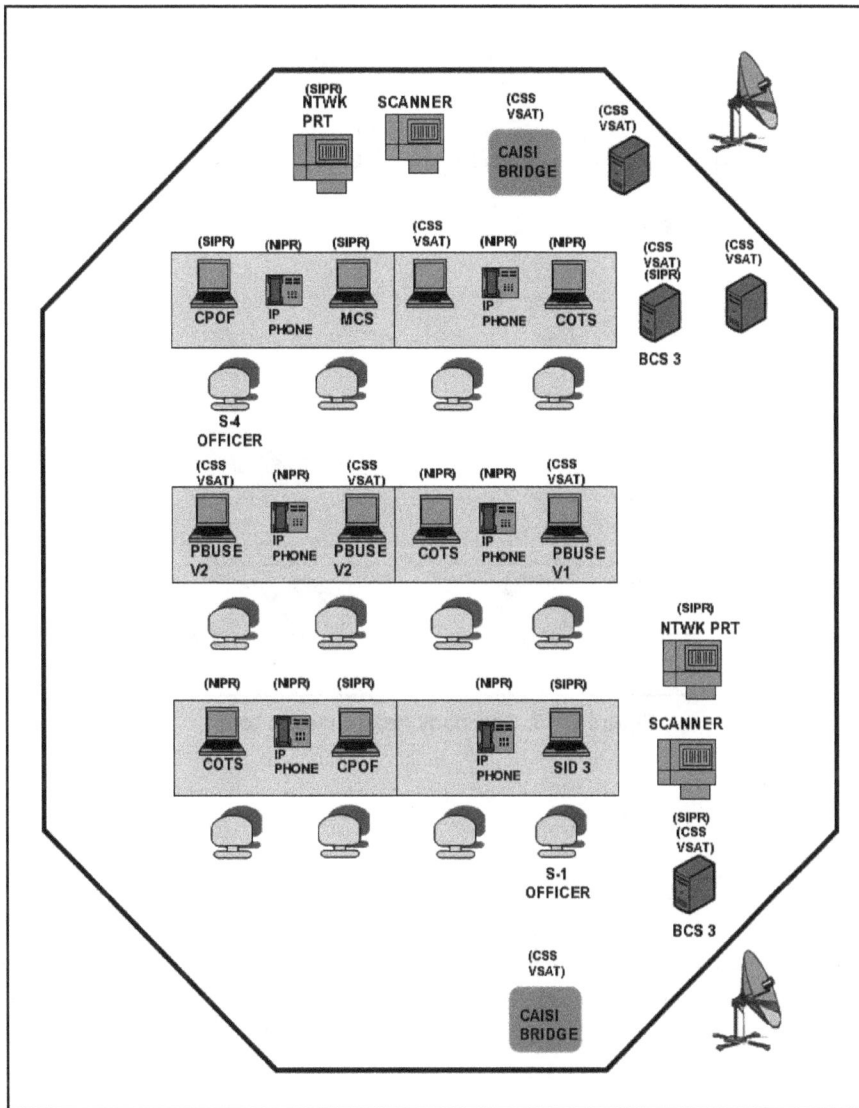

Figure B-9. Network operations cell

B-21. Figure B-10, page B-12, highlights the company headquarters tent. This tent will typically be located in proximity to the main CP. This tent is not a SICPS.

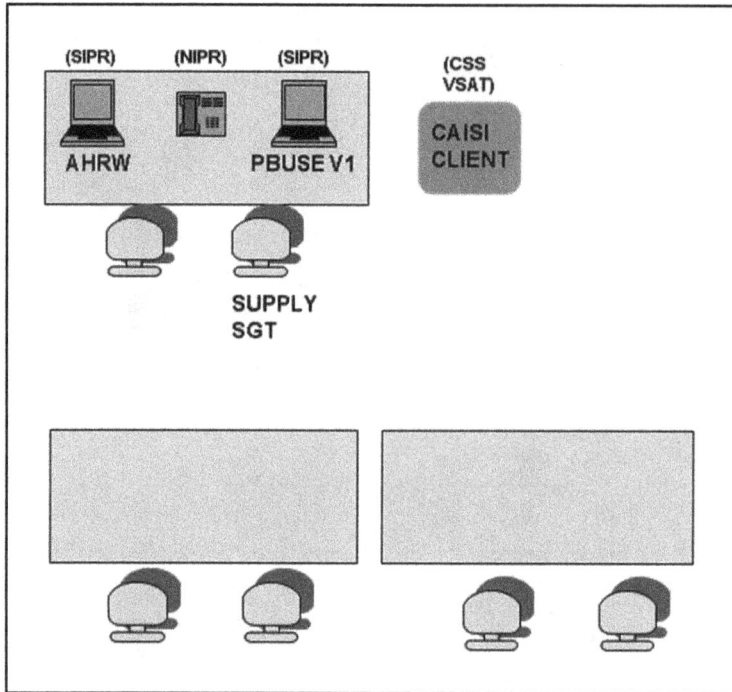

Figure B-10. Company headquarters tent

Appendix C

Army Battle Command System

IS is the advantage derived from the ability to collect, process, and disseminate an uninterrupted flow of information while exploiting or denying an adversary's ability to do the same. *Information systems* are the equipment and facilities that collect, process, store, display, and disseminate information. This includes computers—hardware and software—and communications as well as policies and procedures for their use (FM 3-0). The MEB is equipped with portions of the ABCS to help give it significant advantages in collecting technical information, and distributing information and intelligence rapidly. The ABCS enables commanders to rapidly gain reliable information and therefore, achieve information dominance in their OE. The ABCS satisfies two critical battle C2 requirements—interoperability and SA. ABCS employs networks that are interoperable with theater, joint, and combined C2 systems.

MEB C2 SYSTEMS

C-1. The ABCS consists of 10 battlefield automated systems, which comprise the core for ABCS and provide the capabilities that support the Military personnel's mission needs. Each system aids in planning, coordinating, and executing operations by providing access to a horizontally integrated C2 network and passing of information it.

C-2. The ABCS 6.4 provides a net-centric data management capability on a dedicated server. This ABCS version differs from earlier versions due to the incorporation of the centralized information server. The addition of the ABCS information server (AIS) to the tactical operations center (TOC) structure enables horizontal information exchange. Also, the AIS employs a publish and subscribe server methodology. The AIS helps the ten ABCS systems interoperate as one thus, ABCS is called a system-of- systems

C-3. The MEB may use seven current primary C2 systems. These systems are linked to the global C2 system—Army (GCCS-A), creating seamless connectivity from brigades to corps. Five systems correspond to five battlefield functional areas—maneuver, fire support, AMD, intelligence and electronic warfare (IEW), and battle command sustainment support. The functional staff sections and units assigned to the MEB will have a range of other automated systems; some will stand alone and other must be integrated into the MEB C2 system.

C-4. Current C2 systems include—
- Maneuver control system (MCS)–usually found in the S-3 section.
- Advanced field artillery tactical data system (AFATDS)–usually found in the fires section.
- Air and missile defense workstation (AMDWS)–usually found in the area denial artillery munitions (ADAM) section.
- Distribute Command Ground System —Army (DCGS-A)–usually found in the S-2 section.
- Battle command sustainment support system (BCS3)–usually found in the S4 section.
- Force XXI battle command brigade and below (FBCB2).
- Command post of the future (CPOF).

MANEUVER CONTROL SYSTEM

C-5.   The MCS provides tactical commanders and staffs with an automated, near real time capability for planning, coordinating, monitoring, and controlling tactical operations. MCS operators can tailor the applications to graphically display the picture of the AO they choose. A combination of systems automatically feeds data to the MCS to produce the view of the AO. These ABCS sources can be local and remote. The MCS is primarily used for creating and sending OPORDs in a CP. It also is equipped with digital collaborative tools that commanders and staffs use to plan future operations and review past operations.

C-6.   MCS-light (MCS-L) is a laptop computer system that interfaces with the MCS workstation. MCS-L is a lightweight, user friendly, inexpensive, and operationally flexible workstation that augments the large desktop. MCS-L is used to enhance and shorten the decision-making process, enhance planning operations, and supervise the execution of operations.

ADVANCED FIELD ARTILLERY TARGET DATA SYSTEM

C-7.   The AFATDS provides the Army and United States Marine Corps (USMC) automated fire support (FS) command, control, and communications portion of the ABCS. AFATDS provides integrated automated support for planning, coordinating, and controlling all FS assets such as field artillery, mortars, CAS, naval gunfire, attack helicopter, and offensive electronic warfare (EW). It also provides for counterfire, interdiction, and suppression of enemy targets. The AFATDS enables the maneuver commander to plan and attack using the optimal weapon-target pairing combinations. AFATDS can display FS systems, target types, command guidance, available munitions, and weapons status so that FS planners can make informed decisions based on the commander's guidance.

AIR AND MISSILE DEFENSE WORKSTATION

C-8.   The AMDWS is the C2 component of the AMD planning and control system (AMDPCS). It is the staff planning and SA tool used to integrate sensors (for example, Sentinel radar), air defense fire units (such as Avenger, Patriot), and CPs from the air defense artillery (ADA) battery to theater echelons. AMD planners use AMDWS to display AMD plans, and air SA to ABCS and commanders at all echelons. It is also the AMD planning and control link to joint/multinational C2 systems. It provides visibility of air breather tracks (such as aircraft, UAS, cruise missiles), and tactical ballistic missiles (such as launch point, impact point, and current location).

DISTRIBUTE COMMAND GROUND SYSTEM

C-9.   The DCGS-A is the ABCS intelligence fusion system that provides a timely, accurate, and relevant picture of the enemy situation to Military personnel. DCGS-A provides graphic representations of the enemy situation to ABCS. It provides leaders all source intelligence to support visualization of the AO, and more effectively conduct the land battle. The system capabilities enable the Soldier to collaborate with other systems, process and analyze all source intelligence, support nonstructured threat analysis, provide predictive analysis, produce a correlated ground picture, disseminate intelligence products, and provide target nominations. It also supports management of intelligence, surveillance, reconnaissance assets, intelligence collection, provision of combat intelligence/OPSEC mission support, provision of EW support, and protection. The DCGS-A interoperates with organic IEW sensors; ABCS; joint, theater, and national sensors and preprocessors; as well as other service intelligence processors.

C-10. DCGS-A provides intelligence processing on a laptop computer. DCGS-A users (for example, S-2s) are primarily users of preprocessed intelligence information and graphic IPB products received from MI units.

BRIGADE COMMAND SUSTAINMENT SUPPORT SYSTEM

C-11. The brigade command sustainment support system (BCS3) is the Army's maneuver sustainment C2 system that provides a concise picture of unit logistics requirements and support capabilities. It provides a running estimate of evolving logistics situations, including an assessment of current combat power that is essential for Military personnel to assess their units' capabilities to complete their mission. The BCS3 integrates the logistics common picture as well as in-transit visibility, enabling the Military personnel to view material in the logistics pipeline. Ultimately, BCS3 will be able to provide automated future combat power assessments, (such as projecting changes in asset status in 24-, 48-, and 72-hour representations).

FORCE XXI BATTLE COMMAND BRIGADE AND BELOW

C-12. The FBCB2 is the mobile INFOSYS that provides a battle command capability for units operating at the tactical level. FBCB2 integrates with the ABCS subsystems, and can transmit SA and provide C2 messaging. FBCB2 operates using two forms of communication. FBCB2-terrestrial uses a radio-based tactical mobile network and FBCB2 blue force tracker (BFT) uses satellite communications. FBCB2 is found on platforms down to platoon level and on key leader platforms at battalion and brigade. Current software enables terrestrial and BFT units to share SA. Future software will enable the exchange of some C2 messaging between terrestrial and BFT units.

Force XXI Battle Command Brigade and Below-Terrestrial

C-13. FBCB2-terrestrial is part of the lower TI. It uses the EPLRS, and the single channel ground and air radio system-advanced system improvement program (SINCGARS-ASIP).

Force XXI Battle Command Brigade and Below-Blue Force Tracker

C-14. FBCB2-BFT uses a light band (L-band) satellite link for communications. FBCB2-BFT shares SA (such as blue position reports and geospatial reports) with terrestrial units and ABCS systems that use reach back tunnels found in regional operation centers. Both secure and unsecure system messaging is available using ABCS.

SUPPORTING C2 SYSTEMS

DIGITAL TOPOGRAPHIC SUPPORT SYSTEM

C-15. The digital topographic support system (DTSS) provides automated support for terrain mapping and analysis, and creation of topographic products within the timeframes required by today's Army. DTSS provides S-3 engineer sections with the capability for geospatial data generation, collection, and management; geospatial information processing, presentation, and analysis; and engineer survey and map reproductions for C2 terrain visualization. DTSS manages the digital topographic database for ABCS. It can also create annotated image maps from scanned or digital imagery.

INTEGRATED METEOROLOGICAL SYSTEM

C-16. The integrated meteorological system (IMETS) is a tactical, automated weather data receiving, processing, and dissemination system. It provides timely weather and environmental effects, forecasts, observations, and decision aid information to commanders through ABCS. Selected S-2 sections are fielded with IMETS to provide near real time weather data to conduct IPB. Additionally, IMETS provides information to all ABCS battlefield functional areas.

TACTICAL AIRSPACE INTEGRATION SYSTEM

C-17. The tactical airspace integration system (TAIS) provides a digitized, integrated, and automated system to provide AC2 and air traffic services. TAIS provides the ADAM section with a link to the Joint force air component commander's theater battle management core systems (TBMCS) for total Army airspace integration into the joint fight. TAIS interfaces with joint TBMCS and civil airspace control agencies, and provides input to ABCS.

GLOBAL COMMAND AND CONTROL SYSTEM-ARMY

C-18. The GCCS-A is the interface between the tactical ABCS systems found at brigade and higher levels. The system architecture links users via the SECRET Internet protocol router network (SIPRNET) for worldwide communication. GCCS-A provides COP and associated friendly and enemy status information. It also provides force employment planning and execution tools such as, receipt of forces, intratheater planning, readiness, force tracking, onward movement, and execution status. GCCS-A is not usually fielded to the MEB, but could be found there in contingency operations.

COMMAND AND CONTROL PERSONAL COMPUTER

C-19. The command and control personal computer (C2PC) enables staff sections to interface with GCCS-A using a LAN within the CP. It depicts current locations of friendly and enemy units; creates, imports, and exports maps overlays; and shares overlays and message traffic. C2PC is not a formal part of ABCS, but is used in some units.

COMMAND POST OF THE FUTURE

C-20. The command post of the future (CPOF) is a decision support system, providing situational awareness and collaborative tools for tactical decisionmaking, planning, rehearsal and execution management from battalion through Army service component at the command level. The commander can use CPOF to collaborate with other commanders and key staff to share critical situational awareness information and plan accordingly. CPOF currently relies on several ABCS systems for information feeds and co-hosts MCS on CPOF hardware.

CBRN AUTOMATED SYSTEMS

C-21. The joint CBRN networked applications provide situational awareness and contribute to the COP for incidents involving the intentional or accidental release of CBRN hazards.

C-22. The JWARN provides the MEB and joint forces with a common capability to collect, analyze, identify, locate, report and disseminate warnings about CBRNE or toxic industrial chemicals/toxic industrial materials (TIC/TIM) events. JWARN is employed by CBRN defense specialists and other designated personnel in C2 centers at the appropriate levels of the MEB. JWARN draws data automatically from actual detectors and sensors, and provides commanders with analyzed data to support operational decisionmaking in a CBRN environment. JWARN adds capabilities for data processing, production of plans and reports, and access to specific CBRNE information in order to augment the MEB's CBRN personnel and assets.

C-23. The joint effects model provides a single, validated capability to predict and track CBRNE and TIC/TIM events and effects. The joint effects model resides in MEB C2 information systems and interfaces with warning systems, and geospatial information and weather data and messages. It supports deliberate planning and analysis for operational use. The joint effects model interfaces with JWARN to support plotting and analysis of CBRNE and TIC/TIM events and effects.

C-24. Joint operational effects federation (JOEF) is a joint planning capability that provides operational modeling and simulation for commanders and staffs to accurately predict chemical/biological effects upon personnel, equipment and operations. JOEF determines operational effectiveness and supports development of CBRN operational requirements. JOEF also supports TTP doctrine and contingency operations development and planning; new technology and concept evaluation; specific training; and near real-time decisionmaking as a Battle Management Information System in a combat environment. JOEF interfaces with JWARN to support the analysis of and response to CBRNE and TIC/TIM events and effects.

Glossary

Acronym/Term	Definition
ABCS	Army Battle Command System
AC2	airspace command and control
ACP	air control point
ACR	armored cavalry regiment
ADA	aerial damage assessment
ADAM	area denial artillery munition
ADC	area damage control
ADP	automated data processing
AFATDS	Advanced Field Artillery Tactical Data System
AFSB	Army field support brigade
AHRW	Army human resource workstation
AHS	Army Health System
AIS	Army Battle Command System information server
ALO	air liaison officer
ALT	acquisition, logistics, and technology
AMD	air and missile defense
AMD PCS	Air and Missile Defense Planning and Control System
AMDWS	air and missile defense workstation
AMEDD	Army Medical Department
AO	area of operation
AOR	area of responsibility
APOD	aerial port of debarkation
APOE	aerial port of embarkation
APP SVR	application server
ARFOR	Army forces
ARNG	Army National Guard
ARNGUS	Army National Guard of the United States
AS/FP	area security/protection
ASA (ALT)	Assistant Secretary of the Army for Acquisition, Logistics and Technology
ASCC	Army service component command
ASCOPE	areas, structures, capabilities, organizations, people, and events
ASIP	advanced system improvement program
ASR	alternate supply route
AT	antiterrorism

BAO	brigade ammunition officer
BC SVR	battle command server
BCOC	base cluster operations center
BCS3	Battle Command Sustainment Support System
BCT	brigade combat team
BDE	brigade
BDF	base defense force
BDOC	base defense operation center
BFSB	battlefield surveillance brigade
BFT	blue force tracker
BJA	brigade judge advocate
BLS	brigade legal section
BLST	brigade logistics support team
BP	battle position
BSA	brigade support area
BSB	brigade support battalion
BSS	brigade surgeon section
BSTB	brigade special troops battalion
C2	command and control
C2PC	command and control personal computer
CA	civil affairs
CAF	contractors accompanying the force
CAISI	Combat Service Support Automated Information System Interface
CAS	close air support
CBRN	chemical, biological, radiological, and nuclear
CBRNE	chemical, biological, radiological, nuclear, and high yield explosive
CCIR	commander's critical information requirement
CCT	contingency contracting team
CI	criminal intelligence
CIC	combat information center
CJCSI	Chairman, Joint Chiefs of Staff instruction
CLR PRT	color printer
CM	consequence management
CMO	civil-military operations
CMOC	civil-military operations center
COA	course of action
COL	colonel
COMSEC	communications security
CONPLAN	concept plan
CONUS	continental United States

COP	common operational picture
COR	contract officer representative
COSC	combat and operational stress control
COTR	contract officer technical representative
COTS	cargo offload and transfer system
CP	command post
CPOF	command post of the future
CPT	captain
CRM	composite risk management
CSB	contracting support brigade
CSC	convoy support center
CSM	command sergeant major
CSSAMO	combat service support automation management office
CW2	chief warrant officer 2
CW3	chief warrant officer 3
DA	Department of the Army
DC	dislocated civilian
DCG	deputy commanding general
DCO	deputy commanding officer
DCGS-A	Distribute command Ground System—Army
DHA	detainee holding area
DHS	Department of Homeland Security
DOD	Department of Defense
DOS	Department of State
DS	direct support
DS LAP	Direct Support Logistics Assistance Program
DSCA	defense support of civil authorities
DSS	division surgeon section
DTMS	Digital Training Management System
DTO	division transportation office
DTSS	Digital Topographic Support System
DTSS	Digital Topographic Support System
EAD	echelon above division
EECP	early-entry command post
EOC	emergency operations center
EOD	explosive ordnance disposal
EPLRS	Enhanced Position Location Reporting System
EPW	enemy prisoner of war
ESC	expeditionary support command
ESF	emergency support function

EW	electronic warfare
FBCB2	Force XXI Battle Command Brigade and Below
FC	fires cell
FCM	Foreign Consequence Management
FHA	foreign humanitarian assistance
FHP	force health protection
FM	field manual
FMI	field manual interim
FMV	full motion video
FP	protection
FRAGO	fragmentary order
FS	fire support
FSC	forward support company
FSCM	fire support coordination measure
FSCOORD	fire support coordinator
FSE	fire support element
FSMT	Forward support medical evacuation team
FSO	fire support officer
G-1	assistant chief of staff, personnel
G-2	assistant chief of staff, intelligence
G-3	assistant chief of staff, operations
G-4	assistant chief of staff, logistics
G-5	assistant chief of staff, plans
G-6	assistant chief of staff, communication
G-7	assistant chief of staff, information engagement
G-9	assistant chief of staff, civil affairs
GCC	geographical combatant commander
GCCS-A	Global Command and Control System – Army
GCS	ground control station
GMET	general misson essential task
GRT	ground receiver terminal
GS	general support
HBCT	heavy brigade combat team
HHC	headquarters and headquarters company
HHD	headquarters and headquarters detachment
HLS	Homeland Security
HN	host nation
HQDA	Headquarters, Department of the Army
HR	human resources
HSS	health service support

HVA	high value asset
I/R	internment and resettlement
IBP	intelligence preparation of the battlefield
ICS	incident command system
IED	improvised explosive device
IEW	intelligence and electronic warfare
IM	information management
IMETS	integrated meteorological system
INFOSYS	information systems
IP	internet protocol
IPB	intelligence preparation of the battlefield
IS	information superiority
ISR	intelligence, surveillance, and reconnaissance
JCOB	joint contingency operations base
JDOMS	Joint Director of Military Support
JFC	joint force commander
JNN	joint network node
JOEF	joint operational effects federation
JP	Joint publication
JSA	joint security area
JSAO	joint security area operations
JTF	joint task force
JWARN	Joint Warning and Reporting Network
L&O	law and order
LAN	local area network
LAP	Logistics Assistance Program
LCMC	Life Cycle Management Command
LNO	liaison officer
LOC	line of communications
LOGCAP	Logistic Civil Augmentation Program
LOGNET	logistics data network (aray)
LSD	large screen display
LT	lieutenant
LTC	lieutenant colonel
LZ	landing zone
MAJ	major
MANSCEN	Maneuver Support Center
MANSPT	maneuver support
MBA	main battle area
MCB	movement control board

MCO	major combat operation
MCS	Maneuver Control System
MCS-L	Maneuver Control System-Light
MCT	movement control team
MDMP	military decision-making process
MDSC	medical deployment support command
MEB	maneuver enhancement brigade
MEDBDE	medical brigade
MEDEVAC	medical evacuation
MEF	Marine expeditionary force
METT-TC	mission, enemy, terrain and weather, troops and support available, time available, civil considerations
mgmt	management
MI	military intelligence
MMS	maneuver and mobility support
MOE	measure of effectiveness
MOP	measure of performance
MOS	military occupational skill
MP	military police
MSG	master sergeant
MSO	mission staging operation
MSR	main supply route
MTOE	modified table of organization and equipment
NAI	named areas of interest
NCO	noncommissioned officer
NES	national education super computer
NGO	nongovernmental organization
NIMS	National Incident Management System
NIPR	NIPRNET internet protocal router network
NRF	National Response Framework
NSC	network support company
NWRK	network printer
O-4	major
O-5	lietuenant colonel
O-6	colonel
OE	operational environment
OIC	officer in charge
OP	observation post
OPCON	operational control
OPLAN	operations plan
OPLOGPLN	operations logistics planner

OPORD	operational order
OPSEC	operational security
PA	public affairs
PAO	public affairs office
PBUSE	property book unit supply enhance
PEO	program executive office
PFC	private first class
PIO	police intelligence operations
PM	provost marshal
PME	peacetime military engagement
PMESII	political, military, economic, social, information, infrastructure
PMESII-PT	political, military, economic, social, information, infrastructure, physical environment and time
PSC	AN/PSC-S satellite radio
PSYOP	psychological operations
PTA	patterns, trends, and associations
PVNTMED	preventive medicine
PWS	performance work statement
QA	quality assurance
QC	quality control
RAA	redeployment assembly area
RDSP	rapid decision-making and synchronization process
RI	relevant information
ROC	rear operations center
ROE	rules of engagement
ROI	rules of interaction
S-1	personnel staff officer
S-2	intelligence staff officer
S-3	operations staff officer
S-4	logistics staff officer
S-5	plans staff officer
S-6	signal staff officer
S-7	information operations staff officer
S-9	civil affairs staff officer
SA	situational awareness
SCAMP	single channel antijam manportable
SCOE	software center of excellence
SE	site exploitation
SEMA	state emergency management agency
SFC	sergeant first class
SGM	sergeant major

SGT	sergeant
SICPS	Standard Integrated Command Post System
SID	standard installation and division personnel reporting system
SIF	strategic internment facility
SINCGARS	single-channel ground and airborne radio
SIPR	SIPRNET secure internet protocol router network
SIPRNET	SECRET Internet Protocol Router Network
SMC	support maintenance company
SOF	special operations forces
SOP	standing operating procedure
SOW	statement of work
SPC	specialist
SPO	support operations officer
SRC	special reporting code
SSG	staff sergeant
STAMIS	Standard Army Management Information System
STE	secure terminal equipment
SU	situational understanding
TAA	tactical assembly area
TAC	tactical
TAC CP	tactical command post
TACON	tactical control
TACSAT	tactical satellite
TAIS	Tactical Airspace Integration System
TBMCS	Theater Battle Management Core System
TCF	tactical combat force
TDA	table of distribution and allowance
TF	task force
TI	tactical Internet
TIC	toxic industrial chemical
TIF	theater internment facility
TIFRC	theater internment facility reconciliation center
TIM	toxic industrial material
TLP	troop-leading procedure
TM	team
TO	theater of operations
TOC	tactical operations center
TOE	table of organization and equipment
TRADOC	United States Army Training and Doctrine Command
TRP	target reference point

TSC	theater sustainment command
TTP	tactics, techniques, and procedures
U.S.	United States
UAS	Unmanned Aircraft System
UMT	unit ministry team
UN	United Nations
USACE	United States Army Corps of Engineers
USAMC	United States Army Materiel Command
USAR	United States Army Reserve
USG	United States Government
USMC	United States Marine Corps
VRC	vehicle radio communication
VSAT	very small aperture terminal
WARNO	warning order
WMD	weapon of mass destruction
XMSN	transmission
XO	executive officer

SECTION II – TERMS

antiterrorism

(DOD) Defensive measures used to reduce the vulnerability of individuals and property to terrorist acts, to include limited response and containment by local military and civilian forces. (JP 3-07.2) See FM 3-07.

area damage control

(DOD, NATO) Measures taken before, during, or after hostile action or natural or manmade disasters to reduce the probability of damage and minimize its effects. (JP 3-10) See FM 3-07.

area of influence

(DOD, NATO) A geographical area wherein a commander is directly capable of influencing operations by maneuver or fire support systems normally under the commander's command or control. (JP 1-02)

area of interest

(DOD) That area of concern to the commander, including the area of influence, areas adjacent thereto, and extending into enemy territory to the objectives of current or planned operations. This area also includes areas occupied by enemy forces who could jeopardize the accomplishment of the mission. (JP 2-03)

area of operations

(DOD) An operational area defined by the joint force commander for land and maritime forces. Areas of operations do not typically encompass the entire operational area of the joint force commander, but should be large enough for component commanders to accomplish their missions and protect their forces. (JP 3-0)

area security

A form of security operation conducted to protect friendly forces, installation routes, and actions within a specific area. (FM 3-90)

assessment

    (Army) The continuous monitoring and evaluation of the current situation, particularly the enemy, and progress of an operation. (FM 3-0)

base

    (DOD) 1. A locality from which operations are projected or supported. 2. An area or locality containing installations which provide logistic or other support. 3. Home airfield or home carrier. (JP 1-02)

base cluster

    (DOD) In base defense operations, a collection of bases, geographically grouped for mutual protection and ease of command and control. (JP 3-10)

base cluster operations center

    (DOD) A command and control facility that serves as the base cluster commander's focal point for defense and security of the base cluster. (JP 3-10)

base defense

    (DOD) The local military measures, both normal and emergency, required to nullify or reduce the effectiveness of enemy attacks on, or sabotage of, a base, to ensure that the maximum capacity of its facilities is available to United States forces. (JP 1-02)

base defense operations center

    (DOD) A command and control facility, with responsibilities similar to a base cluster operations center, established by the base commander to serve as the focal point for base security and defense. It plans, directs, integrates, coordinates, and controls all base defense efforts. (JP 3-10)

base defense reaction forces

    Forces comprised of personnel or elements of units assigned to a specific base with the responsibility to rapidly bolster base defenses or react to an unforeseen threat. (FM 3-90)

battle command

    The art and science of understanding, visualizing, directing, leading, and assessing forces to impose the commander's will on a hostile, thinking, and adaptive enemy. Battle command applies leadership to translate decisions into actions—by synchronizing forces and warfighting functions in time, space, and purpose—to accomplish missions. (FM 3-0)

brigade special troops battalion

    A subordinate unit to a brigade combat team that provides command and control to the engineer, military intelligence, network support (signal), and headquarters companies. Found only in the heavy and infantry brigade combat teams.

combat power

    (DOD, NATO) The total means of destructive and/or disruptive force which a military unit/formation can apply against the opponent at a given time. (JP 1-02) (Army) The total means of destructive, constructive, and information capabilities that a military unit/formation can apply at a given time. Army forces generate combat power by converting potential into effective action. (FM 3-0)

combined arms

    (Army) The synchronized and simultaneous application of the elements of combat power to achieve an effect greater than if each element were used separately or sequentially. (FM 3-0) (Marine Corps) 1. The full integration of combat arms in such a way that to counteract one, the enemy must become more vulnerable to another. 2. The tactics, techniques, and procedures employed by a force to integrate firepower and mobility to produce a desired effect upon the enemy.

command

    (DOD) The authority that a commander in the Armed Forces lawfully exercises over subordinates by virtue of rank or assignment. Command includes the authority and responsibility for effectively using available resources for planning the employment of, organizing, directing, coordinating, and controlling military forces for the accomplishment of assigned missions. It also includes responsibility for health, welfare, morale, and discipline of assigned personnel. 2. An order given by a commander; that is, the will of the commander expressed for the purpose of bringing about a particular action. See FM 6-0. 3. A unit or units, an organization, or an area under the command of one individual. See FM 6-0. (JP 1)

command and control

(DOD) The exercise of authority and direction by a properly designated commander over assigned and attached forces in the accomplishment of the mission. Command and control functions are performed through an arrangement of personnel, equipment, communications, facilities, and procedures employed by a commander in planning, directing, coordinating, and controlling forces and operations in the accomplishment of the mission. (JP 1) (Army) The exercise of authority and direction by a properly designated commander over assigned and attached forces in the accomplishment of a mission. Commanders perform command and control functions through a command and control system. (FM 6-0)

command and control system

(Army) The arrangement of personnel, information management, procedures, and equipment and facilities essential for the commander to conduct operations. (FM 6-0)

command group

The commander and selected staff members who accompany commanders and enable them to exercise command and control away from a command post. (FMI 5-0.1)

command post

(DOD, NATO) A unit's or subunit's headquarters where the commander and the staff perform their activities. [Note: the Army definition ends here.] In combat, a unit's or subunit's headquarters is often divided into echelons; the echelon in which the unit or subunit commander is located or from which such commander operates is called a command post. (JP 1-02) See FM 6-0.

commander's intent

(DOD) A concise expression of the purpose of the operation and the desired end state. It may also include the commander's assessment of the adversary commander's intent and an assessment of where and how much risk is acceptable during the operation. (JP 3-0) (Army) A clear, concise statement of what the force must do and the conditions the force must establish with respect to the enemy, terrain, and civil considerations that represent the desired end state. (FM 3-0)

consequence management

(DOD) Actions taken to maintain or restore essential services and manage and mitigate problems resulting from disasters and catastrophes, including natural, manmade, or terrorist incidents. (JP 3-28)

control

(DOD) 1. Authority that may be less than full command exercised by a commander over part of the activities of subordinate or other organizations. (JP 1-02) See FM 3-0. 2. In mapping, charting, and photogrammetry, a collective term for a system of marks or objects on the Earth or on a map or a photograph, whose positions or elevations (or both) have been or will be determined. (JP 1-02) See FM 3-25.26. 3. Physical or psychological pressures exerted with the intent to assure that an agent or group will respond as directed. (JP 1-02) 4. An indicator governing the distribution and use of documents, information, or material. Such indicators are the subject of intelligence community agreement and are specially defined in appropriate regulations. [Note: see AAP-6.] (JP 1-02) See FM 2-0. (Army) 1. In the context of command and control, the regulation of forces and warfighting functions to accomplish the mission in accordance with the commander's intent. (FM 3-0) 2. A tactical mission task that requires the commander to maintain physical influence over a specified area to prevent its use by an enemy. (FM 3-90) 3. Action taken that eliminates a hazard or reduces the risk from that hazard. Part of the third step in risk management. (FM 5-19) 4. In the context of stability mechanisms, to impose civil order. (FM 3-0)

counterintelligence

Information gathered and activities conducted to protect against espionage, other intelligence activities, sabotage, or assassinations conducted by or on behalf of foreign governments or elements thereof, foreign organizations, or foreign persons, or international terrorist activities. [Note: see AAP-6.] (JP 2-0) See FM 3-13. (Marine Corps) The active and passive measures intended to deny the enemy valuable information about the friendly situation, to detect and neutralize hostile intelligence collection, and to deceive the enemy as to friendly capabilities and intentions.

defense support of civil authorities

Civil support provided under the auspices of the National Response Plan. (JP 3-28)

force health protection

(DOD) Measures to promote, improve, or conserve the mental and physical well-being of Service member. These measures enable a healthy and fit force, prevent injury and illness, and protect the force from health hazards. (JP 4-02)

force projection

(DOD) The ability to project the military instrument of national power from the United States or another theater in response to requirements for military operations. (JP 5-0) See FM 3-0.

full spectrum operations

The Army's operational concept: Army forces combine offensive, defensive, and stability or civil support operations simultaneously as part of an interdependent joint force to seize, retain, and exploit the initiative, accepting prudent risk to create opportunities to achieve decisive results. They employ synchronized action—lethal and nonlethal—proportional to the mission and informed by a thorough understanding of all variables of the operational environment. Mission command that conveys intent and an appreciation of all aspects of the situation guides the adaptive use of Army forces. (FM 3-0)

information superiority

(DOD) The operational advantage derived from the ability to collect, process, and disseminate an uninterrupted flow of information while exploiting or denying an adversary's ability to do the same. (JP 3-13) See FM 3-0.

information system

(DOD) The entire infrastructure, organization, personnel, and components for the collection, processing, storage, transmission, display, dissemination, and disposition of information. [Note: see AAP-6.] (JP 3-13) (Army) The equipment and facilities that collect, process, store, display, and disseminate information. This includes computers—hardware and software—and communications, as well as policies and procedures for their use. (FM 3-0)

initiative (individual)

The willingness to act in the absence of orders when existing orders no longer fit the situation or when unforeseen opportunities or threats arise. (FM 3-0)

major operation

(DOD) A series of tactical actions (battles, engagements, strikes) conducted by combat forces of a single or several Services, coordinated in time and place, to achieve strategic or operational objectives in an operational area. These actions are conducted simultaneously or sequentially in accordance with a common plan and are controlled by a single commander. For noncombat operations, a reference to the relative size and scope of a military operation. (JP 3-0) See FM 3-0.

maneuver

(DOD) 1. A movement to place ships, aircraft, or land forces in a position of advantage over the enemy. 2. A tactical exercise carried out at sea, in the air, on the ground, or on a map in imitation of war. 3. The operation of a ship, aircraft, or vehicle, to cause it to perform desired movements.

4. Employment of forces in the operational area through movement in combination with fires to achieve a position of advantage in respect to the enemy in order to accomplish the mission. (JP 3-0)

*maneuver support operations

Integrate the complementary and reinforcing capabilities of key protection, movement and maneuver, and sustainment functions, tasks, and systems to enhance freedom of action.

measure of effectiveness

(DOD) A criterion used to assess changes in system behavior, capability, or operational environment that is tied to measuring the attainment of an end state, achievement of an objective, or creation of an effect. (JP 3-0)

measure of performance

(DOD) A criterion to assess friendly actions that is tied to measuring task accomplishment. (JP 3-0)

mission

(DOD) 1. The task, together with the purpose, that clearly indicates the action to be taken and the reason therefor. See FM 5-0. 2. In common usage, especially when applied to lower military units, a duty assigned to an individual or unit; a task. See FM 5-0. 3. The dispatching of one or more aircraft to accomplish one particular task. See FM 3-04.111. [Note: see AAP-6.] (JP 1-02)

mission command

The conduct of military operations through decentralized execution based upon mission orders. Successful mission command demands that subordinate leaders at all echelons exercise disciplined initiative, acting aggressively and independently to accomplish the mission within the commander's intent. (FM 3-0)

mission orders

A technique for developing orders that emphasizes to subordinates the results to be attained, not how they are to achieve them. It provides maximum freedom of action in determining how to best accomplish the assigned missions. (FM 3-0)

mobile security force

A dedicated security force designed to defeat level I and II threats on a base and/or base cluster. (JP 3-10)

movement and maneuver warfghting function

See **warfighting function.**

movement control

(DOD, NATO) 1. The planning, routing, scheduling, and control of personnel and cargo movements over lines of communications. 2. An organization responsible for the planning, routing, scheduling, and control of personnel and cargo movements over lines of communications. [Note: the Army definition adds "Organizations responsible for these functions are movement control teams, movement control centers, and movement control activities."] (JP 3-10)

*movement corridor

A designated area established to protect and enable ground movement along a route.

mobile security force

A dedicated security force designed to defeat level I and II threats on a base and/or base cluster. (JP 3-10)

mutual support

(DOD, NATO) That support which units render each other against an enemy because of their assigned tasks, their positions relative to each other and to the enemy, and inherent capabilities. (JP 3-31) See FM 3-90.

operational environment

(DOD) A composite of the conditions, circumstances, and influences which affect the employment of military forces and bear on the decisions of the commander. (JP 3-0)

operational theme

The character of the dominant major operation being conducted at any time within a land force commander's area of operations. The operational theme helps convey the nature of the major operation to the force to facilitate common understanding of how the commander broadly intends to operate. (FM 3-0)

personnel recovery

The sum of military, diplomatic, and civil efforts to prepare for and execute the recovery and reintegration of isolated personnel. (JP 3-50)

protection warfighting function

See warfighting function.

reorganization

Action taken to shift internal resources within a degraded unit to increase its level of combat effectiveness. (FM 100-9)

reserve

(DOD) 1. Portion of a body of troops which is kept to the rear or withheld from action at the beginning of an engagement, in order to be available for a decisive movement. See FM 3-90. 2. Members of the Military Services who are not in active service but who are subject to call to active duty. 3. Portion of an appropriation or contract authorization held or set aside for future operations or contingencies and, in respect to which, administrative authorization to incur commitments or obligations has been withheld. (JP 1-02)

response force

(DOD) A mobile force with appropriate fire support designated, usually by the area commander, to deal with level II threats in the rear area. (JP 3-10)

route reconnaissance

(Army/Marine Corps) A directed effort to obtain detailed information of a specified route and all terrain from which the enemy could influence movement along that route. [Note: see AAP-6.] (FM 3-90)

running estimate

A staff section's continuous assessment of current and future operations to determine if the current operation is proceeding according to the commander's intent and if future operations are supportable. (FM 3-0)

sensitive site

A geographically limited area with special diplomatic, informational, military, or economic sensitivity to the United States government. (JP 3-31)

sensitive site exploitation

A related series of activities inside a captured sensitive site to exploit personnel documents, electronic data, and material captured at the site, while neutralizing any threat posed by the site or its contents. (JP 3-31)

situational obstacle

An obstacle that a unit plans and possibly prepares prior to starting an operation, but does not execute unless specific criteria are met. It provides the commander flexibility for emplacing tactical obstacles based on battlefield development. (FM 90-7)

situational understanding

> The product of applying analysis and judgment to relevant information to determine the relationships among the mission variables to facilitate decisionmaking. (FM 3-0)

stability operations

> (DOD) An overarching term encompassing various military missions, tasks, and activities conducted outside the United States in coordination with other instruments of national power to maintain or reestablish a safe and secure environment and provide essential governmental services, emergency infrastructure reconstruction, and humanitarian relief. (JP 3-0) See FM 3-0.

strong point

> (DOD, NATO) A key point in a defensive position, usually strongly fortified and heavily armed with automatic weapons, around which other positions are grouped for its protection. (Army) A heavily fortified battle position tied to a natural or reinforcing obstacle to create an anchor for the defense or to deny the enemy decisive or key terrain. (FM 3-90)

support area

> Is a specific surface area designated by the echelon commander to facilitate the positioning, employment, and protection of resources required to sustain, enable, and control tactical forces. (FM 3-0.1)

survivability operations

> The development and construction of protective positions, such as earth berms, dug-in positions, overhead protection, and countersurveillance means, to reduce the effectiveness of enemy weapon systems. (FM 3-34)

sustainment

> The provision of logistics and personnel services required to maintain and prolong operations until successful mission accomplishment. (JP 3-0)

sustainment warfighting function

> See warfighting function.

tactical combat force

> A combat unit, with appropriate combat support and combat service support assets that is assigned the mission of defeating level III threats. (JP 3-10) See FM 3-90.

task organizing

> (DOD) The act of designing an operating force, support staff, or logistics package of specific size and composition to meet a unique task or mission. Characteristics to examine when task-organizing the force include, but are not limited to: training, experience, equipage, sustainability, operating environment, enemy threat, and mobility. (JP 3-05) (Army) The act of designing an operating force, support staff, or logistics package of specific size and composition to meet a unique task or mission. Characteristics to examine when task-organizing the force include, but are not limited to: training, equipage, sustainability, operating environment, enemy threat, and mobility. For Army forces, it includes allocating available assets to subordinate commanders and establishing their command and support relationships. (FM 3-0)

unified action

> (DOD) The synchronization, coordination, and/or integration of the activities of governmental and nongovernmental entities with military operations to achieve unity of effort. (JP 1)

unmanned aircraft system

> That system whose components include the necessary equipment, network, and personnel to control an unmanned aircraft. (JP 1-02)

warfighting function

A group of tasks and systems (people, organizations, information, and processes), united by a common purpose, that commanders use to accomplish missions and training objectives. The six warfighting functions are: a. **command and control** – the related tasks and systems that support commanders in exercising authority and direction; b. **fires** – the related tasks and systems that provide collective and coordinated Army indirect fires, joint fires, and command and control warfare, including nonlethal fires, through the targeting process; c. **intelligence** – the related tasks and systems that facilitate understanding of the operational enviironment, enemy, terrain, and civil considerations; d. **movement and maneuver** – the related tasks and systems that move forces to achieve a position of advantage in relation to the enemy. Direct fire is inherenet in maneuver, as is close combat; e. **protection** – the related tasks and systems that preserve the force so the commander can apply maximum combat power; f. **sustainment** – the related tasks and systems that provide support and services to ensure freedom of action, extend operational reach, and prolong endurance. (FM 3-0)

References

SOURCES USED

The following sources are either quoted or paraphrased in this publication.

ARMY PUBLICATIONS

AR 40-3, *Medical, Dental, and Veterinary Care,* 22 February 2008.

AR 40-5, *Preventive Medicine*, 25 May 2007.

AR 40-66, *Medical Record Administration and Health Care Documentation*, 17 June 2008.

AR 165-1, *Chaplain Activities in the United States Army*, 25 March 2004.

FM 1-05, *Religious Support*, 18 April 2003.

FM 2-0, *Intelligence*, 17 May 2004.

FM 3-0, *Operations*, 27 February 2008.

FM 3-04.111, *Aviation Brigades*, 12 July 2007.

FM 3-05.40, *Civil Affairs Operations*, 29 September 2006.

FM 3-05.401, *Civil Affairs Tactics, Techniques, and Procedures*, 5 July 2007.

FM 3-06 (90-10), *Urban Operations*, 26 October 2006.

FM 3-07, *Stability Operations*, 6 October 2008.

FM 3-11, *Multiservice Tactics, Techniques, and Procedures for Nuclear, Biological, and Chemical Defense Operations*, 10 March 2003.

FM 3-11.21, *Multiservice Tactics, Techniques, and Procedures for Chemical, Biological, Radiological and Nuclear Consequence Management Operations*, 1 April 2008.

FM 3-13, *Information Operations: Doctrine, Tactics, Techniques, and Procedures*, 28 November 2003

FM 3-19.1, *Military Police Operations*, 22 March 2001.

FM 3-19.4, *Military Police Leader's Handbook*, 4 March 2002.

FM 3-19.17, *Military Working Dogs*, 6 July 2005.

FM 3-19.50, *Police Intelligence Operations*, 21 July 2006.

FM 3-34, *Engineer Operations*, 2 January 2004.

FM 3-34.2, *Combined Arms Breaching Operations,* 31 August 2000.

FM 3-34.210, *Explosive Hazards Operations*, 27 March 2007.

FM 3-34.230, *Topographic Operations*, 3 August 2000.

FM 3-34.400, *General Engineering*, 9 December 2008.

FM 3-52, *Army Airspace Command and Control in a Combat Zone*, 1 August 2002.

FM 3-90, *Tactics*, 4 July 2001.

FM 3-100.4, *Environmental Considerations in Military Operations*, 15 June 2000.

FM 3-100.21, *Contractors on the Battlefield*, 3 January 2003.

FM 4-0, *Combat Service Support*, 29 August 2003.

FM 4-01.30, *Movement Control*, 1 September 2003.

FM 4-02, *Force Health Protection in a Global Environment*, 13 February 2003.

FM 4-02.1, *Combat Health Logistics*, 28 September 2001.

FM 4-02.2, *Medical Evacuation*, 8 May 2007.

FM 4-02.4, *Medical Platoon Leaders' Handbook Tactics, Techniques, and Procedures*, 24 August 2001.

FM 4-02.12, *Health Service Support in Corps and Echelons Above Corps*, 2 February 2004.

FM 4-02.17, *Preventive Medicine Services*, 28 August 2000.

FM 4-02.21, *Division And Brigade Surgeons' Handbook (Digitized) Tactics, Techniques, And Procedures,* 15 November 2000.

FM 4-02.51, *Combat and Operational Stress Control*, 6 July 2006.

FM 5-0, *Army Planning and Orders Production*, 20 January 2005.

FM 5-19, *Composite Risk Management*, 21 August 2006.

FM 5-103, *Survivability,* 10 June 1985.

FM 6-0, *Mission Command: Command and Control of Army Forces*, 11 August 2003.

FM 6-20, *Fire Support in the Airland Battle*, 17 May 1988.

FM 6-20-10, *Tactics, Techniques, and Procedures for the Targeting Process*, 8 May 1996.

FM 6-22, *Army Leadership*, 12 October 2006.

FM 6-22.5, *Combat Stress*, 23 June 2000.

FM 7-0, *Training for Full Spectrum Operations*, 12 December 2008.

FM 7-1, *Battle Focused Training*, 15 September 2003.

FM 7-15, *The Army Universal Task List*, 31 August 2003.

FM 8-55, *Planning for Health Service Support*, 9 September 1994.

FM 22-51, *Leaders' Manual for Combat Stress Control*, 29 September 1994.

FM 34-10, *Division Intelligence and Electronics Warfare Operations*, 25 November 1986.

FM 34-60, *Counterintelligence*, 3 October 1995.

FM 34-130, *Intelligence Preparation of the Battlefield*, 8 July 1994.

FM 63-2, *Division Support Command, Armored, Infantry, and Mechanized Infantry Divisions*, 20 May 1991.

FM 71-100, *Division Operations*, 28 August 1996.

FM 90-7, *Combined Arms Obstacle Integration*, 29 September 1994.

FM 100-8, *The Army in Multinational Operations,* 24 November 1997.

FM 100-9, *Reconstitution*, 13 January 1992.

FM 100-10-2, *Contracting Support on the Battlefield*, 4 August 1999.

FMI 3-0.1, *The Modular Force*, 28 January 2008.

FMI 3-90.10, *Chemical, Biological, Radiological, Nuclear, and High Yield Explosives Operational Headquarters*, 24 January 2008.

FMI 4-93.41, *Army Field Support Brigade Tactics, Techniques, and Procedures*, 22 February 2007.

FMI 5-0.1, *The Operations Process*, 31 March 2006.

JOINT PUBLICATIONS

JP 1, *Doctrine for the Armed Forces of the United States*, 14 May 2007.

JP 1-02, *Department of Defense Dictionary of Military and Associated Terms*, 12 April 2001.

JP 2-0, *Joint Intelligence*, 22 June 2007.

JP 2-03, *Geospatial Intelligence Support to Joint Operations*, 22 March 2007.

JP 3-0, *Doctrine for Joint Operations*, 17 September 2006.

JP 3-05, *Doctrine for Joint Special Operations*, 17 December 2003.

JP 3-07.2, *Antiterrorism*, 14 April 2006.

JP 3-07.6, *Joint Tactics, Techniques, and Procedures for Foreign Humanitarian Assistance*, 15 August 2001.

JP 3-08, *Interagency, Intergovernmental Organization, and Nongovernmental Organization Coordination during Joint Operations Vol I*, 17 March 2006.

JP 3-10, *Joint Security Operations in Theater*, 1 August 2006.

JP 3-10.1, *Joint Tactics, Techniques, and Procedures for Base Defense*, 23 July 1996.

JP 3-13, *Information Operations*, 13 February 2006.

JP 3-28, *Civil Support*, 14 September 2007.

JP 3-31, *Command and Control for Joint Land Operations*, 23 March 2004.

JP 3-33, *Joint Task Force Headquarters*, 16 February 2007.

JP 3-34, *Joint Engineer Operations*, 12 February 2007.

JP 3-35, *Deployment and Redeployment Operations*, 7 May 2007.

JP 3-40, *Joint Doctrine for Combating Weapons of Mass Destruction*, 8 July 2004.

JP 3-41, *Chemical, Biological, Radiological, Nuclear, and High-Yield Explosives Consequence Management*, 2 October 2006.

JP 3-50, *Personnel Recovery*, 5 January 2007.

JP 3-52, *Joint Doctrine for Airspace Control in the Combat Zone*, 30 August 2004.

JP 3-57, *Civil-Military Operations*, 8 July 2008.

JP 3-57.1, *Joint Doctrine for Civil Affairs*, 14 April 2003.

JP 5-0, *Joint Operation Planning*, 26 December 2006.

MULTI-SERVICE PUBLICATIONS

FM 1-02, *Operational Terms and Graphics*, 21 September 2004.

FM 3-11.21, *Multiservice Tactics, Techniques, and Procedures for Chemical, Biological, Radiological, and Nuclear Consequence Management Operations*, 1 April 2008.

FM 3-34.170, *Engineer Reconnaissance*, 25 March 2008.

FM 3-90.12, *Combined Arms Gap-Crossing Operations*, 1 July 2008.

FM 3-100.4, *Environmental Considerations in Military Operations*, 15 June 2000.

FM 4-30.16, *Multi-Service Tactics, Techniques, and Procedures for Explosive Ordnance Disposal in a Joint Environment*, 27 October 2005.

DOCUMENTS NEEDED

These documents must be available to the intended users of this publication.

DA Form 1156, *Casualty Feeder Card*.

DA Form 3953, *Purchase Request and Commitment*.

DA Forms are available on the APD web site (www.apd.army.mil).

Executive Order 13139, *Improving Health Protection of Military Personnel Participating in Particular Military Operations*, 30 September 1999.

READINGS RECOMMENDED

These readings contain relevant supplemental information.

FM 3-19.40, *Internment/Resettlement Operations*, 4 September 2007.

FM 3-90.6, *The Brigade Combat Team*, 4 August 2006.

FM 3-90.61, *The Brigade Special Troops Battalion*, 22 December 2006.

This page intentionally left blank.

Index

This page intentionally left blank.

By order of the Secretary of the Army:

GEORGE W. CASEY, JR.
General, United States Army
Chief of Staff

Official:

JOYCE E. MORROW
Administrative Assistant to the
Secretary of the Army
0903607

DISTRIBUTION:

Active Army, Army National Guard, and U.S. Army Reserve: To be distributed in accordance with the initial distribution number (IDN) 115993, requirements for FM 3-90.31.

www.ingramcontent.com/pod-product-compliance
Lightning Source LLC
Chambersburg PA
CBHW081407270326
41931CB00016B/3408